Lecture Notes in Artificial Intelligence 13499

Subseries of Lecture Notes in Computer Science

Series Editors

Randy Goebel
University of Alberta, Edmonton, Canada

Wolfgang Wahlster
DFKI, Berlin, Germany

Zhi-Hua Zhou
Nanjing University, Nanjing, China

Founding Editor

Jörg Siekmann
DFKI and Saarland University, Saarbrücken, Germany

More information about this subseries at https://link.springer.com/bookseries/1244

Lola Cañamero · Philippe Gaussier ·
Myra Wilson · Sofiane Boucenna ·
Nicolas Cuperlier (Eds.)

From Animals to Animats 16

16th International Conference
on Simulation of Adaptive Behavior, SAB 2022
Cergy-Pontoise, France, September 20–23, 2022
Proceedings

Springer

Editors
Lola Cañamero (iD)
ETIS
CY Cergy Paris Université
Cergy-Pontoise, France

Philippe Gaussier (iD)
ETIS
CY Cergy Paris Université
Cergy-Pontoise, France

Myra Wilson
Aberystwyth University
Aberystwyth, UK

Sofiane Boucenna (iD)
ETIS
CY Cergy Paris Université
Cergy-Pontoise, France

Nicolas Cuperlier (iD)
ETIS
CY Cergy Paris Université
Cergy-Pontoise, France

ISSN 0302-9743   ISSN 1611-3349 (electronic)
Lecture Notes in Artificial Intelligence
ISBN 978-3-031-16769-0   ISBN 978-3-031-16770-6 (eBook)
https://doi.org/10.1007/978-3-031-16770-6

LNCS Sublibrary: SL7 – Artificial Intelligence

© Cover illustration: Jean Solé

This Springer imprint is published by the registered company Springer Nature Switzerland AG
The registered company address is: Gewerbestrasse 11, 6330 Cham, Switzerland

Preface

This book regroups the contributed articles that were presented at From Animals to Animats 16: The 16th International Conference on the Simulation of Adaptive Behavior (SAB 2022), held at CY Cergy Paris University in Cergy-Pontoise, France, on September 21–23, 2022. The workshops took place on September 20, 2022.

The objective of the SAB interdisciplinary conference series is to bring together researchers in computer science, artificial intelligence, artificial life, control, cybernetics, robotics, neuroscience, ethology, evolutionary biology, and many other fields, to further our understanding of the behaviors and underlying mechanisms that allow natural animals and artificial animats to adapt and survive in complex, dynamic and uncertain environments. The conference focuses on models of adaptive behavior and its underlying mechanisms, and on experiments grounded on well-defined models, including robot models, computer simulation models and mathematical models designed to help characterize and compare various organizational principles and architectures underlying adaptive behavior in real animals and in synthetic agents—animats.

The Simulation of Adaptive Behavior conference started in September 1990. After years of great success, SAB has given birth to numerous conferences, e.g., conferences on genetic algorithms, reinforcement learning, swarm intelligence, bio-inspired systems, and developmental robotics. This 16th edition of SAB marks the 30th anniversary of the conference. To celebrate this special event, we wanted to take the opportunity to reflect on the past, present and future of SAB, and we sought to foster self-critical, thought-provoking, and nurturing discussions among specialists to ensure that the conference presented the state of the art and inspired new ideas at the cutting edge of science. In addition to the traditional open call for papers, a larger than usual number of renowned specialists from a broad range of domains were invited to contribute their knowledge, expertise, and critical views. To this end, 6 renowned specialists have been solicited in this 16th edition to organize themed sessions, comprising both invited and contributed presentations. A total of 19 specialists have been invited to present and discuss the new trends in the following areas:

- Collective intelligence
- Affective and social cognition and interaction
- Bio-inspired vision
- Embodiment
- Brain-inspired control architectures for adaptation, and learning
- Bio-inspired navigation

This year was thus marked by numerous colleagues that have accepted our invitation to speak about the simulation of adaptive behaviors and the new trend they see for years to come. Grounded in the constructivist and enactivist paradigms, all the speakers emphasize the importance of the emergent properties related to sensory motor laws. Our field is now mature with precise methodologies to go from the ethology to the robotics experiments while focusing on grabbing the underlying theoretical principles to explain the multiscale organizations and cognitive mechanisms we can observe. The ethical aspect of our works is also discussed not as an ad hoc construction but as a fundamental part of social interactions that is extended to human/machine interactions.

Starting from the general life organization principle, Josh Bongard reviewed recent efforts to create biological robots, and how their protean natures have led us to rethink how we approach soft robotics, embodied cognition, and intelligence in general. Next, as far as collective intelligence is concerned, Guy Theraulaz reviewed our current knowledge of the behavioral mechanisms underlying collective intelligence in animal societies such as social insects, fish schools or flocks of birds. These mechanisms enable a group of individuals to coordinate their actions, solve a wide variety of problems and act as a single superorganism. Collective intelligence emerges from rudimentary and local interactions among individuals during which these exchange information. To study collective intelligence phenomena in animal societies a general methodology is proposed that consists in monitoring and quantifying the behaviors of individuals and, in parallel, the collective organization and behaviors at the group-level, and then connect both levels by means of computational models. In the same session, Heiko Hamann discussed the opportunities of bio-hybrid systems with natural plants. Plants offer many interesting features, such as adaptive behavior, growth, and sensitive physiological systems. He developed data-driven simulators of a plant's growth and motion and exploited natural adaptive behaviors to build, for example, systems that self-repair. In recent works plants are used as sensors to correlate specific forms of air pollution with measurable effects in the plant. On her side, Sabine Hauert, proposed to break down the conventional disciplinary silos. She showed swarm engineering can be adopted across scales and applications, from nanomedicine to treat cancer, to cm-sized robots for large-scale environmental monitoring or sophisticated robots for intralogistics. Sabine Hauert tries to build a unified framework for the engineering of swarms across scales that makes use of machine learning to automatically discover suitable agent designs and behaviors. While most of the works focused on an homogenous set of agents Elio Tuci, discussed how heterogeneity in swarm robotics (design and control of multi-robot systems) can be used as a tool to generate desired collective responses (swarms in which robots differ in their hardware, control software, or both). Finally, Andy Philippides, explained how desert ants learn long paths through complex terrain after only a single exposure to the visual information. Such rapid learning with small brains is possible because learning is an active process scaffolded by specialized behaviors which have co-evolved with the ant's brain and sensory system to robustly solve the single task of navigation. He shows visual information specifies actions and route navigation is recast as a search for familiar views. This simplification allows the information needed to robustly navigate routes to be rapidly and robustly encoded by a single layer neural network making it plausible for small-brained animals and lightweight robots with all computation on-board.

Focusing on individual behavior and the building of sensory motor laws, Jochen Triesch discussed how far we still are from building biomimetic vision systems that autonomously learn to perceive the world. He posited that biological sensory systems strive to learn efficient representations of their sensory inputs while also adapting their behavior, in particular their eye movements, to optimize sensory coding. J. Triesh reviewed the fundamentals of Active Efficient Coding as a theoretical framework that aims to explain such learning based on information theoretic principles and discussed the future challenges. Next, Benoit Cottereau described a novel approach which combines spiking neural networks with a biologically plausible plasticity rule (spike-timing dependent plasticity or STDP) to model the emergence of motion and depth selectivity in primate visual cortex and show how such an approach can be implemented in adaptive artificial systems. On her side, Jenny Read discussed how insect stereopsis likely evolved to produce simple behavior, such as orienting towards the closer of two objects or triggering a strike when prey comes within range, rather than to achieve a rich perception of scene depth. This sort of adaptive behavior can be produced with very basic stereoscopic algorithms which make no attempt to achieve fusion or correspondence, or to produce even a coarse map of depth across the visual field. Such algorithms may be all that is required for insects and may also prove useful in some autonomous applications. Finally, Stéphane Viollet showed the biorobotic approach is a meeting point where robotics and neuroscience are used to try to explain the behavior of animals, especially winged insects (fly, bee, wasp...) and to model the processing of the sensory modalities at work in these outstanding animals. The robots are a kind of embodiment to validate the models. He showed future robotic applications can benefit greatly from the skylight polarization and questions what will future morphing robots look like.

Advances in the understanding of mammal brains also bring a lot of novelties for modelling and the building of new robotics systems. Francesca Sargolini started with a summary of entorhinal grid cells and how they provide the brain with an invariant metric map that allows rats (and more generally mammals) to navigate in space using mainly self-movements. She reviewed recent studies showing that grid cell activity is also modulated by environmental (allocentric) cues. She presented recent data showing that grid cells compute information necessary for both self-motion-based and allocentric navigation. Moreover, her results suggest that grid cells may be implicated in organizing experience according to a specific temporal structure. This function is a key aspect that may reconcile the two opposite views on the role of grid cells in spatial navigation. Next, Caswell Barry showed that hippocampal spatial activity is governed by a small number of simple laws and in particular suggest the presence of an information-theoretic bound imposed by perception on the fidelity of the spatial memory system. Finally, Denis Sheynichovich discussed recent imaging studies suggesting the existence of scene-sensitive areas in the dorsal visual stream that are likely to combine visual information from successive egocentric views, whereas behavioral evidence indicates the memory of surrounding visual space in extraretinal coordinates. His talk explored the idea that a high-resolution panoramic visual representation links visual perception and mnemonic functions during natural behavior. Such a representation can mediate hippocampal involvement in a range of spatial and non-spatial tasks, accounting for the proposed role of this structure in scene perception, representation of physical and conceptual spaces, serial image memorization and spatial reorientation. His model predicts a common role of view-based allocentric memory storage in spatial and visual behavior.

For the control of more complex behavior and their autonomous learning, Mehdi Khamassi reviewed computational models for the coordination of different types of learning algorithms, e.g. model-free and model-based RL. Such coordination seems a promising way to endow robots (and more generally autonomous agents) with the ability to autonomously decide which learning strategy is appropriate in different encountered situations, while at the same time permitting us to minimize computation cost. Next, Jeffrey Krichmar discussed neuromodulation and behavioral trade-offs. Biological organisms need to consider many trade-offs to survive (foraging for food vs fleeing from predators). These trade-offs can also appear in cognitive functions such as introverted or extroverted behavior. Many of these trade-offs are regulated by chemicals in our brain and body, such as neuromodulators or hormones. Neuromodulators send broad signals to the brain that can dramatically change behaviors, moods, decisions, etc. The brain can control these modulatory and hormonal systems by setting a context or making an adjustment when there are prediction errors. J. Krichmar showed how applying these concepts to robots and models results in behaviors that are more interesting and more realistic. Finally, Tony J. Prescott explained how the mammal brains architecture contributes to adaptive behavior, and how it has emerged through evolution, and is constructed during development, among the most challenging questions in science. Our research explores the role of layered brain architectures in two contexts: active touch sensing in mammals and sense of self in humans. Recently, we have also applied the framework of constraint closure, viewed as a general characteristic of living systems, to the problem of brain organization. This analysis draws attention to the capacity of layered brain architectures to scaffold themselves across multiple timescales.

All these results open new avenues to question whether robots can have empathy as done by Christian Balkenius in his talk discussing the importance of grounding robot social interactions according to emotional processes. Kerstin Dautenhahn discussed application areas explored in term of developing robots as socially assistive tools. This includes developing robots to facilitate robot-assisted play for children with upper-limb challenges, as well as using social robots to explore bullying interventions for school-aged children. Finally, AJung Moon questions the design of interactive robots with ethics in mind. Unexpected social, ethical, and legal issues can arise as we design systems that interact with people. How can we begin to integrate ethics into design when discussions about what is 'right' and 'wrong' always seem to lead to more questions than solutions? Her talk presents new ways to ground the discussions of ethics in technical design.

Hence, after more of 30 years of progress Simulation of Adaptive Behavior is still a flourishing domain with now a deeper understanding of the some of the underlying principles and the development of smarter technological applications. Yet we still have issues to understand how learning can be truly autonomous.

These invited contributions for the six sessions were complemented by 7 papers accepted for long oral presentation (acceptance rate of 17.4% and 10 papers presented as posters (acceptance rate of 56.5%), among the 23 submissions received this year.

This book contains the 17 selected papers organized in four chapters. The first part presents five papers [1–5] that bring innovative ideas and results about the notion of embodiment. The second part includes five papers [6–10] that cover theoretical aspect of brain-inspired control, adaptation and learning, as well as a paper [11] presenting a ready-to-use Python programming library to facilitate the implementation of models based on reservoir computing. The third part consists of two papers [12–13] that inspire new perspectives in bioinspired vision, but also two articles [14–15] about navigation models inspired by the functioning of certain brain structures in mammals. This book ends with a part that contains two papers [16–17] opening on the themes of social (affective) cognition and collective intelligence.

Following the trend in the previous SAB 2018 event and many other academic meetings, to minimize paper consumption we decided to distribute the conference proceedings on USB Flash Drives. The review process was organized using the SciencesConf submission and review system. The quality of the review process was high thanks to 6 Area Chairs (ACs) who helped the Program Chairs in defining the Program Committee, and in finding excellent reviewers for each paper.

The enthusiasm and hard work of numerous individuals was essential to the conference's success. Above all, we would like to acknowledge the significant contribution of all the scientific committee, who thoughtfully reviewed all the submissions and provided detailed suggestions on how to improve the articles.

We also wish to express our gratitude to the 6 Session Chairs who kindly accepted to actively participate in the organization of their respective session.

We are indebted to our sponsors for their generous support: the International Society for Adaptive Behavior (ISAB), CY Cergy Paris University, CY Advanced Studies, ETIS, CNRS, ENSEA, and Springer LNAI.

Finally, we would like to thank Jean Solé for the artistic conception of the SAB 2022 poster and the proceedings cover.

We hope readers will enjoy and profit from the articles in this book, and will look forward to the next SAB conference.

September 2022

Lola Cañamero
Philippe Gaussier
Myra Wilson
Sofiane Boucenna
Nicolas Cuperlier

Organization

General Chairs

Lola Cañamero   ETIS, CY Cergy Paris Université, France
Philippe Gaussier   ETIS, CY Cergy Paris Université, France
Myra Wilson   Aberystwyth University, Aberystwyth, UK

Program Committee Chairs

Sofiane Boucenna   ETIS, CY Cergy Paris Université, France
Nicolas Cuperlier   ETIS, CY Cergy Paris Université, France

Steering Committee

Sofiane Boucenna   CY Cergy Paris Université, France
Lola Cañamero   CY Cergy Paris Université, France
Nicolas Cuperlier   CY Cergy Paris Université, France
Philippe Gaussier   CY Cergy Paris Université, France
Mehdi Khamassi   Sorbonne Université, France
Alexandre Pitti   CY Cergy Paris Université, France
Francesca Sargolini   Aix-Marseille University, France
Guy Theraulaz   Université Paul Sabatier, France
Jochen Triesch   Frankfurt Institute for Advanced Studies,
                         Germany
Myra Wilson   Aberystwyth University, Aberystwyth, UK

Program Committee

Hussein A. Abbass   University of New South Wales, Australia
Frederic Alexandre   Inria Bordeaux, France
Ronald Arkin   Georgia Tech, USA
Sofiane Boucenna   CY Cergy Paris Université, France
Nicolas Cuperlier   CY Cergy Paris Université, France
Lola Cañamero   CY Cergy Paris Université, France
Julien Diard   Université Grenoble Alpes, France
Stéphane Doncieux   Sorbonne Université, France
Alexandros Giagkos   Aston University, UK
Philippe Gaussier   CY Cergy Paris Université, France

Alvaro Gutierrez	Universidad Politécnica de Madrid, Spain
Auke Jan Ijspeert	EPFL, Switzerland
Mehdi Khamassi	Sorbonne Université, France
Jeff Krichmar	University of California, Irvine, USA
Eric Medvet	University of Trieste, Italy
Stefano Nolfi	CNR-ISTC Rome, Italy
Anil Ozdemir	University of Sheffield, UK
Alexandre Pitti	CY Cergy Paris Université, France
Andrew Philippides	University of Sussex, UK
Mathias Quoy	CY Cergy Paris Université, France
Andreagiovanni Reina	Université libre de Bruxelles, Belgium
Andrea Roli	University of Bologna, Italy
Nicolas Rougier	Inria Bordeaux, France
Franck Ruffier	Aix Marseille Université, France
Gregor Schöner	Ruhr-Universität Bochum, Germany
Elio Tuci	University of Namur, Belgium
Myra Wilson	Aberystwyth University, UK

Additional Reviewers

Arnaud Blanchard
Ghilès Moustafaoui

Contents

Embodiment

Embodiment

How to Design Morphologies. A Design Process for Autonomous Robots

Vincent Rist[✉] and Manfred Hild

Berliner Hochschule für Technik (BHT), Berlin, Germany
ristv@yahoo.com, manfred.hild@bht-berlin.de

Abstract. We describe a design process for robots in order to study the relationship between the agent's morphology and its behavioral capabilities. The limbs are modeled using circular arcs, resulting in smooth, round body shapes. From those two-dimensional models, a directed graph is generated, which represents the morphological manifold and captures all statically stable postures of the robot. On this graph, motion sequences can be found using abstract key postures properties that are morphologically independent. In a further step, we are investigating the extent to which our virtual 2D morphology is also suitable for a physical 3D robot. For this purpose, 2D morphologies are extruded linearly in the z-dimension so that they can be manufactured with a conventional 3D printer. We can then deploy the motion sequences on a physical robot, assembled using a convenient 3D-printable plug'n'clamp kit. The evaluation showed that with this process, one can either optimize a behavior for a specific morphology or try to optimize the morphology for a specific behavior. Even though the process does not yet find the most efficient motion sequence and more research will have to be conducted on that matter, a stable forward motion could be generated for every robot morphology.

Keywords: Internal models and representations · Dynamical systems approaches · Autonomous robotics

1 Introduction

The morphology of an agent mostly stays constant throughout its lifetime, even though it heavily influences the agent's behavioral diversity. This is due to the time and money consuming venture of designing, assembling and deploying a fully functioning robot and due to the difficulty of engineering a morphologically flexible machine. Those are also the reasons why the study of morphology has usually been constrained to simulation, which allows for enormous amounts of morphologies to be genetically optimized. Even though the artificial evolution has proven to produce diverse morphology and suitable behavior [1,10], the approach has two downsides: Firstly, because of its constraint to simulation it is only partially applicable to the physical world [2]. And secondly, it is difficult to reason why a found solution is optimal, which means changing the task at hand

© The Author(s), under exclusive license to Springer Nature Switzerland AG 2022
L. Cañamero et al. (Eds.): SAB 2022, LNAI 13499, pp. 3–14, 2022.
https://doi.org/10.1007/978-3-031-16770-6_1

usually requires a new evolution. The proposed design process tries to address these downsides.

The morphology and its physical properties turn embodied robots into complex dynamical systems. The postures corresponding to the stable fixed points of these systems create manifolds inside the high-dimensional sensorimotor state space [6,7]. Any state a robot might find itself in is represented as a point on the manifold, and any path along the manifold that connect two of those states corresponds to a motion sequence. Hence, the manifold of a particular robot holds information about all possible motion sequences that it can pursue. They can be explored dynamically and autonomously during runtime [3] and offer an alternative method of planning action than to simulate the body shape and its physical properties onboard in real-time.

2   Proposal of a Design Process

By using the morphological manifold for motion planning, the consequences of changing a morphological parameter can be directly visualized in real-time. The intent of the proposed design process is not necessarily to produce faster, cheaper or more efficient robots, but to have a tool which helps robot designers to reason about their design decision based on the shape of the manifolds and the resulting motion sequences. We created a modular plug'n'clamp kit which allows the designers to reduce the time and resource expenses of assembling and deploying robots, which facilitates rapid evaluation of the morphology and behavior in the physical world. The four-part process is schematically visualized in Fig. 1. The following subsections discuss each part in more detail.

2.1   Arc Representation

Commonly, morphologies are modeled using polygons in 2D or polyhedrons in 3D, which produce shapes with flat edges and sharp corners. We decided to extend our mathematical model to allow for smooth and round contours as well. This means robots could have both flat limbs, like the hooves of ungulate animals, or round limbs, like the paws of felines. Adding smooth, round contours to the pool of possible morphological features has some advantages: The first being

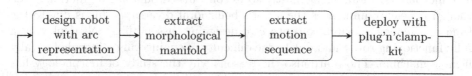

Fig. 1. Schematic visualization of the proposed design process. Morphologies have to be geometrically designed, are analyzed for their morphological manifold and motion sequences and are finally physically deployed with a plug'n'clamp kit. Experiments in the real world deliver insights on how to upgrade the robot design and the next iteration of the process begins.

that flat edges and sharp corners are features of ideal shapes that are never perfectly implemented due to manufacturing constraints, e.g., the nozzle diameter of a 3D-printer. Secondly, smooth shapes are commonly found in nature. Robots with a similar aesthetic might seem more organic and less mechanic to the observer. Thirdly, robots that fall onto a flat edge absorb the kinetic energy of the impact, which might damaged it. A round edge, however, can redirect this energy by rolling off. Robots might even use their round edges to induce rocking by periodically shifting their center of mass, i.e., robots with round limbs can experience interesting dynamical behavior.

One way of mathematically describing smooth, round contours is with the help of circular arcs. A circular arc A is a continuous subset of a circle outline C that is defined by its radius r and its midpoint $m = (m_x, m_y)$:

$$A \subset C = \{(x, y) \in \mathbb{R}^2 \mid r^2 = (x - m_x)^2 + (y - m_y)^2\}$$

By tangentially concatenating those arcs one can model parametrized shapes like seen in Fig. 2. Those arc shapes are particularly well suited as two-dimensional limb models for several reasons: First off, the arc representation requires fewer parameters to model a smooth and round limb than the approximation of the same shape with a polygon or with splines. Additionally, the radius of the arc touching the ground can be used to adjust the friction, an important morphological property for many behaviors like grasping or locomotion. And finally, the continuous property of the arc representation also causes the morphological manifolds to be continuous, whereas the discrete polygon representation creates discontinuous steps in the manifold corresponding to postures where the robot tips over the corners of the polygon.

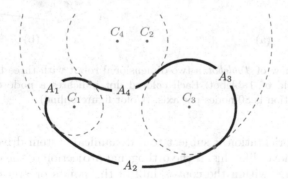

Fig. 2. Example of a limb modeled with four circular arcs A_1 through A_4. The transition from one arc to the next has to be tangential to avoid corners. This particular shape can be defined unambiguously by four parameters: the radii of C_1 and C_3, the distance between their midpoints, and the central angle of the connecting arcs, which is the same for both A_2 and A_4. See [9] for more detail.

We use the arc representation to model two-dimensional robot limbs that can have both the advantages of sharp, flat and of smooth, round contours.

2.2   Morphological Manifold as a Directed Graph

The posture of a robot is defined by its current body configuration, i.e., its degrees of freedom, and by the orientation of the robot in the world. Let us inspect *Tablebot*, the robot from Fig. 3(a). It consists of three limbs: the two legs are connected to the torso by rotary joints. The joints are indicated by black circles in the figure. Tablebot's center of mass is visualized as a black dot, whereas the white dots symbolize the centers of mass of each individual limb. The joint angles φ_l and φ_r define the relative rotation between the legs and the torso, i.e., the configuration. A third angle φ_o specifies the rotation of the torso relative to the ground, which defines the orientation of the robot in its two-dimensional world. For (a) $\varphi_o = 0$ holds, which is why it is omitted in the figure.

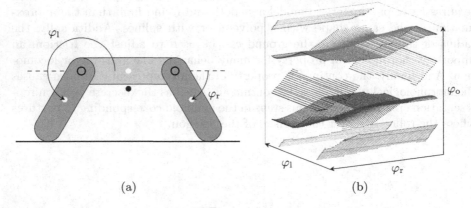

(a)   (b)

Fig. 3. (a) Side-view of *Tablebot*, a two-dimensional robot with three limbs. (b) Morphological manifold of Tablebot. Each colored dot indicates a node of the directed graph. The resolution is 80 nodes per axis. (Color figure online)

The robot's orientation is subject to a dynamical system driven by gravity. In essence, it behaves like this: If the orthogonal projection of the center of mass to the ground lays within the convex hull of the points or areas touching the ground, a stable fixed point attractor is reached. Otherwise, the robot falls, which means it experiences a change in orientation. The stable fixed point attractors of this system correspond to stable postures of the robot. In the case of (a) the x-coordinate of the center of mass lays between the points of ground contact, so the posture is stable. With its degrees of freedom, the robot can manipulate its own ground contact and its center of mass, and thus also the orientation of the stable postures. Considering all possible stable postures, they form a manifold inside the posture space, just like the one in Fig. 3(b).

Even though some parts of the manifold can be formulated as geometrical planes it becomes difficult to describe the manifold analytically. [4] shows how robots can autonomously learn quadrics that represent their manifold during runtime. An alternative approach is to use a discrete model of the manifold structured as a directed graph. The nodes of the graph correspond to discrete stable postures. If a robot that currently holds posture a can transition into posture b by moving its joint by a certain angle, the postures are connected by a directed edge: $(a \rightarrow b)$. The edge has to be a directed one because not all posture transitions are reversible, e.g., if the joint movement caused the robot to fall. This is the reason why the morphological manifold commonly consists of a number of disconnected submanifolds, which are distinguished by color in Fig. 3(b). All postures that are part of the same submanifold are bidirectionally connected, i.e., no falling occurs during transition, if the movement speed is not too fast. The irreversible fall-edges and physical constraints like angle bounds or self collision make up the borders of the submanifolds.

2.3 Algorithmically Determined Motion Sequences

Manifold graphs hold information about all possible stable postures and how (and if at all) the robot can transition between them. Each posture has certain properties, like the positions of the center of mass, of the ground contact points, etc. This data structure enables algorithms to find suitable key postures on the graph and connect them to create motion sequences for certain tasks. In this study, we chose a locomotion sequence consisting of only three key postures. For example, one might want to generate a simple locomotion sequence by periodically transitioning between the three key postures in Fig. 4: The robot starts in posture (a) where the distance between its ground contact points is relatively small. By positively actuating its right leg, a transition to posture (b) is accomplished. Since most of the weight (black dot) is now shifted to the left side, the right leg is more likely to slide across the ground than the left leg. In the transition from (b) to (c) the robot shifts its weight onto the other side while at the

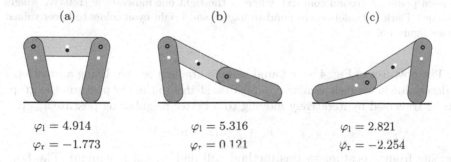

| (a) | (b) | (c) |

$\varphi_l = 4.914$ $\varphi_l = 5.316$ $\varphi_l = 2.821$

$\varphi_r = -1.773$ $\varphi_r = 0.121$ $\varphi_r = -2.254$

Fig. 4. Three key postures for locomotion. By periodically transitioning from (a) through (c) the robot will slide from left to right.

same time keeping a fixed distance between the utmost contact points with the ground, which avoids slipping of the feet. Lastly, the robot intentionally reduces this contact distance by actuating its left leg. The shift in weight will now cause the left leg to slip, and the robot finds itself in posture (a) once again. This coordination of friction and slippage will cause the robot to move forward. The motion resembles a human gait when moving across a slippery surface.

The two posture properties at play here are the distance d between the points of ground contact and the relative weight position w. If the robot splits its legs outwards as far as possible, then $d \approx 1$ and for $d \approx 0$ the points of contact move closer together. $w = 0$ if the center of mass is right on top of the left point of contact and $w = 1$ for the right side, meaning $w = 1/2$ corresponds to an even weight distribution. Figure 5 shows a clipped projection of the cyan colored submanifold from Fig. 3(b) onto the configuration space. The color gradient of the displayed images shows the value of d and w of the corresponding posture. Key posture (a) needs to have a low d and a balanced $w = 1/2$, which is why postures closer to the bottom right corner are well suited. (b) and (c) on the other hand, need postures with a high d value and strongly shifted w (i.e., $w \approx 0$ or $w \approx 1$), which can be found in the upper right or bottom left corner respectively.

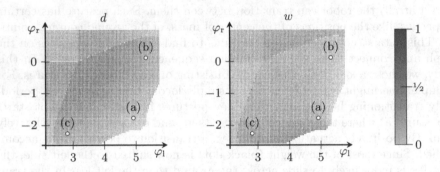

Fig. 5. A projection of the manifold onto the configuration space with a resolution of 90 postures per axis. The color gradient on the left indicates the value of d (distance between points of ground contact), whereas the right one indicates w (relative weight position). Dark red colors correspond to higher and bright cyan colors to lower values. (Color figure online)

The postures in Fig. 4 were found using a gradient search. Using a function f to determine how much similarity a posture shares to the key posture, the graph can be traversed by iteratively moving to a better neighboring posture x_{n+1}:

$$x_{n+1} = x_n + f'(d(x_n), w(x_n))$$

Starting from a posture x_0 this method will find a local maximum. The functions and starting postures x_0 were hand-tuned. This approach leaves room for optimization, but it is a step towards abstracting behavior from morphology through posture properties.

2.4 Plug'n'Clamp Kit

The final step of the design process is assembly and deployment. Through modularity robots can become morphologically flexible machines even during runtime [5]. Inspired by the toy-robot-assembly-kit *Topobo* [8] we created a similar modular plug'n'clamp kit. The limbs that are modeled with the arc representation are extruded linearly in the z-dimension, and then directly converted into printable STL-files, which helps robot designers to reduce time and effort during assembly and deployment of their agents. The kit complies with the following criteria:

1. *Printability*: Limbs and connecting components are designed for optimal 3D-printing. This means that filament and time expenses are reduced, no supporting structures are needed, and predetermined breaking points are avoided.
2. *Pluggability*: The effort involved with assembly and disassembly remains low. Robots can be assembled without screws, tools, or ball bearings by using a plug and clamp system instead.
3. *Modularity*: All modules can be combined with all other modules. The kit tries to constrain the morphology as little as possible.
4. *Simplicity*: The number of different individual parts needed to enable deployment is reduced to a minimum. Standard parts such as the pins can be reused for other morphologies and do not require reprinting.
5. *Aesthetics*: The kit prefers rounded contours over sharp corners and straight edges so that the assembled robots nicely harmonize with the arc representation.

The essential components of the kit are displayed in Fig. 6. The little H-shaped pins (a) are used as universal connecting tools, which can be printed within five minutes. Robot limbs such as (b) consist of two symmetrical parts, which are printed separately and are then plugged together. The advantages of using this method is that firstly only the frame and some connecting structures have to be printed, which reduces filament consumption and printing time. Secondly, motors or other peripherals can be clamped in between the two halves as done in (b) avoiding the need for screws. Here we were using the *Dynamixel XL330-M288-T* motors from *Rotobis*. Plugging multiple limbs together will look like (c), a 3D embodiment of the 2D Tablebot morphology.

3 Evaluation

Two different test series have been conducted to evaluate the utility of the described process. The *OpenCM9.04* from *Robotis* served as a microprocessor and four AA-batteries in series created a supply voltage of 6 V. All other parts were printed with gray PLA-filament, resulting in 279 g of total robot weight. With both legs stretched outward and the torso limb touching the ground, the robot reaches a length of 39 cm. The robot was placed on a medium-density fiberboard plate and then executed three cycles of a given motion sequence,

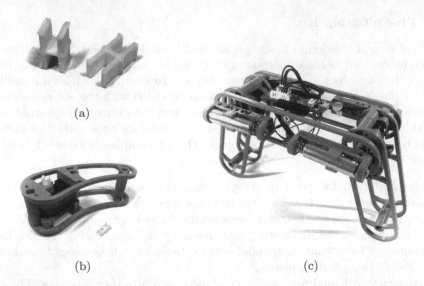

(a)

(b)   (c)

Fig. 6. (a) Universal, H-shaped pins that are used to manually connect and disconnect two components. (b) A limb consisting of two separately printed parts with a motor clamped in-between. (c) A fully assembled and deployable embodiment of the Tablebot morphology with a processor and batteries.

which itself consisted of three key postures. Then the average walking distance per cycle D and the average energy consumption per cycle E was measured.

For the first test series, we described four different motion sequences for Tablebot by tweaking the key posture properties as shown in Fig. 7. Sequences that include posture (a1) caused the robot to pull its legs closer together as compared to (a2). When applying (b1) and (c1) the robot made a big step by maximizing d and by putting less focus on w. For (b2) and (c2) it was the other way around: less d and more w. Each sequence was then evaluated seven times on the robot.

The average results are presented in Fig. 8. They demonstrate that for this morphology, taking big steps seems to increase D and strongly shifting the center of mass seems to decrease E. Motion sequence S2 gets the most walk distance out of its energy consumption. This test series demonstrates how the design process provides a method of optimizing a motion sequence for a certain task and a certain morphology.

As the morphology stayed constant for the first test series, we wanted to see if the key posture properties also apply to different morphologies. So we randomly scattered the shape parameters of Tablebot's legs inside the parameter space and received the four new morphologies seen in Fig. 9. The same torso module was used for the four robots as it had little influence on the task at hand and to avoid reprinting additional modules. Each morphology M_i was analyzed for a motion sequence S_i by using the same key posture properties as sequence S2

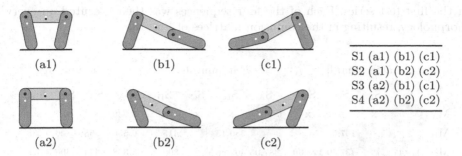

			S1 (a1) (b1) (c1)

Row table on right:

S1 (a1) (b1) (c1)
S2 (a1) (b2) (c2)
S3 (a2) (b1) (c1)
S4 (a2) (b2) (c2)

(a1)   (b1)   (c1)

(a2)   (b2)   (c2)

Fig. 7. Six different key postures. The table on the right combines the postures into motion sequences S1 through S4.

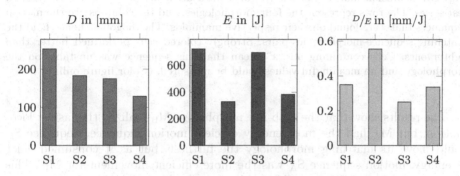

D in [mm] E in [J] D/E in [mm/J]

Fig. 8. The averaged results from testing motion sequence S1 through S4 on the Table-bot morphology. D represents the walking distance that the robot travelled per cycle. E is the energy consumed for that motion.

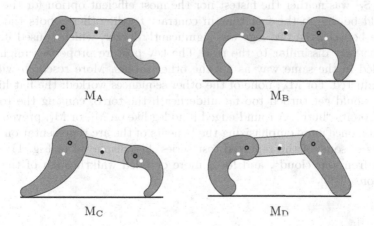

M_A M_B

M_C M_D

Fig. 9. Four new morphologies. They are constructed similarly to Tablebot, but with diversified leg parameters. To be comparable to each other, the overall robot length stays constant. The walking direction is still from left to right.

of the first test series. Each of the four sequences was then executed on every morphology, resulting in the confusion matrices of Fig. 10.

	D in [mm/J]				E in [mm/J]				D/E in [mm/J]			
	S_A	S_B	S_C	S_D	S_A	S_B	S_C	S_D	S_A	S_B	S_C	S_D
M_A	180.00	x	x	x	281.87	x	x	x	0.639	x	x	x
M_B	177.00	215.93	107.53	161.27	322.03	380.15	256.16	415.31	0.550	0.568	0.420	0.388
M_C	119.17	178.93	137.40	128.00	387.05	402.98	338.21	390.65	0.308	0.444	0.406	0.328
M_D	159.60	170.13	75.93	171.40	369.08	443.47	319.12	429.66	0.432	0.384	0.238	0.399

Fig. 10. Confusion matrices of the averaged measurements per cycle for the second test series. The rows represent the four morphologies, and the columns are the motion sequences that were found on their respective manifolds. The diagonals hence hold the matching sequence-morphologies-pairs. Strongly colored cells performed better than lighter ones. Cells containing an "x" mean that this sequence was unstable on the morphology and no meaningful values could be measured. (Color figure online)

The results show that the crab-like morphology M_B realized the fastest locomotion, but M_A had the most energy efficient motion sequence. Sequence S_D could move its matching morphology the furthest, but as it consumed a lot of energy, motion sequence S_A was the more efficient movement for M_D. This demonstrates how different walking behaviors can be designed with the correct key posture properties. Agents might casually prefer a slow but efficient way of moving forward, but in case of an emergency a faster and more energy consuming "sprint" might temporarily be activated. For M_C the process failed as sequence S_C was neither the fastest nor the most efficient option for the robot. This could be due to the fact that in contrary to the other robots the length difference between the two legs was significantly larger, which caused its manifold to be very dissimilar to the rest. The key posture properties might have not applied in the same way as for the other robots. More research will have to be conducted. For M_A, none of the other sequences worked: the flat hind leg (left leg) would get turned too far underneath the torso, causing the robot to easily fall on its "butt". A round-edged hind leg like on M_B or M_D prevents such constraints, once more emphasizing the benefits of the arc representation. Video recordings of some of the reported test series, like displayed in Fig. 11, can be streamed from our cloud[1], and for a more detailed walkthrough of the whole process consult [9].

---

[1] https://cloud.bht-berlin.de/index.php/s/RpHTdf4mLLEByJW.

Fig. 11. Selected screenshots of the video recordings. Here Morphology M_B is executing motion sequence S_B, which was the fastest morphology-motion-pair from the second test series.

4 Discussion and Outlook

In this study, we only looked at 2D quasi-static motion on flat terrain to keep the dimensionality of the manifolds low. This limits the range of possibly generated gaits to the sliding motion we could observe in this paper. Increasing the dimensionality of the agent increases its complexity, and hence it diversifies the range of possible gaits or motion sequences. Transferring the robot into a three-dimensional world, adding more limbs, or enabling dynamic motion are all potential areas of future research, but introduce new dimensions to the system and make it harder to model morphologies, abstract behavior, and generate 3D-printable parts for the plug'n'clamp kit. By adding the derivatives of the static dimensions (φ_0', φ_0'', and so on) to the systems, the momentum of the limbs could be taken into account, allowing for the generation of more dynamical gaits, like galloping. It would be interesting to study how non-flat environments manifest themselves inside the manifold, and if the agent could use these changes to classify the obstacles in order to adapt the previously discovered motions accordingly. But increasing the dimensionality of the manifolds also impairs their visualize-ability, which make it harder for a designer to reason his design decisions. The curse of dimensionality strikes again.

Optimization algorithms could be used to automatize the process of finding gaits or other motion sequences in the morphological manifold superseding, the current hand-tuned gradient search.

Also, we plan to have the agents explore their behavioral possibilities autonomously in the physical world by dynamically generating their manifold graph as done in [3] and by learning their motion sequences themselves.

Our overall goal, is to build an interactive tool that can visualize the relationship between morphology and behavior, ultimately helping the designer to comprehend the consequences of his decisions. Once the correlations are better known, the tool might even and make reasonable design suggestion. But there is still work and research to be done.

References

1. Bongard, J.: Morphological change in machines accelerates the evolution of robust behavior. Proc. Natl. Acad. Sci. **108**(4), 1234–1239 (2011). https://doi.org/10.1073/pnas.1015390108

2. Brodbeck, L., Hauser, S., Iida, F.: Morphological evolution of physical robots through model-free phenotype development. PLoS ONE **10**(6), 1–17 (2015). https://doi.org/10.1371/journal.pone.0128444

3. Hild, M., Kubisch, M.: Self-exploration of autonomous robots using attractor-based behavior control and ABC-learning. In: Eleventh Scandinavian Conference on Artificial Intelligence, pp. 153–162. IOS Press (2011)

4. Hild, M., Kubisch, M., Höfer, S.: Using quadric-representing neurons (QRENs) for real-time learning of an implicit body model. In: Proceedings of the 11th Conference on Mobile Robot and Competitions (2011)

5. Hild, M., Siedel, T., Benckendorff, C., Thiele, C., Spranger, M.: Myon, A New Humanoid, pp. 25–44. Springer, Boston (2012). https://doi.org/10.1007/978-1-4614-3064-3_2

6. Höfer, S., Hild, M., Kubisch, M.: Using slow feature analysis to extract behavioural manifolds related to humanoid robot postures. In: Tenth International Conference on Epigenetic Robotics, pp. 43–50 (2010)

7. Peters, R., Jenkins, O.C.: Uncovering manifold structures in Robonaut's sensory-data state space. In: 5th IEEE-RAS International Conference on Humanoid Robots, pp. 369–374. IEEE (2005)

8. Raffle, H.S., Parkes, A.J., Ishii, H.: Topobo: A constructive assembly system with kinetic memory. In: Proceedings of the SIGCHI Conference on Human Factors in Computing Systems, pp. 647–654. CHI 2004, Association for Computing Machinery, New York, NY, USA (2004). https://doi.org/10.1145/985692.985774

9. Rist, V.: Algorithmische Morphologien für autonome Roboter. Bachelors thesis, Berliner Hochschule für Technik (2022)

10. Sims, K.: Evolving 3D morphology and behavior by competition. Artif. Life (1994). https://doi.org/10.1162/artl.1994.1.4.353

Exploring Sensitization in the Context of Extending the Behavior of an Artificial Agent

Tristan Gillard[1,2], Jérémy Fix[1,3], and Alain Dutech[1,4(✉)]

[1] Loria, UMR 7503, Nancy, France
{tristan.gillard,jeremy.fix,alain.dutech}@loria.fr
[2] Université de Lorraine, Nancy, France
[3] CentraleSupelec, Metz, France
[4] INRIA Nancy Grand-Est, Nancy, France

Abstract. Sensitization, a non-associative learning widely observed across phylogeny, is fundamental for adaptation and, thus, survival of living organisms. This paper investigates one form of sensitization, namely pseudo-conditioning, in order to present a new computational model inspired by its characteristics. We develop this model as part of the Iterant Deformable Sensorimotor Medium (IDSM), a recently developed abstract model of sensorimotor behavior formation. The characteristics of the presented model are studied and analyzed in the light of our long term objective of investigating new unsupervised learning mechanisms for artificial autonomous agents.

Keywords: Non-associative learning · Sensitization ·
Pseudo-conditioning · Artificial agent · Adaptive behavior acquisition ·
Embodiment

1 Introduction

What drives the behavior of an organism? That fundamental question has been addressed in the literature for a variety of organisms and through different angles. For some species, part of the answer lies in the associative learning mechanisms but there also exists more widespread non-associative learning mechanisms [1,2, 7]. Behavior, in its simplest expression, is a spatio-temporal sequence of motor responses triggered by sensory signals. Habituation and sensitization, the first translating behaviorally in a response decrease while the second in a response increase, are two non-associative learning mechanisms so widely observed in the phylogeny that it suggests their fundamental role in behavioral learning [4,6,16,18].

Sensitization, described in more details in Sect. 2, translates as an increase in response with two flavours. It is defined as either the enhancement of the response to a repeated stimulus (*site-specific sensitization*) or as a generalization of this response to another stimulus (*pseudo-conditioning*). Hence, sensitization, rather than habituation, appears as an interesting mechanism to investigate how an agent can broaden its behavioral responses. Moreover, while site-specific sensitization is anchored on a single stimulus, pseudo-conditioning transfers the response to other stimuli. We can then see pseudo-conditioning as a first step toward generalization. For example, in the context of an agent exploring an environment, pseudo-conditioning would permit an agent to test actions on previously neutral stimuli, possibly discovering new opportunities.

In the context of autonomous artificial agents, there are several papers modeling sensitization [3,10,13,17,20,21], some of them reviewed in [15]. However, most of them use the word sensitization to designate site-specific sensitization exclusively. As far as we know, only the sensitization model of [3] deals with pseudo-conditioning.

The works of [10,20], which have been released at the same period of the work of Rescorla on classical conditioning [19], are the first computer models of both habituation and site-specific sensitization. The behavioral responses, consistent with biological measurements, are a mix of habituation and site-specific sensitization where habituation is more pronounced for low intensity stimuli, and sensitization for high intensity stimuli.

In a recent review of cognitive architectures [15], two models of sensitization are mentioned. In the first, Attentive and Self-Modifying cognitive architecture (ASMO, see [17]), habituation and site-specific sensitization essentially use a "significance" function of the stimulus rather than its intensity, which allows habituation to strong stimuli and site-specific sensitization to weak stimuli. This makes it easier for their robot to stay focused on its target, favoring stimuli close to the target (deemed significant) over others that became more easily ignored. In the second, Self-Aware and Self-Effecting agent (SASE, see [21]), the authors formalize six *mental* architectures from the simplest to the most complex, all based on Markov Decision Processes. Starting with architectures type-4, their conceptual models are said to allow for habituation and site-specific sensitization, but this type-4 architecture is also compatible with classical conditioning, instrumental conditioning, planing and reasoning. Besides, only the simplest architectures (up to type-2) are experimented with, habituation and sensitization both requiring at least type-4 architecture.

In [13], both habituation and site-specific sensitization are modeled for a neuromorphic processor. A weak, repeated stimulus leads to habituation of the neuron activity, whereas a strong stimulus leads to the site-specific sensitization of the neuron activity. They show that such architecture lead to more robust hardware with better aging properties.

All these works use site-specific sensitization along with habituation, but do not mention pseudo-conditioning. The neuro-physiological models of Hawkins [11] can account for a variety of learning mechanisms including pseudo-conditioning. They bring in the suggestion that non-associative learning forms the breeding ground for the emergence of other forms of learning, especially associative conditioning. In the "Autonomous Robot Based on Inspirations from

Biology" (ARBIB, see [3]), habituation and pseudo-conditioning are modeled with a spiking neural network, along with classical conditioning. The neurons encode reflexes, and are implemented on a Khepera robot to observe the resulting behaviors. Conscious of the daunting complexity of models too faithful to the physiological modeling, Damper et al. relied on spiking neural networks to abstract the physiological mechanisms, but this is still a rather complex model. It is also unclear to which extend their model can exploit non associative learning without relying on the mechanisms needed for classical conditioning.

In this paper, we propose a new computational mechanism inspired by pseudo-conditioning as described by biologists. As such, the proposed mechanism is centered on the response generalization to other stimuli. We plug our proposition to an existing conceptual model of habits formation called Iterant Deformable Sensorimotor Medium (IDSM, see [5]), more conceptual than spiking neural networks but less than models in the tradition of Rescorla-Wagner. We are interested in artificial agents that can acquire new behaviors and the IDSM framework specifically addresses the problem of using a simple kind of basic behaviors: habits. IDSM performs well for *memorizing* new behaviors and reinforcing them so as to *replaying* them later. But it has some limitations when it comes to *generating* new behaviors. Our motivation is to add learning or adaptation mechanisms to the IDSM framework so as to open the possibility for the artificial agent to produce new behaviors.

This paper is structured as follows. We start by recalling the biological definition of sensitization and its behavioral correlates in Sect. 2. The Iterant Deformable Sensorimotor Medium (IDSM) framework is then described in Sect. 3. The proposed model is detailed in Sect. 4 and various experiments are presented and analyzed in Sect. 5. We conclude the paper with a discussion.

2 Sensitization

Sensitization is a *non-associative* learning observed within numerous and various species, including insects or single cell organisms [4,18]. However, it is important to note that in the literature, unlike habituation (*i.e.* decrease of a response to a repetitive stimulus), sensitization refers to different phenomena [2,4,8,12,14]. Sensitization is defined as the enhancement of a response behavior after the presentation of a stimulus, and can be of two forms: *site-specific* sensitization and *pseudo-conditioning*. By definition, site-specific sensitization is the enhancement of the behavioral response following repeated presentation of the same stimulus.

Pseudo-conditioning is a form of learning allowing a behavioral response to a given *unconditioned* stimulus US to generalize, temporarily, as a response to another *conditioned* stimulus CS. There are major differences with the associative learning *classical conditioning*. In pseudo-conditioning the presentation of the US alone is enough to prepare for the trigger of the unconditioned response to other stimuli. A stimulus triggering this unconditioned response temporarily becomes a CS. The triggered response in pseudo-conditioning is weaker than with classical conditioning.

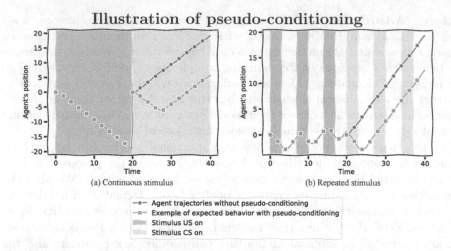

(a) Continuous stimulus   (b) Repeated stimulus

Fig. 1. Illustration of the expected behaviors, with or without pseudo-conditioning learning with continuous stimuli (a) or with repeated stimuli (b, 2 time units on, 2 time units off).

The Fig. 1 illustrates the behavioral response in case of pseudo-conditioning with either a continuous or repeated and shorter stimulation. As shown on the figure, when pseudo-conditioning takes place, a previously neutral stimulus triggers the conditioned response.

3   IDSM

The Iterant Deformable Sensorimotor Medium (or IDSM for short) of [5] is a conceptual model of habits formation from an artificial agent perspective as self-reinforcing sensorimotor behavioral patterns. It is an intermediate model between neuronal models and macroscopic behavior models.

The IDSM works in the sensorimotor space SM of the agent, with $K = dim(SM)$ the number of sensorimotor dimensions. As depicted on Fig. 2a, part of the environment state S_E is abstracted into a sensorimotor state S_{SM}. In the sensorimotor space, the IDSM uses S_{SM} and some *nodes* that store preferred sensorimotor alterations to compute a command μ. This command μ, when applied on the agent in its environment, will alter the environment and the agent.

Formally, a node N of the IDSM is defined as $N = \langle p, v, w \rangle$ with p a vector indicating the node's position in sensorimotor space SM, v a vector indicating the desired velocity in sensorimotor space SM at the position p, and w a scalar indicating the node's weight, which balances its influence relatively to the other nodes within the computation of the dynamic of the agent. The sensorimotor space is normalized and each dimension (either sensor or motor) lies in the range $[0, 1]$.

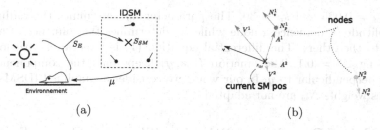

Fig. 2. a) An IDSM works in the sensorimotor space of the agent. According to the current sensorimotor state S_{SM} and to the various nodes of the IDSM, it produces commands μ that control the agent behavior in its environment. S_E is the complete state of the environment. b) An IDSM is built from a collection of nodes N^i which influence the agent dynamics with a velocity V^i and attraction A^i components.

As illustrated on Fig. 2b the influence of each node consists of two components: an attraction component A^i and a velocity component V^i. These components impact the agent's velocity, the attraction component seeking to attract the agent towards its position N_p and the velocity component seeking to align the agent's velocity with N_v. The amplitude of the components is modulated by the distance of the agent to the node (the closer the higher) and by the weight of the node N_w (Eqs. (1)–(8)). The velocity command μ of the agent, normalized in the sensorimotor space SM, is given by[1]:

$$\frac{d\mu}{dt} = \begin{cases} \frac{V(\boldsymbol{x}_{SM}) + A(\boldsymbol{x}_{SM})}{\phi_N(\boldsymbol{x}_{SM})} & \text{if } \phi_N(\boldsymbol{x}_{SM}) > \epsilon \\ 0 & \text{otherwise} \end{cases} \tag{1}$$

$$V(\boldsymbol{x}_{SM}) = \sum_N \omega d_N . [\boldsymbol{N}_v]^\mu \tag{2}$$

$$A(\boldsymbol{x}_{SM}) = \sum_N \omega d_N . [\Gamma(\boldsymbol{N}_p - \boldsymbol{x}_{SM}, \boldsymbol{N}_v)]^\mu, \tag{3}$$

$$\phi_N(\boldsymbol{x}_{SM}) = \sum_N \omega d_N \tag{4}$$

$$\omega d_N = \omega(N_w) . d(\boldsymbol{N}_p, \boldsymbol{x}_{SM}) \tag{5}$$

$$\omega(N_w) = \frac{2}{1 + \exp(-k_\omega N_w)} \tag{6}$$

$$d(\boldsymbol{N}_p, \boldsymbol{x}_{SM}) = \frac{2}{1 + \exp(k_d \|\boldsymbol{N}_p - \boldsymbol{x}_{SM}\|^2)} \tag{7}$$

$$\Gamma(\boldsymbol{a}, \boldsymbol{N}_v) = \begin{cases} \boldsymbol{a} - \left\langle \boldsymbol{a}, \frac{\boldsymbol{N}_v}{\|\boldsymbol{N}_v\|} \right\rangle \frac{\boldsymbol{N}_v}{\|\boldsymbol{N}_v\|} & \text{if } \boldsymbol{N}_v \neq 0 \\ \boldsymbol{a} & \text{otherwise} \end{cases} \tag{8}$$

---

[1] Vectors are depicted in boldface (*e.g.* $\boldsymbol{v}$) or between square brackets (*e.g.* $[f, 0, 0]$), $[\boldsymbol{v}]^\mu$ is the projection of $\boldsymbol{v}$ on the motor dimensions, and $[\boldsymbol{v}]^\sigma$ is the projection on the sensor dimensions. Furthermore, $\mathbb{1}$ is the vector where all components are 1 and $\langle .., .. \rangle$ denotes the dot product.

where $k_\omega = 0.025$ and $k_d = 30$. The parameter k_d determines the radius and the amplitude of influence a node while k_ω determines the influence of a node relative to the others. The differential equation (1) is integrated with forward Euler using $\Delta t = 0.1$. The function $\Gamma(x, y)$ keeps only the component of x which is perpendicular to y. In our work, we consider a simplified IDSM where the nodes weights N_w are not adapted.

4   Model of Pseudo-conditioning Through Generalization of Nodes

Pseudo-conditioning is a form of learning allowing a behavioral response to a given stimulus to be expressed as response to another stimulus. As such, it is a kind of generalization of this response to other stimuli. The following mechanism aims at extending the response dynamics from one sensory dimension of the IDSM to another. We propose to equip every node with an adaptive mask which determines the extend of the influence of a node in the sensorimotor space. Although initially specific to the sensorimotor state of the node, pseudo-conditioning adapts the mask to widen the influence of that node. This adaptation allows the node to become "responsive" to sensorimotor states in which it was not previously responsive.

For the experiments on this model, there are three dimensions in the sensorimotor space SM: one motor dimension and two sensor dimensions: sensor $s1$ perceiving the unconditioned stimulus US and sensor $s2$ perceiving the conditioned stimulus CS. The nodes in the sensorimotor space SM are shown on Fig. 3a, without representation of the second sensor dimension for simplicity (we only plot the subspace $m \times s_1$, which is independent on the specific s_2 value). The two nodes are defined by:

- $N_1 = \langle p = [0.5, 1, 0], v = [-0.5, 0, 0], w = 0 \rangle$,
- $N_2 = \langle p = [0, 0, 0], v = [0.5, 0, 0], w = 0 \rangle$.

Our objective with these two nodes is to produce a default behavior of moving upward without stimuli and downward when the unconditioned stimulus US (perceived by sensor $s1$) is on. Since conditioned stimulus CS is neutral, the dynamics is unchanged on the dimension of sensor $s2$. Thus the dynamics boils down to two blocks, one above the plan $s1 = 0.5$, with the downward behavior activated by the US, and the other below the plan $s1 = 0.5$, with the default upward behavior.

We add a mask component N_m of dimension K with components in $[0, 1]$ to every node N. N_m is used to compute a virtual *masked* distance dm, between the node N and the agent sensorimotor position x_{SM}:

$$dm(N_p, x_{SM}) = \frac{2}{1 + \exp(k_d \| N_p - x_{SM} \|_m^2)} \tag{9}$$

$$\| N_p - x_{SM} \|_m^2 = \sum_i N_{m_i}{}^2 (N_{p_i} - x_{SM_i})^2 \tag{10}$$

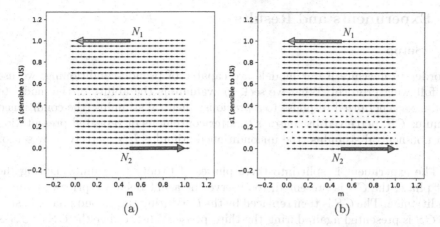

Fig. 3. Motor command variation $(d\mu)$ in the sensorimotor subspace $m \times s_1$ of an IDSM with two nodes used in pseudo-conditioning experiments. Large arrows are nodes, with the base on the N_p and the length of the arrow depicting N_v. a) with a mask $N_m = [1, 1, 1]$. b) with a mask $N_m = [0.5, 0.5, 0.5]$ for N_1 leading to its stronger influence over N_2.

This distance dm, which artificially decrease the sensorimotor distance between the agent and the nodes, is used instead of d in Eq. 2.

It follows that for a given dimension i, the most specific the associated mask component can be is $N_{m\,i} = 1$ (*i.e.* the distance between $N_{p\,i}$ and $x_{SM\,i}$ is fully taken into account). And the most general the associated mask component can be is $N_{m\,i} = 0$ (*i.e.* the distance between $N_{p\,i}$ and $x_{SM\,i}$ is completely ignored, as if $N_{p\,i} = x_{SM\,i}$).

A node starts with its mask equal to $\mathbb{1}$, the most specific possible. Then the mask is modified following:

$$f_{gen} = (\sqrt{K^\sigma} - \|[x_{SM}]^\sigma - [N_p]^\sigma\|)\beta_m \omega d_{mN} \qquad (11)$$

$$\frac{\partial N_m}{\partial t}(x_{SM}, t) = \gamma_m \cdot \mathbb{1} - f_{gen} \cdot N_m \qquad (12)$$

Parameters β_m and γ_m adjust respectively the generalization and the specialization of the masks and are set to $\beta_m = 3$ and $\gamma_m = 0.05$. Each of the mask components is kept in $[0, 1]$.

Thus, the smaller the masked distance between a node N and the sensorimotor position of the agent x_{SM}, the more the mask of the node N_m is decreased (and so becomes generalized). Specialization (*i.e.* increase) of the mask occurs slightly over time. Figure 3b shows the modification of the subspace $m \times s_1$ dynamics when the mask of node N_1 is generalized to $N_m = [0.5, 0.5, 0.5]$. The block of the default behavior is partly reduced to a quarter of ellipsoid with N_2 as its center.

5 Experiments and Results

5.1 Setup

In order to measure if our models are capable of pseudo-conditioning, we use the following protocol. What we seek to evaluate is the ability of the model to produce a generalized response to a previously neutral stimulus (the conditioned stimulus CS, perceived by sensor $s2$), after continuous or repeated presentation of a non-neutral stimulus (the unconditioned stimulus US, perceived by sensor $s1$).

The experiment is split into three phases of twenty time units. During the first phase, the CS is presented, to observe the agent behavior prior to pseudo-conditioning. The CS is then replaced by the US during the second phase. Lastly, the CS is presented again during the third phase. When either the CS or US is active, its value is set to 1. To limit the differences in experimental conditions, at the beginning of each phase, the agent is reset to a null velocity starting position ($x_E = \dot{x}_E = \ddot{x}_E = 0$) and a sensorimotor state $x_{SM} = [0.5, 0, 0]$. Here, the choice of forcing the sensor value to 0 is made to have identical initial conditions between phases, in particular to compare the first and third phases. This can be interpreted as the insertion of a time unit without stimulus between each phase. As explained in Sect. 4, the IDSM is modified accordingly.

In a given experiment, the stimulation follows one of the four patterns below. Note that for every experiment, all the stimulation (whether CS or US) follow the same pattern.

- **(a)**: continuous stimulus;
- **(b)**: repetitions of 3 time units on/1 time unit off;
- **(c)**: repetitions of 2 time units on/2 time units off;
- **(d)**: repetitions of 1 time unit on/3 time units off.

5.2 Results

The results can be seen on Figs. 4 and 5. For the control agent, the default behavior (upward motion) is observed during the first and third phase, with presentation of the CS. During the second phase, with presentation of the US, a response behavior (downward motion) is observed.

Each figure is composed of four subplots, one for each stimulation pattern. Each subplot has the same layout. The top plot displays the learning agent trajectory and the control agent trajectory. The second plot from the top gives information regarding perception of both stimuli by the agent. The third plot from the top shows the normalized motor value of the agent in the sensorimotor space (the first component of x_{SM}), and the velocity command μ. In order not to overload the figure unnecessarily, the last plot shows the evolution of the nodes masks reduced only to their motor component (the mask of other dimensions, i.e. first sensor sensible to the US and second sensor sensible to the CS, having exactly the same values).

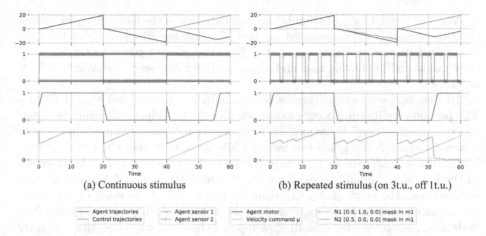

(a) Continuous stimulus   (b) Repeated stimulus (on 3t.u., off 1t.u.)

—— Agent trajectories   ·····+ Agent sensor 1   —— Agent motor   ····· N1 [0.5, 1.0, 0.0] mask in m1
—— Control trajectories   ·····+ Agent sensor 2   ···· Velocity command μ   —— N2 [0.5, 0.0, 0.0] mask in m1

Fig. 4. Results for activation patterns (a) and (b). From top to bottom: agents trajectories, sensory activation, motor command and masks. After time 40, the stronger generalisation of N_1 compared to N_2 (see masks plot), leads to pseudo-conditionned behavior of the agent, seen as "learning" to move downward when the CS is perceived.

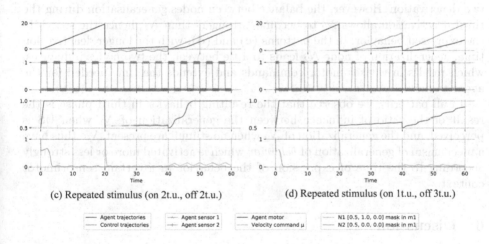

(c) Repeated stimulus (on 2t.u., off 2t.u.)   (d) Repeated stimulus (on 1t.u., off 3t.u.)

—— Agent trajectories   ·····+ Agent sensor 1   —— Agent motor   ····· N1 [0.5, 1.0, 0.0] mask in m1
—— Control trajectories   ·····+ Agent sensor 2   ···· Velocity command μ   —— N2 [0.5, 0.0, 0.0] mask in m1

Fig. 5. Results for activation patterns (c) and (d) where the activation time equal or superior to the deactivation time. From top to bottom: agents trajectories, sensory activation, motor command and masks. These patterns highlight that in phase 2 the generalization of masks leads to equal contributions of the 2 nodes and so, to the immobility of the agent. In phase 3, masks values strongly inhibit the expression of the moving down behavior.

With all the patterns of stimulation, the behavior of the learning agent during the third phase (*i.e.* presentation of the CS following presentation of the US) is a mix between its behaviors of the first and second phases, starting as a "US influenced" behavior and ending as a "CS influenced" behavior (default behavior).

In Fig. 4a, pseudo-conditioning has no influence in first and second phases. The pseudo-conditioning occurs as expected in the last phase, allowing the agent to experiment a "new" behavior (*i.e.* temporarily modified dynamics in the sensorimotor space SM): going downward while perceiving only the CS. The evolution of the masks shows that only the node N_1, responsible for the response to the US, is maximally generalized. At all times, the mask of N_1 is more generalized than the mask of N_2. Constant specialization of the mask of N_1 allows the default behavior to be expressed again at the end of the third phase. The node N_2, responsible for default downward behavior, only generalizes slightly and temporarily following the reset of the agent at the start of each phase.

In all repeated patterns (see Figs. 4b and 5), the mask of node N_2 generalizes each time there is no active stimulus. In the pattern (**b**), with the shorter deactivation time between stimulus activation, the learning agent in the second phase does not respond to deactivation of the stimulus since N_1 stays more generalized than N_2 and behaves as if the US was activated continuously during the first two deactivation. However, the balance between nodes generalisation during the third deactivation allows N_2 to become "stronger" than N_1, hence the switch in the expressed behavior. In the patterns (**c**) and (**d**), with the longer deactivation time, generalization of node N_2 leads to a tie between the two nodes influences, which results in weaker motor commands and extends the time needed for the agent to move.

In all patterns, we observe that the resulting behavior in third phase is the result of the ratio of influence between the generalization of N_1 when US is perceived, and the generalization of N_2 when no stimuli are present. We thus have a mechanism of generalization of *behavior* which is activated more or less strongly according to the time of expression of the behavior in a certain sensorimotor context.

6   Discussion

We have proposed a model to provide pseudo-conditioning (with nodes masks) to an agent based on the IDSM. Since IDSM is a conceptual model, our model is easier to read than models based on neural networks.

The generalization of the nodes through the masks results in a transfer of the behavioral response from the stimulus initially triggering it to other stimuli. Nevertheless, our model also allows for the generalization of masks of nodes which are "linked" to no stimuli (sensori components of the position of such nodes are all set to 0). We do not know if it makes sense from the point of view of biology, since by definition pseudo-conditioning occurs after a stimulus has induced a response behavior.

The mask mechanism we propose for pseudo-conditioning leads to a widespread generalization: once a node is fully generalized it impacts the behavior of the agent equally everywhere in the sensorimotor space. This generalized behavior is only counterbalanced by the existence of other nodes (through the usual IDSM equations). This "competition" between nodes may not be sufficiently strong to preserve other existing behaviors. In such a case, it may be needed to introduce a specialization mechanism shaping the sensorimotor regions where the node should actually generalize, or restrict the dimensions on which to do so. For example, specialization could be triggered by the discrepancy between the component N_v of node N and the last movement of the agent in the sensorimotor space SM, since such difference would mean that the motor command stored in N is not in line with the current environment. Adding another non-associative learning like habituation (*i.e.* inhibition of the response to a repeatedly presented stimulus) could also help prevent over-generalization by minimising the impact of the repetitions of low-intensity stimuli. We started to work on those non-associative learning [9]. Moreover the dual-process theory (see [10]) and the behavioral homeostasis theory (see [6,8]) are works studying how non-associative learning fit together and what could be the impacts of such association.

Alternatively to the masks model, even in the context of the IDSM, we may have proposed other mechanisms allowing the same pseudo-conditioning as experimented in this paper. As the aim is to adapt the sensorimotor region of influence of a node, we could have simply defined and adapted one k_d per node, which would have resulted in similar results. However, the mask mechanism is strictly more general in the sense that it allows (although not illustrated here) to generalize along certain dimensions while still being specific along others.

Note that the results of our experiments depend strongly on many parameters. The number of nodes, their positions, the various IDSM parameters are very inter-dependant and were carefully chosen. We considered a very simple IDSM for experimenting the mask mechanism and more complex settings with more nodes and more complex behaviors remain to be studied. In addition, the original IDSM model includes an evolution of the weights and the generation of new nodes which were here removed to ease the analysis. The idea is that the mask mechanism should allow the agent to experiment known behaviors in unknown situations, which will eventually be memorized by the creation of new nodes.

To conclude, the presented mechanisms could be seen as a first step to allow a reflex-based agent to "experiment" different behaviors in various situations depending on its recent experience. Further studies are needed to explore to which extend such non-associative mechanisms allow for an agent to extend its behavioral repertoire. Our work is a proof of concept since we considered very simple environments and we still need to explore the applicability of these mechanisms in more complex and challenging environments.

References

1. Alex, J.Y., Rankin, C.H.: Nonassociative learning in invertebrates. In: The Oxford Handbook of Invertebrate Neurobiology. Oxford University Press, Oxford (2017)
2. Byrne, J.H., Hawkins, R.D.: Cold Spring Harb. Perspect. Biol. Cold Spring Harbor perspectives in biology **7**(5) (2015)
3. Damper, R.I., French, R.L., Scutt, T.W.: ARBIB: an autonomous robot based on inspirations from biology. Robot. Autonom Syst. **31**(4), 247–274 (2000)
4. Dussutour, A.: Learning in single cell organisms. Biochem. Biophys. Res. Commun. **564**, 92–102 (2021)
5. Egbert, M.D., Barandiaran, X.E.: Modeling habits as self-sustaining patterns of sensorimotor behavior. Front. Hum. Neurosci. **8**, 590 (2014)
6. Eisenstein, E.M., Eisenstein, D.L., Sarma, J.S., Knapp, H., Smith, J.C.: Some new speculative ideas about the "behavioral homeostasis theory" as to how the simple learned behaviors of habituation and sensitization improve organism survival throughout phylogeny. Commun. Integrat. Biol. **5**(3), 233–239 (2012)
7. Eisenstein, E., Brunder, D., Blair, H.: Habituation and sensitization in an neural cell: some comparative and theoretical considerations. Neurosci. Biobehav. Rev. **6**(2), 183–194 (1982)
8. Eisenstein, E., Eisenstein, D., Smith, J.C.: The evolutionary significance of habituation and sensitization across phylogeny: A behavioral homeostasis model. Integrat. Physiol. Behav. Sci. **36**(4), 251–265 (2001)
9. Gillard, T., Dutech, A., Fix, J.: Non-associative learning and the Iterant Deformable Sensorimotor Medium. Research Report 9472, Inria Nancy - Grand Est, May 2022
10. Groves, P.M., Thompson, R.F.: Habituation: a dual-process theory. Psychol. Rev. **77**(5), 419 (1970)
11. Hawkins, R.D.: A biologically based computational model for several simple forms of learning. In: Hawkins, R.D., Bower, G.H. (eds.) Computational Models of Learning in Simple Neural Systems, Psychology of Learning and Motivation, vol. 23, pp. 65–108. Academic Press (1989)
12. Hawkins, R.D., Kandel, E.R.: Is there a cell-biological alphabet for simple forms of learning? Psychol. Rev. **91**(3), 375 (1984)
13. Hong, Q., Yan, R., Wang, C., Sun, J.: Memristive circuit implementation of biological nonassociative learning mechanism and its applications. IEEE Trans. Biomed. Circ. Syst. **14**(5), 1036–1050 (2020)
14. Kimble, G.A.: Hilgard and Marquis Conditioning and learning, 2nd edn. Prentice-Hall, Englewood Clifs (1961)
15. Kotseruba, I., Tsotsos, J.K.: 40 years of cognitive architectures: core cognitive abilities and practical applications. Artif. Intell. Rev. **53**(1), 17–94 (2018). https://doi.org/10.1007/s10462-018-9646-y
16. McSweeney, F.K., Murphy, E.S.: Sensitization and habituation regulate reinforcer effectiveness. Neurobiol. Learn. Memory **92**(2), 189–198 (2009)
17. Novianto, R., Johnston, B., Williams, M.-A.: Habituation and sensitisation learning in ASMO cognitive architecture. In: Herrmann, G., Pearson, M.J., Lenz, A., Bremner, P., Spiers, A., Leonards, U. (eds.) ICSR 2013. LNCS (LNAI), vol. 8239, pp. 249–259. Springer, Cham (2013). https://doi.org/10.1007/978-3-319-02675-6_25
18. Perry, C.J., Barron, A.B., Cheng, K.: Invertebrate learning and cognition: relating phenomena to neural substrate. Wiley Interdiscip. Rev. Cogn. Sci. **4**(5), 561–582 (2013)

19. Rescorla, R.A.: A theory of Pavlovian conditioning: variations in the effectiveness of reinforcement and nonreinforcement. In: Classical conditioning: Current Research and Theory, pp. 64–99. Appleton-Century-Crofts (1972)
20. Stanley, J.C.: Computer simulation of a model of habituation. Nature **261**(5556), 146–148 (1976)
21. Weng, J.: On developmental mental architectures. Neurocomputing **70**(13–15), 2303–2323 (2007)

Investigating a Minimal Categorical Perception Task with a Node-Based Sensorimotor Map

Felix M. G. Woolford[(✉)] and Matthew D. Egbert

School of Computer Science, University of Auckland, Auckland, New Zealand
fmg.woolford@gmail.com

Abstract. We present a variation on a classic evolutionary robotics experiment using an unorthodox controller model, a Node-Based Sensorimotor Map (NB-SMM) – a stateless, deterministic, continuous-time controller which directly maps an animat's sensorimotor state to a change-in-motor-state command. Our investigation illustrates how such a simple model can be used in an evolutionary robotics context in place of a more typical neural network model, but offers its own set of practical and theoretical points of difference. Previous work has likened the role of the internal state of a recurrent neural network to the role of the brain in the brain-body-environment system. It is often assumed that in order to produce adaptive behaviour, our control systems require some internal state which modulates the dynamics of the animat's sensorimotor loop. Our results challenge this received view by demonstrating that a stateless controller can also perform tasks that may be considered cognitive.

1 Introduction

A key benefit of the evolutionary robotics approach is the ability to strip away all but the most essential requirements of a model of cognitive behaviour. Seth's animats, for example, illustrated a counterpoint to the assumption that an internal arbitration mechanism was required for action selection, by presenting a model with only a "set of independent sensorimotor links, and the influence of some internal state" [7]. What exactly is the role and nature of such an internal state though? How does it relate to the role of knowledge and representation in sensorimotor perception [8]? One way to clarify this is to investigate models which have no internal state whatsoever and evaluate their capabilities. To this end, we use a stateless controller model to revisit a previous investigation of a minimal categorical perception behaviour [3].

Node-Based Sensorimotor maps (NB-SMM) are a class of continuous-time controller models which operate by deterministically mapping the instantaneous sensorimotor state of an animat to a change-in-motor state output. The defining feature of an NB-SMM is that the parameters of the mapping function are determined by a limited number of *nodes* in a sensorimotor space. A benefit of the node-based approach is that the process of generating and adjusting these nodes can be altered to allow targeted investigation of particular aspects of cognitive behaviour. One approach is for nodes to be generated dynamically while the controlled animat goes about its activity. These dynamic NB-SMMs are *stateful* – the parameters of the nodes and mapping function change in response to the model's internal state. Alternatively, nodes may be placed through some optimisation process while the animat is offline. These static NB-SMMs are *stateless* and always give the same output for a particular sensorimotor input. Varieties of dynamic NB-SMM models have been used to explore habit-based behaviour [4,5] and goal-oriented behaviour [10]. Our previous work with a static NB-SMM enumerated all possible configurations of 1- and 2-node NB-SMM's and demonstrated that even those minimal systems provided a foundation of functional behaviour [9].

In this investigation, we present an example of how a simple, static NB-SMM can be used in the context of an evolutionary robotics-style experiment. We then compare the behaviour produced by the NB-SMM-controlled animats with animats controlled by stateful continuous-time recurrent neural networks (CTRNNs) evolved to perform the same behaviour.

2 Model

2.1 NB-SMM

We use the same kind of NB-SMM that we defined in [9], which in turn uses the same functions to determine a change-in-motor-state output as a related *iterant deformable sensorimotor medium model* [4,5].

An NB-SMM generates a map in sensorimotor space, which is a construct which defines all possible sensory and motor states of an animat, with each spatial dimension representing a single motor or sensor variable of the animat. This map defines a change-in-motor-state output for every possible sensorimotor state, and thus the controller operates by continuously outputting new change-in-motor-state commands as the animat's sensorimotor state changes. Crucially, the controller has no internal state which modulates over time the relationship between sensorimotor state and output. In other words, the only relevant property in determining the output behaviour at any moment is the immediate state of the simulated "body". Such a system is in contrast to a *stateful* controller such as a CTRNN-based system, in which the state of internal hidden neurons typically influence the relationship between input and output.

The mapping itself is defined in terms of *nodes* which are localized in sensorimotor space. Each node has a *position* in sensorimotor space, around which its influence is strongest, and a *velocity* component which determines the direction and speed of its influence on the change-in-motor-state of the controlled animat.[1] Finally each node has a *weight* which determines its relative influence compared to other nodes. Thus each node can be expressed as a tuple $N = \langle \vec{p}, \vec{v}, w \rangle$

---

[1] Note that this "velocity" of the node does not refer to a rate at which the node moves through sensorimotor space – its position is fixed.

This particular architecture has been chosen for the sake of consistency with related work, but the motivation for its specific design principles is of limited relevance here – further discussion and explanation of the following functions may be found in [5] and [9]. The key point is that the nodes are used determine the mapping via the following function:

$$\frac{d\mu}{dt} = f(\vec{r}) = \tau \frac{\sum_N \left((\omega(N_w) d(N_{\vec{p}}, \vec{r}))^2 \cdot (N_{\vec{v}} + \Gamma(N_{\vec{p}} - \vec{r}, N_{\vec{v}}))^{\vec{\mu}} \right)}{\sum_N (\omega(N_w) d(N_{\vec{p}}, \vec{r}))} \tag{1}$$

which itself is composed of the following:

$$d(\vec{x}, \vec{y}) = \frac{2}{1 + \exp(k_d ||\vec{x} - \vec{y}||^2)} \tag{2}$$

$$\Gamma(\vec{a}, \vec{V}) = \vec{a} - (\vec{a} \cdot \frac{\vec{V}}{||\vec{V}||}) \frac{\vec{V}}{||\vec{V}||} \tag{3}$$

$$\omega(N_w) = \frac{2}{1 + \exp(-k_\omega N_w)} \tag{4}$$

In these functions, $N_{\vec{p}}$ is the position in SM-space for each node, $N_{\vec{v}}$ is the velocity for each node, N_w is the weight of the node, and $\vec{r}$ is the animat's current position in SM-space. The superscript μ in Eq. 1 indicates taking only the motor component of the vector. The fixed parameters k_d and k_ω respectively scale the range of influence of all nodes in SM-space and the influence of node weight. τ scales the output relative to the animat's velocity.

2.2   Experiment Setup

The NB-SMMs are evolved to guide a animat through a task involving distinguishing between two curves, one classed as "narrow" and one as "wide". The animat must demonstrate its ability to distinguish the curves' widths by consistently stopping at the peak of the designated target curve (i.e. always atop the narrow curve or always atop wide). The challenge to

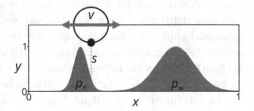

Fig. 1. Illustration of the task environment.

this task is that the sensor only detects the distance to the point of the curve immediately in front of it, and thus a particular sensory state is associated with multiple points in the environment, over both curves. The animat must therefore employ an exploratory strategy over time in order to distinguish between the objects, which provides an interesting challenge for a stateless controller.

The experimental setup is illustrated in Fig. 1. The environment consists of a animat in a two-dimensional arena with a stimulus in the shape of two bell-shaped curves. The arena has a width and height of size 1 and periodic boundaries on the horizontal axis. The stimulus a shape such that

$$y = \max \left(\exp \left(\frac{(x - p_n)^2}{2\sigma_n^2} \right), \exp \left(\frac{(x - p_w)^2}{2\sigma_w^2} \right) \right) \tag{5}$$

where p_n and p_w are the x-positions of the centers of the narrower and wider curves and $\pm\sigma_n$ and $\pm\sigma_w$ are the maxima of the function's derivative for the narrower and wider curves. During the evolutionary process $\sigma_n = 0.03$ and $\sigma_w = 0.08$, but evolved animats are subsequently exposed to a range of widths. In each trial p_n and p_w are set randomly, with a minimum distance of 0.3 between the two to avoid significant overlap.

In each trial the animat is initially positioned with its sensor at $y = 1$ and with a random x-position. It can move along the x-axis with a velocity of v units per second such that $-0.25 \leq v \leq 0.25$. Its sensor is activated as the distance d between it and the shape at the point directly below the animat, such that its state is

$$s = 1 - d \tag{6}$$

This means that the animat's sensor state is at its maximum when it is at exactly the peak of either of the curves. The animat is controlled by an NB-SMM with a two-dimensional sensorimotor space corresponding to the single motor and single sensor. The motor state μ of the animat corresponds to its velocity but is scaled such that its value is on the interval $[0, 1]$, i.e. $\mu = 0.5$ corresponds to $v = 0$.

The parameters of the NB-SMM are defined through a genome which is optimised via a microbial genetic algorithm [6] with a population size of 100 evaluated over 220 generations with a deme size (a property specific to the microbial GA variant) of 15. The NB-SMM has 11 nodes, and the position, velocity, and weight of each node are defined in the evolutionary genome for a total of 5 genes per node. Additionally the k_d and k_ω parameters are also defined in the genome. The τ parameter is fixed at $\tau = 10$. This requires a genome with $5 * 11 + 2 = 57$ genes to be evolved, where each gene is a 64-bit float from the range $[0, 1)$. The genes for k_d and k_ω are scaled so that the parameter values are $2 \leq k_d \leq 20$ and $0.01 \leq k_\omega \leq 0.05$, and node weights are scaled so that $-300 \leq w \leq 600$. Position and velocity genes do not need scaling.

We present results for variations of the task where either the wide or narrow curve is the one that should be approached (hereafter the *approach*-curve) while the other is avoided (*avoid*-curve), and we refer to these different tasks as the wide-approach and narrow-approach variants. Each genome is tested in 108 trials lasting for 40 s, with the initial conditions of animat starting position and velocity selected systematically across their ranges. Trials are evaluated with a fitness function which calculates the root-mean-square error between the animat's position and the peak of the *approach* curve (either p_n or p_w), averaged over the last eight seconds of each trial, and then averaged over those 108 per-trial fitnesses.

For the last 20 generations, the fitness function is adjusted such that the root-mean-square error is also multiplied by the animat's velocity. Simulations were run using Euler integration with a step size of 0.01.

2.3 CTRNN Comparison

We compare the results of the NB-SMM-controlled animats with some that are controlled by minimal CTRNNs evolved to solve the same task. An explanation of CTRNNs and their use may be found in [1]. Our CTRNNs are 2-neuron networks where the first neuron receives an input and the second neuron's state is mapped to determine the animat's motor state. The first neuron is connected to itself, and the second is connected to itself and to the first. The input is the animat's absolute sensor value. Note that differs from the version of the experiment presented in [3] where the CTRNN input is the time-derivative of the sensor. Ranges for biases, connection weights, and time constants are $[-32, 32]$, $[-16, 16]$, and $[0.5, 10]$ respectively. Apart from the use of CTRNNs, the experimental setup is consistent with that used with the NB-SMMs, however as the optimisation process for these experiments proved more difficult, we doubled the population and deme sizes, and the number of generations.

3 Results

3.1 NB-SMM Results

An effective solution (fitness less than 0.008) was found in all 10 runs for each task variant. Wide-approach variants consistently had a superior fitness to the narrow-approach variants (0.007 versus 0.004 average fitness). All evolved NB-SMM-controlled animats display a more or less consistent behavioural strategy: When approaching either curve from one particular side (either left or right) the animat will turn back before reaching the peak, and when approaching from the other side it will pass over the peak of the *avoid* curve or come to stop at the peak of the *approach* curve. Figures 2 and 3 present visualisations of an example solution's sensorimotor map and the phase spaces of the coupled system of the animat and its environment. Specific trajectories are highlighted on each figure for a single trial beginning from the initial conditions ($x = 0.9, \mu = 0.75$). In the sensorimotor trajectories, there are several overlapping points from which the trajectory progresses in different ways from a single state. This is possible because there are multiple states in the coupled system which produce the same sensorimotor state – when the animat is in particular positions over both the wide and narrow curve. The challenge of the task of course is that the animat must respond to these different environmental contexts appropriately, despite having a controller which reacts only to the sensorimotor state.

How do the evolved NB-SMMs solve the task? Essentially, they exploit the regularity that for any given non-zero motor state, the rate of change for the sensor state is greater as the animat passes over the narrow curve compared

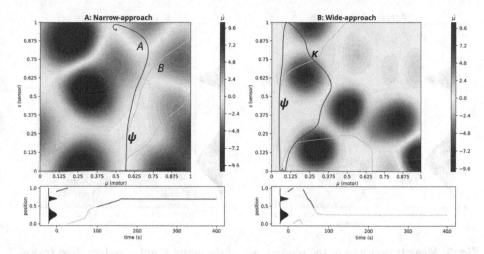

Fig. 2. Visualisations of the sensorimotor maps generated by two example NB-SMMs. For each, a sensorimotor trajectory is shown for a single trial in which the animat performs the task correctly, and a time series plot of the animats' position during each is shown below. These same trajectories are also highlighted in Fig. 3 in the coupled systems' phase spaces. ψ, κ, A, B are discussed in the text. Note that the dark green trajectory indicates that the animat is nearer to the narrow curve than the wide. (Color figure online)

to the wide curve. In Fig. 2 this can be seen occurring after points ψ. At each ψ we have two instances where the animat is in the same sensorimotor state, but is interacting with different curves. Furthermore the animat is in a similar position relative to each peak (i.e. to left of both in Fig. 2A, and to the right of both in 2B). In other words, the divergence of the two trajectories from state ψ onwards is entirely a consequence of the way in which the animat interacts with different-width curves. Contrast this to point κ on Fig. 2B, where the two segments of the trajectory intersect again, but the animat is on the left side of the narrow peak but on the right side of the wide peak, meaning that the difference in sensorimotor response following κ is primarily due to the contrast between moving toward a curve's peak as opposed to moving away.

In the figures, the part of the trajectory associated with the *approach*-curve continues to approach the stable point after ψ, never intersecting with the *avoid* part again in the same way. Since the controller is stateless, it follows that the process of discriminating narrow and wide curves occurs entirely after point ψ. This is not to say that all preceding behaviour is redundant, nor the other parts of the map, which do not directly influence this aspect of the behaviour. We find that all evolved animats display a general strategy in which the animat establishes a particular sensorimotor state, (mostly) regardless of initial conditions, and from that state takes advantage of the different environmental sensory response while passing over the different curves. This can be seen in Fig. 3, where trajectories from many initial conditions rapidly tend to converge.

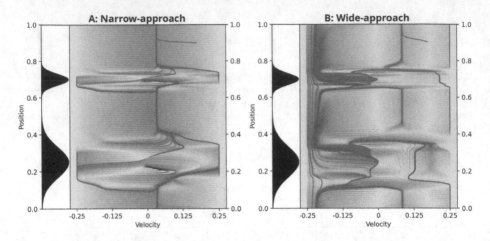

Fig. 3. Many trajectories in the phase space of the entire coupled system. Red trajectories indicate that the trajectory approaches a state which corresponds with successful task performance, while blue indicates a failure. The green trajectories match those in Fig. 2. (Color figure online)

As for the process of discriminating between the curves after ψ, how does this work within the constraints of an NB-SMM, which by definition always gives the same motor output for a particular sensorimotor state? This process is illustrated by the annotated points in Fig. 2. At a given point, $\frac{d\mu}{dt}$ is consistent regardless of the environmental context, but $\frac{ds}{dt}$ varies depending on the environmental context. Therefore even as the animat makes the same motor actions, so long as $\frac{d\mu}{dt} \neq 0$, from a particular sensorimotor state ψ, a trajectory over a fixed time interval will arrive at different points in sensorimotor space, A and B, depending on the shape of the curve. Further, if the mapping is such that the animat always reaches state ψ, or at least approximates it, then it is guaranteed that the animat will only reach state A when it is over the narrow curve, and state B when it is over the wide curve. Ultimately, the NB-SMM's mapping can take advantage of this by producing different motor activity for states A and B. As appropriate, one of these states can lead to the end of the *approach* part of the behaviour (i.e. come to a stop), while the other can lead to the *avoid* part of the behaviour (i.e. move away from the current curve). To take advantage of these regularities, a sensorimotor map that can solve this task must have two parts: One part of the mapping ensures that there is a region of sensorimotor space such that when the animat's sm-state is in that region it will move to stop at the peak of the currently sensed curve; The rest of the mapping ensures that the animat's sensorimotor state will only enter that region in the correct context for the given task. As seen in Fig. 3, there is a caveat to this solution, in which the animat will fail to solve the task if it begins with initial conditions which violate the aforementioned guarantee about states A and B.

Although the general strategy is consistent, we observe a fundamental difference between the two task variants in the behaviour which occurs after ψ. In the wide-approach case, the animat immediately decelerates toward an oscillation around $v = 0$. In the narrow-approach case however, the animat first accelerates before decelerating. These differences can be seen in Fig. 2 and are consistent across all evolved solutions. This highlights the peculiarities of the relationship between sensorimotor maps and the specific dynamics of each task variant. Why does this behavioural distinction develop? As we have established, the total change in motor state will always be greater in the case of passing over the wider curve compared to passing the narrower. In the wide-approach variation, this means that an effective animat can simply decelerate from its ψ state until it approaches $v = 0$ around the same moment that it reaches the peak of the curve. The same map will cause the animat to pass over the top of the narrow curve before it has reached $v = 0$, as occurs in Fig. 2B. In contrast, the narrow-approach variation uses an acceleration to distinguish the curves. When it passes over the narrow curve it accelerates slightly, but then decelerates as it passes over the top and eventually reverses before coming to a stop. When the same animat passes over the wide curve however, it accelerates more, such that it avoids the region of sensorimotor state where the mapping causes it to decelerate and double back. That the narrow-approach variation requires both an acceleration and a deceleration suggests that there is an added degree of complexity to the narrow-approach variation compared to the wide-approach.

3.2 Categorical Perception

The NB-SMMs are only exposed to a particular pair of curve widths during evolution. However the evolved animats also display an ability to respond to various

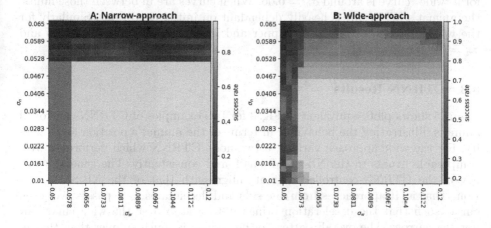

Fig. 4. Frequency with which the animat ends a trial above the approach-curve's peak for different pairings of curve. Each pairing is systematically evaluated across 900 different initial conditions.

pairings of widths, tested between $0.01 < \sigma_N < 0.065$ and $0.05 < \sigma_W < 0.12$. This ability produces emergent categories of "wide" and "narrow" curves defined in terms of how the animats respond to each. The boundaries of these categories are not objective, but rather they vary from animat to animat depending on the precise dynamics of each map. Figure 4 illustrate the fitness of narrow-approach and wide-approach animats across a range of width pairings. We can see that there are thresholds within which the animat's task performance is near perfect, but beyond those thresholds there are regions where the animat's fitness is lower but not indicative of complete task-failure. There are two factors which cause the fitness of the animat to drop off past those limits. Firstly, the set of initial conditions which cause the animat to incorrectly stop atop the avoid curve becomes larger. This is because, as the widths become more similar, the deviation between trajectories after ψ become less pronounced, and this means that more initial states fall within the conditions which the NB-SMM has implicitly established as states which should only be reached when over the approach-curve. Eventually the *avoid* curve becomes so similar to the original approach curve that the animat will always stop at the avoid peak if it encounters it first. In the narrow-approach variant, this limit establishes the lower bound of "wide" curves, and similar establishes the upper bound of "narrow" in the wide-approach variant. Secondly, when the *approach* curve width breaches its own limit, the animat will no longer stop at the correct peak. However it will typically still move relatively slowly near the peak and therefore spend a larger amount of time in that area. Therefore depending on initial conditions, the animat is still likely to be near the peak of the approach curve at the end of the trial, but may also have moved away again. These two factors leads to the fuzziness of the success rates outside of the yellow regions of the plot which describe correct behaviour.

We can see that in the example narrow-approach case, the upper limit for a curve to be considered "narrow" is around $\sigma_n = 0.051$, whereas the lower bound for a "wide" curve is around $\sigma_w = 0.06$. When curves are in between those limits, the animat's behaviour is heavily dependant on initial conditions. Similarly for the wide-approach example, the upper and lower bounds are $\sigma_n = 0.045$ and $\sigma_n = 0.056$ respectively.

3.3   CTRNN Results

Figure 5 shows plots equivalent to Fig. 3 for two examples of CTRNN-controlled animats, illustrating the behaviour in terms of the animat's position and velocity. For the wide-approach variant, a two-node CTRNN which performed with comparable fitness to the NB-SMM was found consistently. The general strategy of the CTRNN-controlled animats align with that of the NB-SMM version. That is, it approaches from one side and decelerates as it passes over each curve, such that the deceleration brings it to a stop over the wide curve but not the narrow. The overall pattern of behaviour is much simpler than that of the NB-SMM-controlled animat, with the animat rapidly achieving a maximum leftward-velocity from most initial conditions.

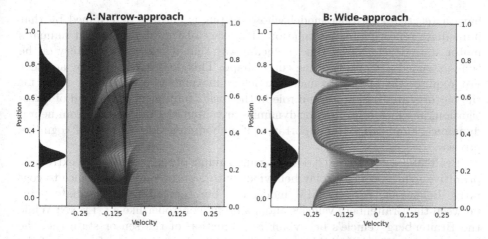

Fig. 5. For two evolved CTRNNs, trajectories of the same variables as plotted in Fig. 3. Note that in these systems there is an additional variable in the internal state of the first neuron, which is not plotted here. In the narrow-approach case, the evolutionary algorithm has failed to find an effective solution.

The narrow-approach variant failed to converge on an effective solution in 10 runs. This failure is consistent with what we observed in the NB-SMM animats regarding the need for both an acceleration and deceleration in the performance of the of the narrow curve variant – resulting in a slightly more complex task – and the relative simplicity of the function approximated by the CTRNN. This result provides a contrast to that in [3], in which a time-derivative of the sensor state is used as the input to a CTRNN with the same topology, producing an effective solution with an oscillatory behaviour.

For the wide-approach variant, Fig. 6 illustrates the performance over various width pairs. Unlike the NB-SMM version, there is essentially no gap between the upper bound of the perceived "narrow" curve and lower bound of the "wide" curve.

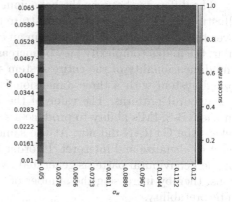

Fig. 6. Fitness results for the CTRNN wide-approach task, equivalent to Fig. 4.

4 Discussion

At first glance, it may seem surprising that the NB-SMM-controlled animats are capable of performing the task. On the one hand, we have a task in which the immediate sensorimotor information that is available to the animat is insufficient to distinguish between the widths of the curve. On the other, we have a reactive controller model whose output is entirely determined by that immediate sensorimotor information. The crux of the matter is that animat's motor state develops over time in such a way that it reflects the history of the time-extended perception of the curve shape. This does not happen by accident – it requires the animat to make particular movements at particular times for the motor state to play a useful role in the task's fulfillment. This kind of investigation, in which sensorimotor dynamics are simulated in isolation from neural dynamics, emphasizes the importance of embodiment in this kind of cognitive process.

Braitenberg's *Vehicles* [2] served as an example of the way in which extremely primitive models could display behaviour with a surprising resemblance to cognitive behaviour. An NB-SMM model can be seen as an intermediate point between the Braitenberg vehicles and a stateful controller like a CTRNN: While the Braitenberg vehicle's behaviour is a function of the sensor state (i.e. the environment); The NB-SMM-controlled animat's behaviour is a function of the sensor and motor state (i.e. environment and body); and the CTRNN-controlled animat's behaviour is a function of the sensor, motor, and internal state (i.e. environment, body, and brain). Exploring the behaviours that are possible with the NB-SMM, and those that are not, is a method for understanding the exact roles of the body and the brain in the context of adaptive behaviour and embodied cognition. Buhrmann, et al. analysed a CTRNN-controlled animat performing another variant of this task [3], and part of their discussion highlighted the role of the internal state of the hidden neuron which causes the system to alternate between an approach regime and an avoid regime. In this context, the controller's internal stayed played a role analogous to a nervous system which modulates the sensorimotor response in accordance with the agent's goal. By the same token, the NB-SMM model can be interpreted as simulating a system which lacks a nervous system, but which nonetheless displays the same goal-oriented property.

The difference between the behaviour of the NB-SMM and CTRNN versions, illustrated in Figs. 3 and 5, demonstrate that the NB-SMM has some advantages over the more typical model, even in an evolutionary robotics context. In particular, the map's complexity may be increased by adding nodes, without increasing the dimensionality of the entire system's state space. Meanwhile, the CTRNN-based system with a three dimensional state space produced relatively simple behavioural patterns. The value of the NB-SMM in this case is demonstrated in the NB-SMM's ability to produce a solution for the narrow-approach variant where the CTRNN did not. At the same time, system's behaviour is relatively easy to visualize and interpret. In order for a CTRNN to match the complexity of the behavioural patterns generated by the NB-SMM it would need more neurons, thereby increasing the number of variables in the system and reducing its interpretability.

Finally, the difference in fitness and behavioural patterns between the two task variants is an unintuitive outcome. Each variant would seem to be simple inversions of each other, with similar performance expected. This is perhaps a misleading aspect of describing the task in functionalist terms such as identifying the curve type and moving to the top of one – it would seem to follow from this that it would be an equivalent process to identify the curve type and move to the top of the other one. However although it is attractive to interpret the behaviour of the animat as first distinguishing the curve type (i.e. moving into a particular sensorimotor state) and then responding appropriately (slowing to a stop or passing over the peak), these delineations only serve to aid the description of what is in practice a single continuous act. Over the course of this act, the sensorimotor dynamics associated both with distinguishing the curves, and with traversing to the peak, are intertwined. The way that the two properties of the task description interact, i.e. which curve to approach, and how a successful approach is measured, appears to have made the wide-approach variant simpler than the other.

A consequence of this in terms of modelling is that seemingly trivial decisions of task specification have the potential to impact the final behaviour of the model, and this raises issues of how abstractions of sensorimotor dynamics affect our ability to extrapolate our results to natural systems. Consider for example the use of wheeled-animat styles of models as abstractions of moving organisms. It is critical to the performance of the two-curves task that the animat be altering its motor speed as it passes over each curve, so that it can use its motor state as a proxy for the time it has spent over the curve. A wheeled-robot style animat has a particular type of relationship between its motor and sensor dynamics, which would be different from that of, say, a more naturalistic legged-robot. Would such an animat be able to utilise its motor state in the same way as the one presented here?

References

1. Beer, R.D.: On the dynamics of small continuous-time recurrent neural networks. Adapt. Behav. **3**(4), 469–509 (1995)
2. Braitenberg, V.: Vehicles, Experiments in Synthetic Psychology. MIT Press, Cambridge (1984)
3. Buhrmann, T., Di Paolo, E.A., Barandiaran, X.: A dynamical systems account of sensorimotor contingencies. Front. Psychol. **4**, 285 (2013)
4. Egbert, M., Cañamero, L.: Habit-based regulation of essential variables. In: Artificial Life 14: Proceedings of the Fourteenth International Conference on the Synthesis and Simulation of Living Systems, pp. 168–175, New York, NY, United States (2014)
5. Egbert, M.D., Barandiaran, X.E.: Modeling habits as self-sustaining patterns of sensorimotor behavior. Front. Human Neurosci. **8**(August), 1–15 (2014)
6. Harvey, I.: The microbial genetic algorithm. In: Kampis, G., Karsai, I., Szathmáry, E. (eds.) ECAL 2009. LNCS (LNAI), vol. 5778, pp. 126–133. Springer, Heidelberg (2011). https://doi.org/10.1007/978-3-642-21314-4_16
7. Seth, A.K.: Evolving action selection and selective attention without action, attention, or selection. In: Proceedings of the 5th Conference on the Simulation of Adaptive Behavior, pp. 1–8 (1998)
8. Silverman, D.: Bodily skill and internal representation in sensorimotor perception. Phenomenol. Cogn. Sci. **17**(1), 157–173 (2017). https://doi.org/10.1007/s11097-017-9503-5

9. Woolford, F.M.G., Egbert, M.D.: Behavioural variety of a node-based sensorimotor-to-motor map. Adapt. Behav. **28**, 425–440 (2019). (Special issue on Approaching Minimal Cognition)
10. Woolford, F.M.G., Egbert, M.D.: Goal oriented behavior with a habit-based adaptive sensorimotor map network. Front. Neurorobot. **16**, 846693 (2022)

Deep Gaussian Processes for Angle and Position Discrimination in Active Touch Sensing

Pablo J. Salazar[✉] and Tony J. Prescott

Department of Computer Science, University of Sheffield, Sheffield S1 4DP, UK
{pjsalazarvillacis1,t.j.prescott}@sheffield.ac.uk

Abstract. Active touch sensing can benefit from the representation of uncertainty in order to guide sensing movements and to drive sensing strategies that operate to reduce uncertainty with respect to the task at hand. Here we explore learning approaches that can acquire task knowledge quickly and with relatively small datasets and with the potential to be exploited for active sensing in robots and as models of biological sensory systems. Specifically, we explore the utility of deep (hierarchical) Gaussian Process models (Deep GPs) that have shown promise as models of episodic memory processes due to their low-dimensionality (compactness), generative capability, and ability to explicitly represent uncertainty. Using data obtained in a robotic active touch task (contour following), we show that both single-layer and Deep GP models are capable of providing robust function approximations from tactile data to angle and sensor position, with Deep GPs showing some advantages in terms of accuracy and uncertainty quantification in angle discrimination.

Keywords: Active touch · Deep Gaussian process · Contour following · Tactile sensing

1 Introduction

Active and exploratory capabilities of tactile perception can overcome the limitations of acquiring tactile information in a spatially constrained sensory apparatus. The active component of touch involves a modulation of attentional systems, requires decision making and performs purposeful movements to optimally obtain relevant tactile information [8,11,20]. In addition, psychophysical studies have characterised the execution of exploratory movement patterns of the sensory apparatus in the extraction of material and geometric properties of objects [9]. According to these studies, the perception of exact shape of an object through tactile sensing relies on a dynamic edge following exploratory procedure. Following the contour of an object depends on correctly perceiving the angle between the edge and the sensory apparatus. An accurate angle perception permits the detection of changes in curvature to maintain contact with

© The Author(s), under exclusive license to Springer Nature Switzerland AG 2022
L. Cañamero et al. (Eds.): SAB 2022, LNAI 13499, pp. 41–51, 2022.
https://doi.org/10.1007/978-3-031-16770-6_4

the edge of the object whose contour is being explored [10]. Studies on angle perception with the index finger on human subjects have observed the tendency of the execution of movements of the sensory apparatus for the improvement of angular perception [24,25]. Thus, the active component of contour following may be contingent on localising the sensory apparatus with respect to the edge of an object and modifying the sensor position to achieve better estimations of the assessed angle. An accurate angle perception would lead to the execution of exploratory movements taking into consideration the relative orientation between the perceiving organ and the edge of the test object.

The utility of exploratory procedures is not limited to specific end-effectors or contact types, highlighting that active touch strategies, as identified in biological systems, could be usefully implemented in robotic systems [21]. The need to deploy robots in unstructured environments requires the integration of multiple modalities to provide the embodied agent with a good understanding of the outside world [5]. Tactile sensing contributes to the direct detection of physical information, for instance surface shape and texture, that can otherwise only be inferred indirectly. A variety of reliable, and small, biomimetic tactile sensors have been developed leading to an upsurge in research on touch in robots [3]. These sensors deliver measurements in the presence of noise which translates into uncertainty that learning models must deal with to make decisions about future actions.

Inspired from the biology of active touch, the execution of the contour following exploratory procedure has relied on methods for localisation of the sensor relative to the object and identification of the edge orientation [12,16,21]. Perception of these magnitudes has been subject on applying Bayesian models along with sequential analysis to make decisions under uncertainty to complete the task [14,15,17]. Similarly, in [1] it was proved that the implementation of Gaussian process models can result in obtaining more accurate predictions of angle and position magnitudes compared to the use of Bayesian models under the same circumstances. However, the use of Deep Gaussian Process models [6] in the representation of angle and position information from tactile data remains to be assessed. GPs operate to infer the correlation of the training data, which, compared, for instance, to deep learning approaches, can present an advantage in building reliable models with relatively small training data. This can also be useful in understanding biological organisms in which learning can take place rapidly based on limited experience. GPs also grow in complexity to suit the data being therefore robust to overfitting [22]. By explicitly representing uncertainty in the data they can guide exploratory procedures aimed at reducing uncertainty [19], and, as a means of representing the data, they can be more transparent in terms of inspecting the low-dimensional manifold that is acquired by the trained system. In the current paper, we compare GP model with a newer variant, Deep GPs, that exploits hierarchical composition to create a deep belief network based on Gaussian process mappings [6]. Deep GPs can overcome some of the disadvantages of standard GPs, being more robust, analogous to the relationship between deep neural networks and generalized linear models [23].

In the current study, the feasibility of identifying the position and angle of the sensor with respect to the edge of a test object using GP models is evaluated using a tactile dataset consisting of evenly distributed palpations of a biomimetic fingertip against the surface proximal to the edge of a circular object. The dataset, developed in [2], and using the TacTip sensor [4], is intended for applications that require the discrimination between angle and perceptual classes such as tracing the contour of the object. In the current work, we seek to demonstrate that discrimination of angle and position perceptual classes can be assessed by implementing non parametric models that provide explicit quantification of uncertainty suitable for use in active sensing strategies such as exploratory procedures. Specifically, we train Gaussian Processes and Deep Gaussian Processes models to learn angle and position percepts from tactile information and to assess the accuracy of those predictions. We demonstrate that both methods work effectively with this dataset with the Deep GPs showing some advantages in terms of accuracy and uncertainty quantification.

2 Methods

2.1 Dataset

Lepora and colleagues have systematically collected sets of tactile data to enable the study of active touch strategies both for biomimetic artificial whiskers and fingertips [13]. These datasets also enable the analysis of regularities in the data when transformed into lower dimensional latent spaces [2]. In the current work, we used a subset of the data obtained with the TacTip biomimetic fingertip mounted on a UR5 robot arm. The sensor is composed of a compliant dome with 127 internal markers whose behavior is captured by a camera located inside the sensor case. The shear displacement of the markers corresponds to the deformation of the compliant component contingent on contacting a surface. The collection procedure followed a series of discrete taps on evenly distributed locations close to the edges of a circular object. The taps were executed along radial frame of reference with respect to the perpendicular angle of the edge. In that sense, position classes consisted of palpations on the surface from −12 mm to 5 mm in increments of 0.5 mm, where the 0 mm position corresponds to a palpation on the edge of the object. Nevertheless, in the present work, we used the data from −9 mm to 5 mm in steps of 1 mm. The use of a batch of the data allowed the assessment the capabilities of GP models to learn from a reduced amount of data, and also for discarding position classes in which the sensor does not provide relevant data due to lack of contact with the object. The angle classes in the original dataset were collected in a range of 0 to 360° with increments of 12°. However, in this work, we used the data from the perceptual classes that can be related to the perception of edges of objects consisting of right angles, i.e.: 0, 180, 86, and 264°, being the last two classes utilised as a proxy for classes of 90 and 270°. The tactile data for the 0° perceptual class is depicted in Fig. 1. The data represents the horizontal (Fig. 1a) and vertical (Fig. 1b) displacement of the internal markers, where each tap corresponds to a single radial position class, along with the marker distribution of the tip of the sensory apparatus (Fig. 1c). The data used in this work consists of four angular classes consisting of fifteen taps, where each tap is consistent with a position class for the localisation of the sensor and identification of the angle between the sensing device and the edge of the object.

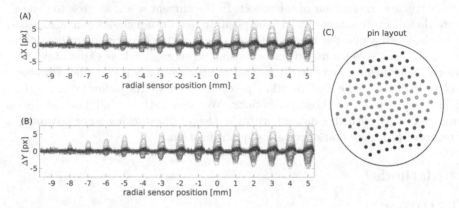

Fig. 1. Tactile data for 15 position classes corresponding to angle perceptual class: $0°$. A) Tracking of horizontal marker displacement (ΔX). B) Tracking of vertical marker displacement (ΔY). C) Layout of 127 internal markers of the TacTip sensor, colours on each plot correspond to the shown marker position

2.2 Dimensionality Reduction

Following the work from [2], the transformation of the data from a discrete tap consisting of a stream of the tracking of each of the 127 markers for the x and y axes along the duration of the tap can be an effective method to observe the intrinsic invariances and regularities in systematically collected data. As Fig. 2 displays, spatial commonalities in the real world are transferred to the latent space without requiring a supervised learning method. Angular classes occupy specific spaces and follow a clockwise distribution on the manifold (Fig. 2a). Similarly, position classes are evenly distributed in the latent space maintaining the spatial neighbouring from the space of observations. This dimensionality reduction represents a reduction in computational load for the Gaussian Process based models that require the inversion of the covariance matrix of training points to obtain the conditional distribution of test datapoints given the training set. The selection of data reduction to three dimensions was determined due to the 78% of the explained variance contained in the transformed data. The variance explained for each principal component was of a 41.49%, 27.21%, and 10.14%, providing a reasonable representation for the discrimination of angular and position perceptual classes.

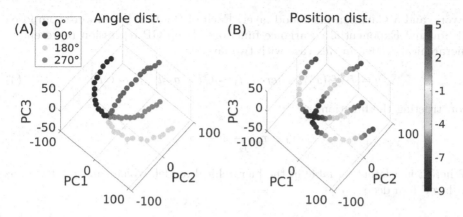

Fig. 2. Dimensionality reduction of tactile data. (A) Representation of angular classes. (B) Representation of position classes

2.3 Gaussian Process Based Models

Gaussian process [22] and Deep Gaussian process [6] models were implemented with the dimensionality-reduced tactile data. Training data consisted of each tap represented in three dimensions. 60 datapoints corresponding to 15 evenly distributed positions for each of the 4 angular percepts were used as an input to the models. Specifically, the non-parametric models were used for regression of angle and position of the sensor with respect to the edges of objects composed of right angles. The Gaussian Process model implementation and optimisation were carried out using the methods provided by the GpFlow library [18]. The model consists of a Matern 52 covariance function, replicating the studies performed in [1] with the difference that we used less training samples to train the GP and Deep GP models. The covariance function was used as a kernel for its combination with the data to form the regression model, with X^* describing previously unseen data, being f^* the approximation of $f(X^*)$:

$$f^*|X^*, X, y \sim \mathcal{N}(m, C), \tag{1}$$

where m and C, the mean and covariance of the function approximation for the test data are obtained as follows:

$$m = K_{*x}(K_{xx} + \sigma^2 I)^{-1} y, \tag{2}$$

$$C = K_{**} - K_{*x}(K_{xx} + \sigma^2 I)^{-1} K_{*x}^T, \tag{3}$$

The covariance matrices used to perform the calculation of Eqs. 2 and 3 consist of the covariance between training points: $K_{xx} = k(XX)$; the covariance between training and test points: $K_{*x} = k(X^*, X)$, and the covariance between test points $K_{**} = k(X^*, X^*)$. In addition, a Deep Gaussian Process regression model with a variational stochastic inference method [23] was implemented with the offered tools from the GPflux library [7]. The model consisted of two G.P layers, and a Gaussian likelihood layer. Each of the G.P layers were composed of Squared Exponential covariance functions. Deep GP regression represents a hierarchical model, in this case with two layers:

$$y = f_1(f_2(x)), \ where \quad f_1 \sim GP \quad and \quad f_2 \sim GP, \tag{4}$$

constructing the function,

$$f : x, \xrightarrow[f_2]{} z \xrightarrow[f_1]{} y, \tag{5}$$

Where z is a latent variable in the hierarchical model, which can be referred as a 'layer' in a deep model.

3 Results

In this section, a comparison between the implemented models is carried out. We present the learned mean function values along with the 95% confidence interval for the predictions of each model for a given input X^* representing previously unseen tactile data. Additionally, the performance of the regression using each method is evaluated through the obtention of the mean absolute error, and the coefficient of determination. The MAE provides a quantification of the assessed magnitude corresponding to each regression model, i.e.: angle and position. The coefficient of determination, known as R^2 score provides a representation of the proportion of variance of the evaluated variables explained by the independent variables in the model. This coefficient measures goodness of fit and therefore provides and indication of the capacity to predict unseen samples (through the amount of explained variance).

3.1 Position Discrimination

The implementation of Gaussian Process and Deep Gaussian Process regression models for the localisation of the sensor in the radial axis with respect to the perpendicular angle of a right-angled object can serve as a method for implementing movement policies to actively follow the contour of the object. In that sense, as can be seen in Fig. 3, both models provide a similar outcome in predicting the position of the sensor given the tactile data acquired at the specific position relative to the edge. However, it can be observed that the confidence interval, translated into the uncertainty of the prediction tends to be slightly higher with the Deep GP model (Fig. 3b) with respect to the GP model (Fig. 3a). A higher variance in the prediction may result in inaccuracies on the perception of sensor position; nevertheless, the provided variance can be used to determine a fixation point or set of points in which the perception of the respective angle could be predicted with higher accuracy.

The performance of the predictions on test data for each model is presented in Table 1. The coefficient of determination metric indicates that both models will provide accurate predictions in further unseen samples. Even though the

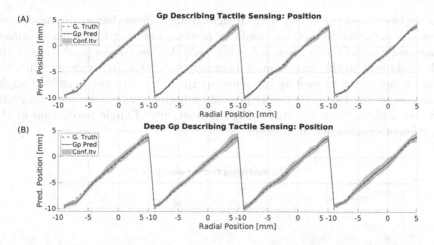

Fig. 3. Prediction of radial position of the sensor relative to the edge of a right-angled object (y axis) using tactile data collected at the corresponding position relative to the edge (x axis). (A) Predictions from Gaussian Process model. (B) Predictions from Deep Gaussian Process model

mean absolute error of the Deep GP model is 0.013 mm greater than the error from the predictions with the GP model, both models display an error of less than 0.2 mm. This relatively low mean absolute prediction error for the studied models would imply a robust localisation of the sensor with respect to the edge of the object. Consequently displaying a potential to effectively modify the position state parameter for the correct perception of the angle relative to the edge of objects comprised of right angles.

Table 1. Performance metrics for Gaussian process and deep Gaussian process for position prediction

Metric	GP	Deep GP
R^2	0.9971	0.9967
MAE	0.1772 [mm]	0.1910 [mm]

3.2 Angle Discrimination

The discrimination of the angle in which the sensor is located with respect to the edge of an object has been proved to be relevant in the execution of exploratory movements in tasks such as following the contour of an object [21]. The predictions provided by both evaluated models are presented in Fig. 4. It can be observed that the predictive expected value for angle perception tends to be relatively accurate for both models. However, the Gaussian process model presents a higher variance in the prediction (Fig. 4a) with respect to the variance obtained from the Deep model (Fig. 4b). This higher variance shows that a diminished consistency in accurate predictions would be present, inducing a significant impact in the execution of the contour following task. An inaccurate prediction of the angle could lead to the execution of incorrect exploratory movements when the motion policy is set to moving the sensor perpendicular to the perceived angle. In that sense, the Deep GP model presents a better performance and potential to better achieve the task considering the relevance of angle perception in the execution of exploratory movements.

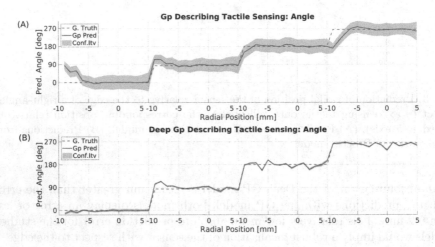

Fig. 4. Prediction of perpendicular angle of the sensor relative to the edge of a right-angled object (y axis) from tactile data obtained at the corresponding radial position relative to the edge (x axis). (A) Predictions from Gaussian Process model. (B) Predictions from Deep Gaussian Process model

Higher variance in the prediction of test datapoints from the GP model is reflected in the R^2 performance metric as detailed in Table 2, which is lower than the coefficient of determination obtained from the Deep model prediction. The best possible R^2 score is 1, thus the Deep GP model tends to provide more certain predictions than when using the Gaussian Process model. Additionally, through the quantification of the mean absolute error we can demonstrate that the Deep Gaussian process model outperforms its shallow counterpart with an error reduction of approximately five degrees.

Table 2. Performance metrics for Gaussian process and deep Gaussian process for angle prediction

Metric	GP	Deep GP
R^2	0.9495	0.9912
MAE	11.03°	6.11°

4   Discussion and Future Work

The execution of exploratory movements to maintain the contact with an object in a contour following setting relies on the accuracy of the perception of the angle between the sensing device and the edge of the object. This perception can be enhanced by positioning the sensor in locations where the angle can be perceived with more accuracy (fixation point). In this work, Gaussian Process and Deep Gaussian Process models were implemented for the discrimination of angle and position of the sensor with respect to the edge of right-angled objects with tactile data. For the position discrimination, both models provide a mean absolute prediction error of less than 0,2 mm, which represents an advantage in localising and positioning the sensor in places where the angle can be perceived with more accuracy. With regards to angle discrimination, it was shown that the Deep GP model provided a better performance with respect to the GP model. This outperforming was reflected in the capability to provide less variability in the predictions of previously unseen data. In addition, the deep model presents the potential to produce more accurate predictions as demonstrated in a mean absolute predictive error reduction of five degrees compared to the shallow model. The results from the angle discrimination provide directions about the policy that ought to be followed to perform active touch, i.e. to locate the sensor in a fixation point. It would be straightforward to determine a fixation point in which the sensor needs to be placed by only taking into account the values of the mean function provided by both models. However, the higher variance of the predictions obtained from the GP model suggests that the angle perception is prone to present a higher perception error as opposed to its deep counterpart which indicates that the predictions will be closer to the predicted mean function values. Therefore, the obtained accuracy and reduction in the uncertainty of the predictions of the Deep GP model can directly influence the performance of exploratory movements to successfully follow the contour of objects comprised of right angles.

The application of this type of models have demonstrated the requirement of a relatively small dataset comprised of 60 datapoints to correctly characterise the evaluated magnitudes. Additionally, the quantification of uncertainty becomes a beneficial metric for decision making to perform active touch. Future work will be directed to integrate the studied models in action-perception loops to allow robotic systems actively perform dynamical edge following of objects with different curvatures under practical scenarios where the quantification of uncertainty and accuracy of the predictions could eventually be essential for the completion of the task.

Acknowledgments. The authors would like to thank N. Lepora and collaborators collecting and making available the dataset used in this work. This work is supported by European Union's Horizon 2020 MSCA Programme under Grant Agreement No 813713 NeuTouch.

References

1. Aquilina, K.: Tactile perception and control of a soft shear-sensitive optical tactile sensor. Ph.D. thesis, University of Bristol (2021), https://research-information.bris.ac.uk/en/studentTheses/tactile-perception-and-control-of-a-soft-shear-sensitive-optical

2. Aquilina, K., Barton, D.A.W., Lepora, N.F.: Principal components of touch. In: 2018 IEEE International Conference on Robotics and Automation (ICRA). pp. 4071–4078. IEEE (5 2018). https://doi.org/10.1109/ICRA.2018.8461045

3. Bartolozzi, C., Natale, L., Nori, F., Metta, G.: Robots with a sense of touch. Nat. Mater. **15**(9), 921–925 (2016). https://doi.org/10.1038/nmat4731

4. Chorley, C., Melhuish, C., Pipe, T., Rossiter, J.: Development of a tactile sensor based on biologically inspired edge encoding. In: 2009 International Conference on Advanced Robotics, pp. 1–6 (2009), https://ieeexplore.ieee.org/document/5174720

5. Dahiya, R.S., Metta, G., Valle, M., Sandini, G.: Tactile sensing-from humans to humanoids. IEEE Trans. Robot. **26**(1), 1–20 (2010). https://doi.org/10.1109/TRO.2009.2033627

6. Damianou, A.C., Lawrence, N.D.: Deep Gaussian processes. J. Mach. Learn. Res. **31**, 207–215 (2012). http://arxiv.org/abs/1211.0358

7. Dutordoir, V., et al.: GPflux: a library for deep Gaussian processes. arXiv:2104.05674 (2021), https://arxiv.org/abs/2104.05674

8. Gibson, J.J.: Observations on active touch. Psychol. Rev. **69**(6), 477–491 (1962). https://doi.org/10.1037/h0046962

9. Lederman, S.J., Klatzky, R.L.: Hand movements: a window into haptic object recognition. Cogn. Psychol. **19**(3), 342–368 (1987). https://doi.org/10.1016/0010-0285(87)90008-9

10. Lederman, S.J., Klatzky, R.L.: Extracting object properties through haptic exploration. Acta Psychol. **84**(1), 29–40 (1993). https://doi.org/10.1016/0001-6918(93)90070-8

11. Lepora, N.: Active tactile perception. In: Prescott, T.J., Ahissar, E. (eds.) Scholarpedia of Touch, pp. 151–159. Atlantis Press, Paris (2016). https://doi.org/10.2991/978-94-6239-133-8_11

12. Lepora, N., Martinez-Hernandez, U., Prescott, T.: Active Bayesian perception for simultaneous object localization and identification. In: Robotics: Science and Systems IX. Robotics: Science and Systems Foundation (2013). https://doi.org/10.15607/RSS.2013.IX.019

13. Lepora, N.F.: Biomimetic active touch with fingertips and whiskers. IEEE Trans. Hapt. **9**(2), 170–183 (2016). https://doi.org/10.1109/TOH.2016.2558180

14. Lepora, N.F., Aquilina, K., Cramphorn, L.: Exploratory tactile servoing with active touch. IEEE Robot. Autom. Lett. **2**(2), 1156–1163 (2017). https://doi.org/10.1109/LRA.2017.2662071

15. Martinez-Hernandez, U., Dodd, T., Prescott, T.J., Lepora, N.F.: Active Bayesian perception for angle and position discrimination with a biomimetic fingertip. In: 2013 IEEE/RSJ International Conference on Intelligent Robots and Systems, pp. 5968–5973. IEEE, November 2013. https://doi.org/10.1109/IROS.2013.6697222

16. Martinez-Hernandez, U., Dodd, T.J., Prescott, T.J.: Feeling the shape: active exploration behaviors for object recognition with a robotic hand. IEEE Trans. Syst. Man Cybern. Syst. **48**(12), 2339–2348 (2018). https://doi.org/10.1109/TSMC. 2017.2732952

17. Martinez-Hernandez, U., Rubio-Solis, A., Prescott, T.J.: Learning from sensory predictions for autonomous and adaptive exploration of object shape with a tactile robot. Neurocomputing **382**, 127–139 (2020). https://doi.org/10.1016/j.neucom. 2019.10.114

18. Matthews, A.G.d.G., et al.: GPflow: a Gaussian process library using TensorFlow. J. Mach. Learn. Res. **18**(40), 1–6 (2017), http://jmlr.org/papers/v18/16-537.html

19. Prescott, T.J., Camilleri, D., Martinez-Hernandez, U., Damianou, A., Lawrence, N.D.: Memory and mental time travel in humans and social robots. Philos. Trans. R. Soc. B Biol. Sci. **374**(1771), 20180025 (2019). https://doi.org/10.1098/rstb. 2018.0025

20. Prescott, T.J., Diamond, M.E., Wing, A.M.: Active touch sensing. Philos. Trans. R. Soc. B Biol. Sci. **366**(1581), 2989–2995 (2011). https://doi.org/10.1098/rstb. 2011.0167

21. Prescott, T.J., Lepora, N., Mitchinson, B., Pearson, M., Martinez-Hernandez, U., Grant, R.A.: Active touch sensing in mammals and robots. In: The Senses: A Comprehensive Reference, pp. 79–109. Elsevier, January 2020. https://doi.org/10. 1016/B978-0-12-805408-6.00031-2

22. Rasmussen, C.E.: Gaussian processes in machine learning. In: Bousquet, O., von Luxburg, U., Rätsch, G. (eds.) ML -2003. LNCS (LNAI), vol. 3176, pp. 63–71. Springer, Heidelberg (2004). https://doi.org/10.1007/978-3-540-28650-9_4

23. Salimbeni, H., Deisenroth, M.P.: Doubly stochastic variational inference for deep Gaussian processes. In: Proceedings of the 31st International Conference on Neural Information Processing Systems, NIPS 2017, pp. 4591–4602. Curran Associates Inc., Red Hook, NY, USA (2017)

24. Voisin, J., Benoit, G., Chapman, C.E.: Haptic discrimination of object shape in humans: two-dimensional angle discrimination. Exp. Brain Res. **145**(2), 239–250 (2002). https://doi.org/10.1007/s00221-002-1117-6

25. Yang, J., Wu, J.: Human characteristics on tactile angle discrimination by object movement condition. In: The 2011 IEEE/ICME International Conference on Complex Medical Engineering, pp. 514–519. IEEE, May 2011. https://doi.org/10.1109/ ICCME.2011.5876795

Neural Body Bending Control with Temporal Delays for Millipede-Like Turning Behaviour of a Multi-segmented, Legged Robot

Nopparada Mingchinda[1], Vatsanai Jaiton[1], Binggwong Leung[1],
and Poramate Manoonpong[1,2]($\boxtimes$)

[1] Bio-inspired Robotics and Neural Engineering Laboratory, School of Information Science and Technology (IST), Vidyasirimedhi Institute of Science and Technology (VISTEC), Rayong, Thailand
poramate.m@vistec.ac.th
[2] Embodied AI and Neurorobotics Laboratory, SDU Biorobotics, The Mærsk Mc-Kinney Møller Institute, University of Southern Denmark, Odense, Denmark

Abstract. In the real world, the turning behaviour of millipedes enables them to navigate through challenging environments, including narrow spaces. Biological studies reveal that their turning behaviour shows temporal delays as the gradual propagation from the anterior to posterior body segments. However, the realization of control mechanisms underlying the complex behaviour and their translation to a robot for efficient narrow space navigation have not been fully addressed. Thus, this study aims to develop neural body bending control (BBC) based on the turning behaviour of millipedes in a millipede-inspired robot with multiple body segments. To implement temporal delays between segments, the BBC exploits the neurodynamics of a series of self-excitatory single neurons to propagate signals from the anterior to posterior body segments in response to external stimuli. The temporal delays between the signals projecting to the anterior and posterior segments enable the robot to bend its body and turn away from an obstacle in a similar manner as observed in millipedes. We further tested the efficiency of the BBC induced turning behaviour performance in different environments with narrow paths. To this end, this study not only proposes neural body bending control based on a neurodynamics approach, but also suggests a possible solution of millipede nervous systems for complex turning behaviour with temporal delays and sensory memory.

Keywords: Bio-inspired robotics · Millipede · Recurrent neural network · Walking robots · Neurodynamics · Temporal delays · Hysteresis

L. Cañamero et al. (Eds.): SAB 2022, LNAI 13499, pp. 52–63, 2022.
https://doi.org/10.1007/978-3-031-16770-6_5

1 Introduction

The millipede is a myriapod under the class Diplopoda with segmented bodies [6,16]. The body of the millipede forms a complex system, which includes the sensory organs located at the antennae [14], and bodily joints that regulate the turning of its body when detecting an obstacle [7]. During turning, each body segment of the millipede bends/turns in succession, enabling it to turn away from the obstacle. This successive propagation of body bending means that the segments bend with temporal delays from the anterior to the posterior portion of the millipede's body, resulting in smooth turning behaviour [7]. Furthermore, after the initial encounter, the segments closer to the head remain bent away from the obstacle. This demonstrates a type of sensory memory that allows body bending to be prolonged. The turning mechanism in the millipede can provide a fascinating insight into the development of a multi-segmented, legged robot that requires obstacle avoidance and navigation through narrow and winding paths. Thus, the current study aims to develop a neural body bending mechanism that translates the turning behaviour of the millipede to a multi-segmented robot by i) implementing temporal delays to the neural signals that propagate from the anterior to posterior segments in response to external stimuli and ii) introducing sensory memory that can extend the duration of body bending.

Previous works used various methods to generate body bending in myriapod-like robots [4,6,10,16]. For example, the implementation of turning motions of a centipede-inspired robot by varying the torsional stiffness of the springs at each passive body joint enables the robot to approach a target [4]. While the work was able to emulate the body bending motions of centipedes, the body joints implemented were passive and body bending direction was dependent on the turning of the first segment in the yaw direction. This approach poses limitations in scenarios where the robot needs to adapt its body shape according to environmental conditions, such as a narrow space. As the versatility and stability of a millipede-inspired robot has been implicated in search and rescue scenarios [10], it is essential to establish control for active body bending of a millipede-inspired robot to make it possible for the robot to navigate challenging environments, e.g., rubble and narrow space. While impressive, previous studies have not yet incorporated temporal delays and sensory memory into their robot systems to generate millipede-like turning behaviour, which is a possible method for smooth obstacle avoidance and narrow space navigation as proposed here.

One way of implementing temporal delays and sensory memory is via self-excitatory single neurons. While being simple and computationally inexpensive, these neurons can exhibit a hysteresis effect derived from their neurodynamics [13]. Previously, it has been exploited for tasks including sensory pre-processing and insect-like behaviour control of an insect-inspired robot with six legs and one body segment [12]. In contrast, we hereby propose for the first time the utilisation of the hysteresis effect of a series of self-excitatory single neurons, to implement temporal delays and sensory memory for complex body bending control of a millipede-inspired robot with twenty legs and ten body segments. Although other approaches, like reservoir computing [5], can be also applied for implementing temporal delays and sensory memory, they are difficult to analyze and understand their internal dynamics. Our neural control approach here with a modular structure is analyzable and understandable. This can pave the way for the development of a neural system toward explainable AI systems (XAI).

2   Materials and Methods

2.1   Millipede-Inspired Robot

The millipede-inspired robot was simulated using CoppeliaSims version 4.3.0 [15] (Fig. 1(a)). The robot is a simplified model of the millipede species *Cylindroiulus caeruleocinctus*[1] [14]. It has one pair of legs per uniform body segment. One active revolute joint connects each body segment, and each body joint has minimum and maximum turning angles of −11 and 11 to the left and right, respectively (Fig. 2). The minimum and maximum turning angles were set such that there are no collisions between each neighbouring leg and segments when the body joint turns in the yaw direction.

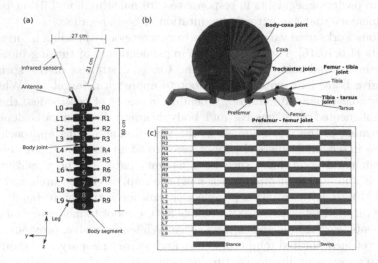

Fig. 1. (a) The morphology of the millipede-inspired robot, which is the simplified morphology of the millipede [14]. (b) The cross-section of the robot, with the leg segments (yellow) and the joints (red). (c) The tripod-like gait showing the alternating swing and stance phases between each leg in a pair (L = left, R = right). (Color figure online)

The robot body segments are indexed from zero to nine, starting from the head. At the head (segment 0), the antennae with two infrared sensors (IR) are

---

[1] Note that the morphology of the millipede has non-uniform body segments and two pairs of legs per segment.

attached for obstacle detection (Fig. 1(a)). Each IR based antenna can provide sensory feedback that is mapped to a range of $[-1, ..., 1]$, where -1.0 means no obstacle detected (i.e., the distance between the sensor and obstacle is larger than 21 cm), and 1.0 means very near obstacle detected (i.e., the distance between the sensor and obstacle is 0 cm). The other values between -1.0 and 1.0 mean that obstacle is in a range between 21 and 0 cm. The closer the obstacle, the higher the sensor signal.

The leg projection from the body segment was simplified from the millipede morphology [6], where each leg with a total length of approximately 7 cm consists of five segments (coxa, prefemur, femur, tibia and tarsus), and five joints (body-coxa, coxa-prefemur (trochanter), prefemur-femur, femur-tibia, and tibia-tarsus joints) (Fig. 1(b)). The active trochanter joint enables the forward (+) and backward (−) movements. The active prefemur-femur joint enables the upward (+) and downward (−) movements (Fig. 1(b)). The two leg joints have the minimum and maximum angles of −57 and 57°, respectively. In total, there are ten pairs of legs or twenty individual legs, ten body segments, and nine body joints[2]. For simplicity, the positions of the body-coxa, femur-tibia, and tibia-tarsus joints were fixed. The total length and the width of the robot, including the IR antennae, are approximately 80 cm and 27 cm, respectively. This is a minimal setup for our control development and experiments. We use a tripod-like gait where ten legs stance and ten opposite legs swing (Fig. 1(c)). This is a minimal setup for our control development and experiments. We use a tripod-like gait where ten legs stance and ten opposite legs swing (Fig. 1(c)). As the focus is on the body joint control, the gait is used instead of other gaits for simplicity. Note that this gait is different from a typical millipede gait (metachronal gait) where the legs ripple in a wave propagating from the posterior to anterior [2].

2.2   Neural Control System for Millipede-Like Turning Behaviour

We employed neural control mechanisms with a modular structure as our control system to generate the millipede-like turning behaviour of our robot (Fig. 2). While different control methods can be used for this task [4,9], we considered the neural control method since it is flexible, and we can later apply neural learning for control parameter adaptation [8].

In this study, the neural control system for turning behaviour (involving body bending and walking) is manually designed based on three generic neural modules previously developed [8,11], and one neural body bending control module (BBC) newly proposed here. The generic neural modules include a central pattern generator (CPG), a CPG post-processing module (CPM), and a sensory processing module (SPM). In this section, we briefly describe the three modules below (see [11] for more details) since they are not our main focus and are employed here for essential leg coordination and gait generation. Next, we

---

[2] Note that the number of legs was limited in order to be able to simulate and run the robot on a standard PC.

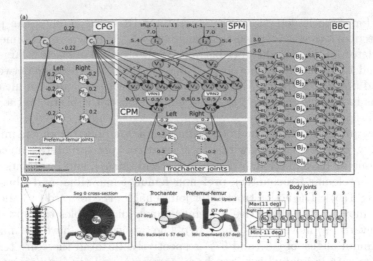

Fig. 2. (a) The neural control system that governs the millipede-inspired robot, consisting of the central pattern generator (CPG), the sensory processing module (SPM), the CPG post-processing module (CPM), and the body bending control module (BBC). The final outputs of the CPG and velocity regulating networks (VRNs) of the CPM are transmitted to the prefemur-femur ($Pf_{0,...,19}$) and trochanter ($Tc_{0,...,19}$) joints of the robot, respectively. (b) A cross-section of the millipede robot showing the body segment and leg joints. (c) The moving directions of the leg joints driven by the neural control system. (d) The top view of the millipede robot showing each body joint's moving directions and their respective joint numbers.

describe the BBC with temporal delays and sensory memory, which is the central contribution of our work in Sect. 2.3.

All neurons of the modules (CPG, CPM, SPM, and BBC) are modeled as discrete-time non-spiking modules. The activity a_i of each neuron develops according to:

$$a_i(t) = \sum_{j=1}^{n} W_{ij} o_j(t-1) + B_i, i = 1, ..., n, \qquad (1)$$

where n refers to the number of units. B_i is a fixed bias term of the neuron i. W_{ij} denotes the synaptic connection from neuron j to neuron i. o_i denotes the output of neuron i, which is calculated using a hyperbolic tangent (tanh) activation function ($o_i = tanh(a_i) \in [-1,1]$) except for the propagation to motor neurons ($Pf_{0,...,19}$, $Tc_{0,...,19}$, $Bj_{0,...,8}$) which are calculated using a linear activation function. All connection strengths together with bias terms are indicated by the small numbers (Fig. 2), except for the self-connection weights (ws) in the BBC, which are investigated in this study.

The CPG is realised by using discrete-time dynamics of a simple 2-neuron oscillator network with full connections (Fig. 2). It generates periodic signals to drive the leg joints with periodic movements. The synaptic weights were adjusted empirically to achieve a proper walking frequency, with the final weights shown in Fig. 2. The prefemur-femur joints are controlled directly by the CPG, while the trochanter joints are indirectly controlled by the CPM. While the CPG generates periodic signals to generate cyclic leg movements, the CPM controls the walking directions by reversing the CPG outputs with respect to the sensory feedback before sending final signals to the trochanter joints. The CPM has two subnetworks (velocity regulating networks (VRNs)) for controlling the left and right trochanter joints. The VRNs taken from [11] are simple feedforward networks with two input neurons $(V_{1,2}) \in [-1, 1]$ (see [11] for more details). The VRNs receive pre-processed sensory inputs via V_1 and V_2, which further propagate their output signals to eight neurons $(V_{3,...,10})$, and finally transmit the output signals to the corresponding leg joints (Fig. 2(a)).

For the SPM, there are two IR-based antennae at the robot's head. They provide sensory inputs when detecting an obstacle within the robot's vicinity. The raw sensory inputs are fed to two recurrent neurons $(I_{1,2})$, which filter sensory noise [11]. The CPM controls the walking directions by reversing the CPG outputs with respect to the sensory feedback from SPM. This enables the robot to turn away from the obstacle. By doing so, the robot can perform obstacle avoidance behaviour. The presence of an obstacle on the left reverses the robot's right legs, making it turn to the right and vice versa.

2.3   Neural Body Bending Control with Temporal Delays

Garcia et al. [7] showed that temporal delays of body segments propagating from anterior to posterior sections during millipede turning enable the millipede to turn itself smoothly away from the obstacle (see Fig. 9 in [7]). Inspired by this, we developed the BBC to implement temporal delays to achieve the body bending/turning behaviour seen in real millipedes for our robot. The fundamental principle behind the structure of the BBC is neurodynamics (i.e., the hysteresis effect) of a series of self-excitatory recurrent neurons [13] (Fig. 3(a, b)), where different excitatory recurrent weight values $(ws > 1.0)$ can generate different hysteresis loops (Fig. 3(b)), resulting in different temporal delays (Fig. 3(c)). The hysteresis loop can also maintain its output signal, despite the diminishing sensory input signal, thereby providing sensory memory (i.e., short-term memory that stores sensory information). Typically, when the weights of self-excitatory single neurons are increased, the temporal delays between each body joint are also increased due to a larger hysteresis loop.

The BBC consists of two series of single neurons with ws (Fig. 2(a)) that control left and right body bending behaviours. The bending to the left or right is controlled by inputs from V_1 and V_2. The input signals are projected through connections, each with a weight of 3.0. Every twentieth pair of neurons from both series projects their output signals to each body joint with the weights of 0.1 (left series) and -0.1 (right series). Moreover, each neuron in a series is connected via an excitatory connection with a weight of 3.0. This represents the progression of body bending from anterior to posterior body segments.

The activation of each single recurrent neuron follows Eq. 1, with the output calculated using a hyperbolic tangent (tanh) activation function. The output

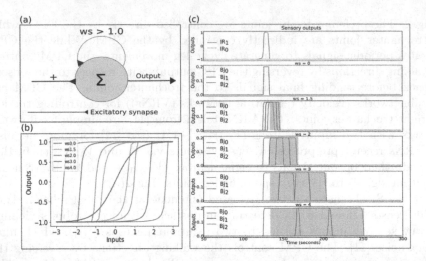

Fig. 3. (a) A single neuron with a self-excitatory connection (ws). (b) Different hysteresis loop sizes for different self-connection weights $ws = [1.5, 2.0, 3.0, 4.0]$. Note that a hysteresis loop does not occur for $ws < 1.0$; thereby $ws = 0.0$ does not show the loop. Here, we explore the weight up to 4.0 since a larger value will lead to an excessive hysteresis loop, resulting in excessive temporal delays and turning behaviour. (c) The preprocessed sensory outputs that drive body joints and the body joint control signals from the first three body joints of the robot across different ws values. The grey areas show the sensory memory as a result of hysteresis effect. (Color figure online)

from the left series is described as $o_{L_i} = tanh(a_{L_i}) \in [-1, 1]$, while the right one is described as $o_{R_i} = tanh(a_{R_i}) \in [-1, 1]$. The left and right outputs are combined for final body joint control as:

$$a_{Bj_k} = 0.1 \times (o_{L_i}) - 0.1 \times (o_{R_i}), \ k = 0, 1, ..., 8, \ i = 0, 20, ..., 160, \quad (2)$$

where a_{Bj_k} stands for the activation of each body joint (Bj_k) as a function of the outputs from the left (o_{L_i}) and the right (o_{R_i}) series. Note that 0.1 is a scaling weight to prevent collision between each body segment and leg during turning. Here the body-leg coordination is achieved via the predefined neural connections (Fig. 2). When the robot detects an obstacle on its left, the neuron I_1 of the SPM will be activated and transmit its output to drive the robot body to bend to the right and at the same time reverse all right trochanter joints; thereby making the robot turn to the right and vice versa.

3   Experiments and Results

To evaluate the use of BBC in producing temporal delays and sensory memory in our millipede-inspired robot, we first observed the changes in the absolute angles of body segments against the world frame of the simulation during turning away from a wall. The turning behaviour is expected to be different across different ws

due to different hysteresis loops, and thus different periods of temporal delays and sensory memory. We based the likeness of the turning behaviour of our robot to that of a real millipede by comparing the absolute joint angles (see Fig. 9 in [7]). Then, we demonstrated the robot turning behaviour and compared it with real millipede turning behaviour. Finally, we tested the performance of the control approach in different narrow environments.

3.1 Millipede-Like Turning Behaviour

To validate the BBC-induced turning behaviour and compare it to millipede turning behaviour, we positioned the robot against a solid 200-centimetre wall (Fig. 4(a)). At the start of the simulation, we let the robot walk freely toward the wall. As soon as the robot detected the wall, it bent its body to avoid the wall. Once the robot's entire body passed the wall after turning, the simulation was terminated. Note that since the robot freely walked without straight walking control as such one of its antennae could hit the wall/obstacle first. As a consequence, it could turn to the opposite direction. In this experiment, we explored different weight values for all self-excitatory connections (ws) in the BBC to observe different time delays of body bending control signals. The weights were all set to either 0.0, 1.5, 2.0, 3.0, or 4.0. The hysteresis effect of these weight values ($ws > 1.0$) can be seen at Fig. 3(b).

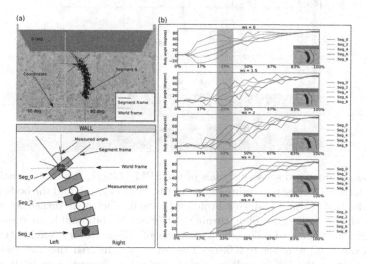

Fig. 4. (a) The measurement of the absolute body segment angles at every second body segment of the millipede against the world frame. (b) The absolute body segment angles across different ws values, along with the shapes of the robot during the highlighted period. Only five segments are shown for clarity. Note that 0% represents the beginning (i.e., the robot walked toward the wall) and 100% represents the end of the body bending behaviour (i.e., the robot successfully avoided the wall). A video of this experiment can be seen at www.manoonpong.com/BBC/video1.mp4

During each trial, we measured the absolute body turning angles of robot body segments as the robot approached and turned away from the wall. We set the reference points at the zeroth, second, fourth, sixth, and eighth segments of the robot (Fig. 4(a)). Figure 4(b) depicts the changes in the absolute angles of the zeroth, second, fourth, sixth and eighth segments during turning behaviour for $ws = 0.0, 1.5, 2.0, 3.0,$ and 4.0. It can be seen that there are variations in the absolute body segment angles at different segments. If ws is zero, all body joints

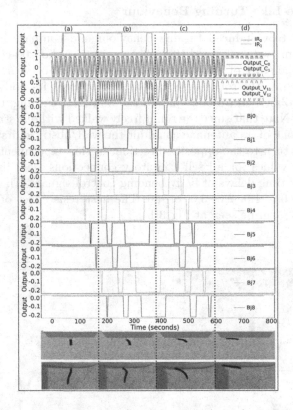

Fig. 5. The preprocessed sensory signals of the SPM ($IR_{0,1}$), the CPG signals of the CPG ($C_{0,1}$), the CPG postprocessing signals of the CPM ($V_{11,12}$), and the body bending signals of the BBC ($Bj_{0,...,8}$) during avoiding the wall. The robot turned left to avoid collision with the wall. The robot turning behaviour is comparable to the observed turning behaviour of a real millipede. The values of self-excitatory weights (ws) of all neurons in the BBC were set to 3.0. (a) The robot encountered the wall and started to slightly turn to the left as well as slightly walked backward since both antennae sensed the wall (high outputs of IR_0 and IR_1). (b) The robot turned left according to the high activation of IR_1. (c) The gradual activation of each body joint as the right antenna (IR_1) shortly detected the wall once again. The robot turned towards the left. (d) The robot resumed straight body. A comparison of robot and millipede turning behaviours is shown in the snapshots below. A video of this comparison can be seen at www.manoonpong.com/BBC/video2.mp4

activate/turn simultaneously (i.e., no temporal delay), resulting in C-shaped body bending. The temporal delays occur and increase as ws increases, resulting in L-shaped body bending. Among these, $ws = 3.0$ bears the most resemblance to the turning angles of a real millipede.

According to this result, we further used $ws = 3.0$ to monitor the sensory and body bending signals during obstacle avoidance (Fig. 5). We also visually compared the robot turning behaviour with real millipede turning behaviour.

We can clearly see temporal delays and successive propagation of body bending signals from the anterior to posterior body joints ($Bj_{0,...,8}$). We also observed sensory memory when the outputs of the body joints remained activated despite the deactivation of sensory inputs.

3.2   Navigation in Different Environments with Narrow Paths

We created a narrow zigzag environment to test the BBC with $ws = 3.0$ and observe robot turning behaviour. The robot performance was evaluated using the task completion time. The completion time (seconds) was measured once all body parts were away from the zigzag environment. The completion time was restricted to 300 s, after which a trial would be considered 'failed'. We timed the robot's walking duration, beginning when the legs started to move inside the environment until all of the legs exited the environment (Fig. 6(a)). We ran the trial five times with random initial heading angles. The robot completed the task with 100% success rate. During navigation, we can see that the robot

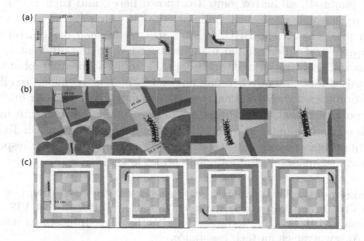

Fig. 6. The navigation behaviour with millipede-like turning of the multi-segmented, legged robot in three different environments. (a) A narrow zigzag environment where a narrow space ratio is 1.0. The narrow space ratio is calculated from the maximum width of the path divided by the total robot width (see Fig. 1(a)). (b) A cluttered environment filled with random objects, where a narrow space ratio is approximately 1.6 in average. (c) A square shaped maze, where a narrow space ratio is 1.9. A video of these experiments can be seen at www.manoonpong.com/BBC/video3.mp4.

bent itself in an L-shaped millipede-like bending pattern around corners. The average completion time was about 80 s. We also tested the robot in a cluttered environment with a narrow path through a cluster of objects (Fig. 6(b)), and a square shaped maze (Fig. 6(c)), where the robot also successfully completed with 100% success rate. The average completion times were about 76 s for the cluttered environment and 271 s for the full square maze.

4   Conclusion

In this study, we introduced the neural body bending control module (BBC). Using the BBC in combination with other generic control modules, including the CPG, CPM, and SPM modules, we successfully coordinated multi body joints and generated a millipede-like turning behaviour in our multi-segmented robot. We further demonstrated the performance of the approach for robot narrow space navigation. The BBC's core is based on simple single recurrent neurons with self-excitatory connections that exhibit neurodynamics, like hysteresis effect. The effect can be exploited to generate temporal delays and sensory memory for motor control. This emphasises that the exploitation of neurodynamics is a powerful method to solve sensorimotor coordination problems [1,8] of complex systems (like multi-segmented robots). While the robot shows a millipede-like turning/body bending behaviour, the number of body segments of the robot used in this study is still lower than real millipedes. In the future, we will add more body segments and legs as well as investigate different body joint setups (e.g., all passive joints [4], all active joints (as shown here), and their combination). Furthermore, we will implement online neural learning [8] for self-excitatory connection plasticity of the BBC; i.e., ws will be learned or controlled in an online adaptive and differentiated manner according to the different body segments. This will lead to a versatile and adaptable multi-segmented robot that can autonomously adapt its body bending angles of different segments to efficiently deal with complex obstacles and narrow paths. Lastly, based on our findings, we further hypothesize that a hysteresis mechanism might also exist in millipede locomotion control systems, as found in other animal locomotion [3]. To address this open question, one may investigate sensory stimuli and motor responses of different body segments during millipede obstacle avoidance.

Acknowledgements. This research was supported by the BrainBot project (I22POM-INT010) and the startup grant on Bio-inspired Robotics of VISTEC. We thank Worasuchad Haomachai, Jettanan Homchanthanakul, Rujikorn Charakorn and Chaicharn Akkawutvanich for their assistance.

References

1. Aguilera, M., Bedia, M.G., Santos, B.A., Barandiaran, X.E.: The situated HKB model: how sensorimotor spatial coupling can alter oscillatory brain dynamics. Front. Comput. Neurosci. **7**, 117 (2013)

2. Ambe, Y., Aoi, S., Tsuchiya, K., Matsuno, F.: Generation of direct-, retrograde-, and source-wave gaits in multi-legged locomotion in a decentralized manner via embodied sensorimotor interaction. Front. Neural Circuits **15** (2021)

3. Aoi, S., et al.: A stability-based mechanism for hysteresis in the walk-trot transition in quadruped locomotion. J. R. Soc. Interface **10**(81), 20120908 (2013)

4. Aoi, S., Tanaka, T., Fujiki, S., Funato, T., Senda, K., Tsuchiya, K.: Advantage of straight walk instability in turning maneuver of multilegged locomotion: a robotics approach. Sci. Rep. **6**(1), 1–10 (2016). https://doi.org/10.1038/srep30199

5. Calandra, M., Patanè, L., Sun, T., Arena, P., Manoonpong, P.: Echo state networks for estimating exteroceptive conditions from proprioceptive states in quadruped robots. Front. Neurorobot. 118 (2021)

6. Garcia, A., Krummel, G., Priya, S.: Fundamental understanding of millipede morphology and locomotion dynamics. Bioinspir. Biomim. **16**(2), 026003 (2020). https://doi.org/10.1088/1748-3190/abbdcc

7. Garcia, A., Priya, S., Marek, P.: Understanding the locomotion and dynamic controls for millipedes: part 1-kinematic analysis of millipede movements. In: Smart Materials, Adaptive Structures and Intelligent Systems, vol. 57304, p. V002T06A005. American Society of Mechanical Engineers (2015). https://doi.org/10.1115/SMASIS2015-8894

8. Grinke, E., Tetzlaff, C., Wörgötter, F., Manoonpong, P.: Synaptic plasticity in a recurrent neural network for versatile and adaptive behaviors of a walking robot. Front. Neurorobot. **9**, 11 (2015). https://doi.org/10.3389/fnbot.2015.00011

9. Hoffman, K.L., Wood, R.J.: Myriapod-like ambulation of a segmented microrobot. Auton. Robot. **31**(1), 103–114 (2011). https://doi.org/10.1007/s10514-011-9233-4

10. Ito, K., Ishigaki, Y.: Semiautonomous centipede-like robot for rubble-development of an actual scale robot for rescue operation. Int. J. Adv. Mechatron. Syst. **6**(2–3), 75–83 (2015). https://doi.org/10.1504/IJAMECHS.2015.070709

11. Manoonpong, P., Parlitz, U., Wörgötter, F.: Neural control and adaptive neural forward models for insect-like, energy-efficient, and adaptable locomotion of walking machines. Front. Neural Circuits **7**, 12 (2013). https://doi.org/10.3389/fncir.2013.00012

12. Manoonpong, P., Worgotter, F., Pasemann, F.: Neural preprocessing of auditory-wind sensory signals and modular neural control for auditory-and wind-evoked escape responses of walking machines. In: 2008 IEEE International Conference on Robotics and Biomimetics, pp. 786–793. IEEE (2009). https://doi.org/10.1109/ROBIO.2009.4913100

13. Pasemann, F.: Dynamics of a single model neuron. Int. J. Bifurc. Chaos **3**(02), 271–278 (1993). https://doi.org/10.1142/S0218127493000209

14. Reboleira, A.S.P., Enghoff, H.: First continental troglobiont cylindroiulus millipede (Diplopoda, Julida, Julidae). ZooKeys **795**, 93 (2018). https://doi.org/10.3897/zookeys.795.27619

15. Rohmer, E., Singh, S.P., Freese, M.: V-REP: a versatile and scalable robot simulation framework. In: 2013 IEEE/RSJ International Conference on Intelligent Robots and Systems, pp. 1321–1326. IEEE (2013). https://doi.org/10.1109/IROS.2013.6696520

16. Yasui, K., Kano, T., Standen, E.M., Aonuma, H., Ijspeert, A.J., Ishiguro, A.: Decoding the essential interplay between central and peripheral control in adaptive locomotion of amphibious centipedes. Sci. Rep. **9**(1), 1–11 (2019). https://doi.org/10.1038/s41598-019-53258-3

Brain-Inspired Control, Adaptation, and Learning

Yoking-Based Identification of Learning Behavior in Artificial and Biological Agents

Manuel Baum[1,2(✉)] [ID], Lukas Schattenhofer[1] [ID], Theresa Rössler[3] [ID],
Antonio Osuna-Mascaró[3] [ID], Alice Auersperg[1,3] [ID], Alex Kacelnik[1,4] [ID],
and Oliver Brock[1,2(✉)] [ID]

[1] Science of Intelligence, Research Cluster of Excellence,
Marchstr. 23, 10587 Berlin, Germany
[2] Robotics and Biology Laboratory, Technische Universität Berlin, Berlin, Germany
{baum,oliver.brock}@tu-berlin.de
[3] Comparative Cognition Group, University of Veterinary Medicine Vienna,
Vienna, Austria
{theresa.roessler,Antonio.OsunaMascaro,alice.auersperg}@vetmeduni.ac.at
[4] Behavioural Ecology Group, University of Oxford, Oxford, UK
alex.kacelnik@zoo.ox.ac.uk

Abstract. We want to understand how animals can learn to solve complex tasks. To achieve this, it makes sense to first hypothesize learning models and then compare these models to real biological learning data. But how to perform such a comparison is still unclear. We propose that yoking is an important component to such an analysis. In yoking, two agents are made to experience the same inputs, rewards or perform the same actions – possibly in combination. We use yoking as an analytical tool to identify the algorithm that drives learning in a target agent. We evaluate this approach in a synthetic task, where we know the ground truth learning algorithm. Then we apply it to biological data from a physical puzzle task, to identify the learning algorithm behind physical problem solving in Goffin's cockatoos. Our results show that yoking works, and can be used to identify the target algorithm more reliably, with less variance and assumptions, than a more unconstrained approach to identify learning algorithms.

Keywords: Learning · Yoking · Off-policy · Reinforcement learning

1 Introduction

Behavioral biology aims to understand how animals learn to solve novel tasks. AI wants to use such knowledge to build general artificial agents. To gain insights into the mechanisms underlying biological learning, we can compare observed

Funded by the Deutsche Forschungsgemeinschaft (DFG, German Research Foundation) under Germany's Excellence Strategy – EXC 2002/1 "Science of Intelligence" – project number 390523135.

behavior to that of artificial agents for which we know the learning method. Agreement between learned behaviors serves as evidence for agreement in the mechanisms that drive behavioral adaptation. But to identify behavioral agreement requires meaningful comparisons of the behavioral trajectories of several agents. We will discuss why this is a challenging problem and show how *yoking*—an experimental technique from behavioral biology—enables such comparisons.

Behavioral trajectories can exhibit substantial variability. Reasons for this include inter-individual differences in embodiment, knowledge, and skills as well as variability in the environment. As a result, the space of action sequences and learning trajectories is extremely large, already for moderately complex tasks and environments. Two learning trajectories may explore entirely different regions in this space, even when they are generated by the same learning algorithm. To gain insights into biological behavior, we therefore must find ways to perform meaningful comparisons in spite of this variability.

We propose a method for identifying learning behaviors based on a set of hypothesized model algorithms, even when behavioral trajectories are sampled from very large spaces. We assume that the agent whose learning behavior we seek to understand (usually a biological agent we call the *target agent*) follows some learning method we would like to identify. The target agent produces behavioral trajectories that sample only a small, but highly relevant subset of all possible behaviors. To identify the mechanisms implemented in the target agent, we compare its behavior to that of a set of alternative agents, each implementing a different learning method. To effectively compare these agents, we *yoke* the other agents to the target agent. This leads to meaningful comparisons, identifying learning models that resemble the target agent's learning behavior.

The term *yoking* originates in behavioral biology. In the classical yoking setting, two animals are aligned so that both experience the outcomes of the

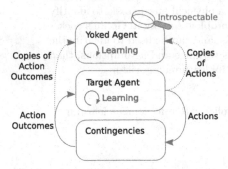

(a) A yoked, introspectable agent receives copies of a target agent's actions and action outcomes. Learning in the yoked agent is evaluated as model for learning in the target agent.

(b) A Goffin's cockatoo opens a baited mechanical puzzle, called lockbox. The lockbox consists of a cashew reward behind an acrylic door, a metal bar blocking that door, and a metal disk blocking the metal bar.

Fig. 1. We evaluate and apply the yoking experimental paradigm with to identify the learning mechanisms that enable animals to solve complex problems.

behavior of just one of them (the target agent). This serves to isolate the role of contingent behavior from the effect of receiving rewards. Whereas it is difficult to yoke perception and actions of biological agents, we have full control over synthetic models. We can enforce their experience to align with respect to rewards, percepts, and actions. Figure 1a shows a schematic of this approach. Yoking causes the artificial agent to mimic the behavior of the target agent, effectively confining learning to plausible behavioral trajectories, rendering the comparison meaningful in spite of large unexplored regions of the behavioral space.

We develop and evaluate a methodology for yoking-based identification of learning algorithms. We apply the yoking paradigm to learning a physical puzzle task, the lockbox depicted in Fig. 1b. To solve this task, an agent must open several mechanical locks in sequence to obtain a reward. We evaluate the proposed method in two sets of experiments. First, we evaluate the yoking approach by successfully identifying the learning algorithm of an artificial target agent for which we know the true learning algorithm. The yoking-based comparison between the target agent and other artificial agents successfully identifies the learning method of the target agent from a set of candidate models. Our experiments show that yoking does this with fewer assumptions and less variance than a more unconstrained approach. We apply yoking to data obtained with real-life cockatoos performing the same task. Our results show that yoking is an important tool in identifying learning behavior in artificial and biological agents.

2   Related Work

We discuss applications of yoking in biological learning experiments and then describe recent applications based on machine learning.

In the biological learning literature, the dominant application of yoking is as a "yoked control." Here, two animals are placed inside identical skinner boxes, where both animals can act and perceive their environments independently, however, they are yoked with respect to the rewards they receive. The release of rewards in both boxes is contingent only on the actions of the *target* animal. This setup reveals if changes in behavior are due to operant conditioning or purely due to a changing frequency of reward or punishment [10]. Yoked control has been criticized because it can bias results towards conclusions in favor of the operant conditioning hypothesis [5]. It seems the main source for bias in yoked controls are individual differences [3]. In this paper we use simulated experiments to evaluate the effect that inter-individual differences have on the yoking procedure. In contrast to the classical application of yoking as a control, we use it with the goal to directly identify a target learning algorithm.

Yoking an animal to another animal's rewards is simple, but yoking perceptual inputs is more difficult. The classical kitten carousel experiment [6] is an example of yoking two animals together so that they get the same sensory inputs. Besides yoking through mechanical linking, powered mobility devices could also be used to yoke two subjects perceptually [1].

To yoke the perception of synthetic agents to real animals, we must know the percepts of the animal. An interesting approach to this problem is a controlled rearing approach, in which newborn chicks are motion-tracked and raised in a mostly virtual environment [13]. This setting was used to train artificial neural networks on the same visual input that the birds received [7].

It is practically impossible to yoke two animals such that they perform the same *actions*. But this can be easily done if the yoked agent is a computational model. Recently, a so-called tandem learning setting was used to yoke deep Q-Learning agents to one another [9]. This was done to analyze the difficulty of off-policy learning problem. Off-policy learning means that an agent learns using data that was not generated by the behavior it executes to solve the task, but by another behavior. Results showed that difficulties in off-policy learning mainly stem from the use of non-linear function approximators and the inherent misfit of target agents' data distributions to yoked agents policies. As it turns out, this insight is not only relevant to machine learning, but also to biological research. The yoked experimental design necessarily involves off-policy learning. And because we likely need complex, non-linear learning models to explain learning in complex animals, biological analysis needs to be aware of the challenges involved in the off-policy learning problem. In this paper we circumvent this issue by using tabular models that are capable of off-policy learning.

There are also other approaches in machine learning where a target agent, potentially human, is copied by another learning agent. Behavioral cloning [12], inverse reinforcement learning [8] and generally the learning-from-demonstration setting [2] are related areas of research. However, the common goal in those cases is to copy the target agent and to achieve high reward, not to identify the target agent's learning algorithm.

3   Comparing Synthetic Learning Models to Target Data

We want to understand how animals learn to solve novel problems. Our approach is to compare their learning to the adaptation of artificial learning models in similar settings. Because the artificial models are introspectable, we learn which mechanisms in artificial models are most likely to explain the observed biological learning. We use two different ways to perform the required comparisons: one in which the behavior of the agent is yoked and one in which it is unconstrained.

3.1   Problem Formalization

We assume that the underlying learning problem can be formalized as reinforcement learning (RL) problem on a discrete Markov Decision Process (MDP). A discrete MDP is a four-tuple (S, A, T, R) that consists of a set of states S, a set of actions A, a probabilistic state-transition function $T = p(s'|s, a)$ and a reward function $R(s, a)$. The probabilistic state-transition function T captures the probability that an action a will cause the system to transition from state s to state s'. The goal of the reinforcement learning problem then is to learn a policy $\Pi(s) = p(a|s)$ that maximizes the expected reward in the MDP. The problem this paper tackles is the question: Given sequences of actions that a reinforcement learning agent performed as it learned to solve the task, can we identify the ground truth learning algorithm that adapted the behavior?

To answer this question we assume an episodic RL setting, where the target agent acts in the MDP during a sequence of m sessions $D_1, ..., D_m$ (episodes). In each session the agent performs n_m actions $a_m = a_m^1...a_m^n$ using its policy Π_m^* which is adapted after each session using the ground truth learning algorithm. As we generally do not have access to the ground truth policy P^* or its output distribution over actions $p_m^*(a_m)$, we can only infer the learning algorithm from the actions a that were performed. Our approach is to compare the actions performed by the target policy Π^* to the output distributions p_m^k of k different policies Π^k that are each adapted by a different candidate learning algorithm. For this comparison we use the Sørensen-Dice similarity [4] between each candidate policy's posterior over actions p_m^k and a categorical distribution fit to the actions performed by the ground truth policy. Given a set of candidate learning algorithm models, this lets us compute a per-session similarity measure between the policy adapted by the target learning algorithm and several candidate policies – each adapted by a different candidate learning algorithm.

3.2 *Unconstrained* Approach to Identify Learning Algorithms

A straightforward approach to this problem is to simulate the MDP using the state-transition function $T = p(s'|s, a)$ and to choose actions based on the candidate policy Π^k. This yields sequences of actions and rewards that can be used to adapt the policy using the candidate learning algorithm in between sessions.

But this approach has drawbacks. The first drawback is that modelling errors accumulate, as the actions performed by the agent depend on the changes made by the learning algorithm, and those changes, in return, depend on the performed actions. If either the simulation (state-transition function T) or the candidate model for the learning algorithm are not exactly correct, errors accumulate significantly over time. The simulation and the learning algorithms are models, so in any case both will be at least slightly wrong. The accumulated errors will lead to high variance not only in the outcomes of the simulations, but also in the metric used to compare those data to the actions performed by the target agent. The second drawback is that we need a full model of the domain in which the behavior is observed. Especially a state-transition function T can be challenging to obtain in contact-rich, real world scenarios.

3.3 *Yoked* Approach to Identify Learning Algorithms

High variance and the need for a state-transition model are challenging problems that can be avoided with a yoking-based approach. The idea of yoking is simple, yet powerful. Instead of using a full simulation to generate actions, we can instead directly use the actions a^* that were performed by the target policy Π^* and align the state to follow the same trajectory as encountered by the ground-truth agent.

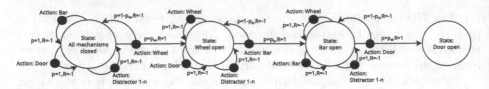

Fig. 2. The lockbox task, modelled as a finite Markov Decision Process with four discrete states. Actions with their probabilistic outcomes and rewards are depicted as branching arrows.

Using this approach, we cannot avoid *all* modeling aspects that come with an MDP model. We still need a set of states S, a set of actions A and a reward function R. However we can avoid modelling the state-transition function T. This approach significantly reduces variance as it avoids randomness introduced by the simulation. Instead, the yoked model is closely aligned to the target agent.

4   Evaluation in a Synthetic Lockbox Task

To assess the performance of both approaches we need an experiment where the ground-truth learning algorithm is known. Thus, we implemented a simulated experiment, similar to the biological one we will use for evaluation in Sect. 5. In this environment we simulate several learning agents and assess how well each of the two approaches can identify the ground truth learning algorithm.

The task we consider is the physical puzzle depicted in Fig. 1b, called a lockbox. This lockbox represents a sequential manipulation problem where the agent has to first remove a metal disk, so that it can then push a bar to the side, which makes it possible to finally open a door and retrieve a reward. This lockbox task can be modelled as a dicrete MDP with four states and three actions shown in Fig. 2. The transition probabilities depend on the agent's mechanical skills p_w, p_b, p_d to open the wheel, bar and door respectively. The reward function yields a reward of 1 for every action that could successfully open a lock, and -1 otherwise. Importantly, opened locks can not be closed again.

We consider five different candidate learners. Two of these learners use tabular Q-Learning [11], but with different learning rates. The model *QLearn (slow)* uses a learning rate $\alpha = 0.1$ and the model *QLearn (fast)* uses a learning rate $\alpha = 0.9$. Two other models follow a custom learning algorithm, we call *Myopic RL*. For each state, this model has a parameter vector ω with as many elements as the number of available actions. In each state, actions are sampled from the categorical distribution $\sigma(\omega)$, where $\sigma(.)$ is the soft-max function. Whenever this agent successfully performs an action i to change the state of the lockbox, then the respective entry ω_i is increased by a constant amount β. The two *Myopic RL* learners differ in this learning rate β, where *Myopic RL (slow)* uses $\beta = 1$ and *Myopic RL (fast)* uses $\beta = 100$. Finally, we also use a baseline algorithm which implements no learning whatsoever, called *No Learning*.

4.1 Identifying Known Ground Truth Learning Algorithms

We cannot use biological data to compare the performance of the *yoked* and *unconstrained* approach, as we don't know what the ground-truth learning algorithm is behind real animals' learning. Thus we will simulate the aforementioned algorithms as the ground-truth learning algorithms and evaluate which of the approaches identifies the target algorithm more reliably.

To generate the ground-truth learning data, we simulated each of the algorithms 32 times on a synthetic lockbox experiment. This lockbox experiment had three states and three relevant actions, as described above, however we added seven additional distractor actions that do not have an effect on the state. The initial action selection probabilities $p(a|s)$ for each policy were sampled from a Dirichlet distribution with $\alpha_1^{dir} = \ldots = \alpha_{10}^{dir} = 1.0$, and blackbox optimization was used to find corresponding parameters for *QLearn* and *Myopic RL* that map to such an initial distribution. We constrained learning to 12 sessions of maximally 200 actions each. As can be seen in Fig. 3, both *Myopic RL* conditions can learn to solve the task, *QLearn (fast)* also shows adequate performance while *QLearn (slow)* manages to only slightly outperform *No Learning* with the very restricted number of actions and sessions. The expected number of required actions for a perfect agent would be 30, given the mechanical skill setting of 0.1.

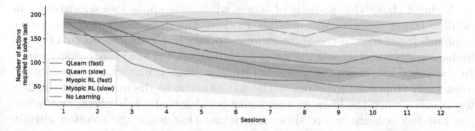

Fig. 3. Mean and $\frac{1}{2}$ standard deviation of the learning curves for different agents in a simulated lockbox task. The Myopic RL agent learns the task the quickest on average, with both sets of parameters. Q-Learning also learns the task with high learning rate, while the learning rate of *QLearn (slow* is too small to learn the task reliably in 12 sessions. Each model was simulated 32 times, sessions limited to a length of 200 actions and the mechanical skill was set as $p_w, p_b, p_d = 0.1$.

Next we perform a comparison of the *yoked* and *unconstrained* approach. We use each of the five previously simulated models individually as the ground truth target algorithm to be identified. In that identification problem, all five models also serve as a candidate model that may be the underlying ground truth algorithm. So, for example, when *QLearn (fast)* is the target, all 5 learning models are used as hypotheses and the goal would be to identify that *QLearn (fast)* is indeed the most probable learner behind the observed changes in behavior.

For each of the 32 runs per target algorithm, we either yoke or simulate each candidate algorithm ten times. These ten models are initialized so that they follow the same distribution of actions as the target algorithm in its first session. We cannot directly use the probabilities $p(a|s)$ of the target algorithm's policy, as in a setting where the target agent is biological we would not have access to this information. Instead we use the relative frequency of actions the target agent performed and, again, use blackbox-optimization to find parameters for the candidate models that yield a $p(a|s)$ according to these frequencies. After this initialization, agents in the *unconstrained* condition are simulated and learn independently, while agents in the *yoked* condition learn from the same actions and receive the same action outcomes as the target model.

Next, we assess which of the agents best explain the target agent's behavior. The following procedure is applied to all pairs of target models and candidate learning models, irrespective of how the candidate models were trained. The similarity measure is computed per session.

For each of the 32 instances of the target agent, there are ten *yoked* and ten *unconstrained* candidate model executions. For each instance i of the target agent, we fit a categorical distribution $\mathbf{p}_i$ its performed actions. Then we compare this distribution to the known action distribution $\mathbf{p}_{ij}(a|s)$ of the $j \in [1, \ldots, 10]$ candidate models using Sørensen-Dice similarity [4]. For each instance of the target agent, this yields ten similarity scores for which we compute mean μ_i and standard deviation σ_i. Finally, to ensure statistical support, we average these statistical moments over the 32 instances such that $\overline{\mu} = \mathbb{E}_i(\mu_i)$ and $\overline{\sigma} = \mathbb{E}_i(\sigma_i)$.

Figure 4 shows this statistic of scores when it is applied session-wise to all pairs of target models and candidate models. The data shows that the *yoking* approach is superior to the *unconstrained* approach. *Unconstrained* suffers from higher variance and reveals the ground-truth algorithm less clearly than *yoking*. In the *yoked* condition, the ground truth algorithm is almost at all points the most likely (topmost) hypothesis. The results are most distinctive after the first few sessions when the learning algorithms could actually take effect, and before the last few sessions where those algorithms that learn the solution already converged to that very same solution.

4.2   Comparison over Size of Action Space

We compare the analytical performance of the *yoked* and *unconstrained* approaches when we vary the size of the action space. In the analysis in the previous subsection, we increased the number or possible actions to ten, by introducing seven actions without effect. In Fig. 5, we assess the performance of the approaches when we vary the number of additional, effect-less actions to between 0 and 17. We measure analytical performance of either approach as follows. First, we compute the probability to identify the correct algorithm on a per-session basis. We do this by computing the probability $p_c^i = p(m_t \geq m_0 \wedge \ldots \wedge m_t \geq m_i)$ that the correct model is the most probable explanation for each session i, using monte-carlo inference based on the distributions $\mathcal{N}(\overline{\mu}, \overline{\sigma})$ described above. Then we average these session-wise scores into an overall score. Figure 5 shows that yoking is generally superior to the unconstrained condition, but the performance does not vary with increasing number of actions. We believe this is because the

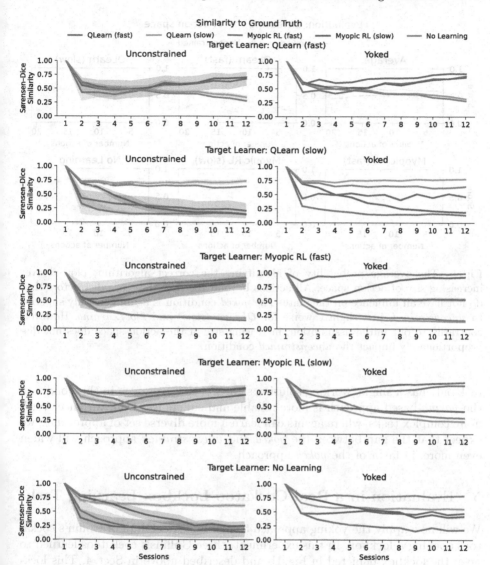

Fig. 4. A comparison of the *unconstrained* approach (left column) to the *yoked* approach (right column). For all five target algorithms, the *yoked* approach identifies the target algorithm as the most likely one (it is the topmost line). It does so with less variance and a larger margin than the *unconstrained* approach. Yoking can even differentiate variants of *QLearn* and Myopic RL with different learning rates. In contrast, the *unconstrained* condition suffers from higher variance which makes conclusions more difficult.

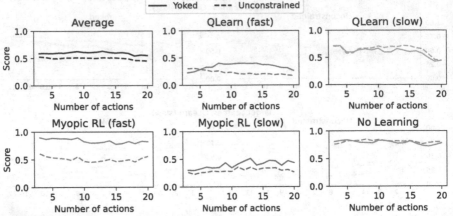

Fig. 5. The average probability of identifying the correct algorithm, plotted over increasing size of action space. All actions beyond the first three are distractors that do not have an influence on the state. The *yoked* condition is again generally superior to *unconstrained*, just slightly worse for *QLearn (slow)* and *No Learning*. However, contrarily to our initial assumption, increasing size of the action space does not disproportionately impact the *unconstrained* condition.

task only has a single, working solution strategy. However even in this condition the *yoking*-based approach is more reliable and suffers less from variance. With more complex tasks, where agents can learn a more diverse set of approaches, we expect that the gap between the *yoked* and *unconstrained* approach will widen even more, in favor of the *yoked* approach.

5   Evaluation in a Real Cockatoo Lockbox Learning Task

We will now apply the yoking approach to real biological data of Goffin's cockatoos opening a lockbox. In this experiment, three Goffins's cockatoos learned to open the lockbox depicted in Fig. 1b and described above in Sect. 4. This lockbox is baited with a cashew reward behind the final plexi-glass door. To obtain the cashew, the birds need to unlock the individual mechanism in the described sequence. For each bird, the data consists of 12 sessions with a maximum of duration of 15 minutes per session. The birds were habituated and pre-trained to open the last two-stages of this lockbox, the door and the bar, so the main learning problem considered here is learning to open the lockbox with the additional metal disk that needs to be unlocked first.

While we acknowledge that none of our candidate algorithms is realistically implemented in the birds, it is still worthwhile and informative to see how the models' adaptation compares to learning in the birds. Due to space constraints we cannot explain the bird experiments in detail, but the most important feature

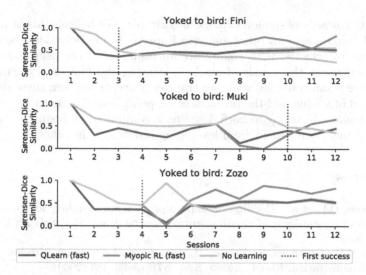

Fig. 6. Similarity of three candidate learning algorithm hypotheses to real bird data. Over the course of 12 sessions, all three birds are first best explained by the *No Learning* hypothesis, until the *Myopic RL* model becomes the best explanation. These switching points also align with the sessions where the real birds made learning progress in the experiments. The *First success* line indicates the session when the birds solved the lockbox for the first time.

of these experiments is that the birds rapidly improve in the task after they discovered the solution to the lockbox for the first time. Figure 6 shows the results of a *yoked* analysis, and indeed their (not) learning in the first sessions seems to be best explained by the *No Learning* model until the *Myopic RL (fast)* model takes over as the best explanation. This inflection point is largely synchronous with those sessions where the birds learn to open the lockbox for the first time. *Myopic RL (fast)* is the fastest candidate learning model in our analysis, which suits the rapid learning we observe in the birds.

6   Conclusion

If we aim to understand how animals learn to solve complex tasks, we need tools to compare biological learning data to synthetic learning models. In this paper, we show that yoking should be an important ingredient to such a comparison. In this context, yoking means that synthetic learning algorithms directly makes use of the actions, percepts, and rewards that the target agent experienced. Our analysis demonstrates that yoking is an appropriate tool to for identifying the learning algorithm underlying an observed learning behavior. But this approach also faces a challenge, namely the off-policy learning problem. Not all reinforcement learning algorithms are equally capable of learning from data generated by another agent [9]. Thus, analyses like ours need to take great care to not bias results towards off-policy capable algorithms. We believe this is a highly significant insight, also for other analytical approaches in behavioral biology.

Our results achieved with yoking are an example for the deep connections that exists between the worlds of machine learning and biological learning. We believe there is much to gain when we transfer concepts between these domains. The method of yoking and the problem of off-policy learning, both, are relevant in either domain. Learning in both domains is confronted with similar problems and each domain can benefit from leveraging insights of the other.

References

1. Anderson, D.I., et al.: The flip side of perception-action coupling: locomotor experience and the ontogeny of visual-postural coupling. Hum. Mov. Sci. **20**(4–5), 461–487 (2001)
2. Argall, B.D., Chernova, S., Veloso, M., Browning, B.: A survey of robot learning from demonstration. Robot. Auton. Syst. **57**(5), 469–483 (2009)
3. Church, R.M.: Systematic effect of random error in the yoked control design. Psychol. Bull. **62**(2), 122 (1964)
4. Dice, L.R.: Measures of the amount of ecologic association between species. Ecology **26**(3), 297–302 (1945)
5. Gardner, R.A., Gardner, B.T.: Feedforward versus feedbackward: an ethological alternative to the law of effect. Behav. Brain Sci. **11**(3), 429–447 (1988)
6. Held, R., Hein, A.: Movement-produced stimulation in the development of visually guided behavior. J. Comp. Physiol. Psychol. **56**(5), 872 (1963)
7. Lee, D., Gujarathi, P., Wood, J.N.: Controlled-rearing studies of newborn chicks and deep neural networks. Preprint arXiv:2112.06106 (2021)
8. Ng, A.Y., Russell, S.J.: Algorithms for inverse reinforcement learning. In: Proceedings of the Seventeenth International Conference on Machine Learning, pp. 663–670. Morgan Kaufmann Publishers Inc., San Francisco (2000)
9. Ostrovski, G., Castro, P.S., Dabney, W.: The difficulty of passive learning in deep reinforcement learning. In: Advances in Neural Information Processing Systems, vol. 34 (2021)
10. Salkind, N.J.: Encyclopedia of Research Design, vol. 1. Sage, Thousand Oaks (2010)
11. Sutton, R.S., Barto, A.G.: Reinforcement Learning: An Introduction. MIT Press, Cambridge (2018)
12. Torabi, F., Warnell, G., Stone, P.: Behavioral cloning from observation. Preprint arXiv:1805.01954 (2018)
13. Wood, S.M., Wood, J.N.: Using automation to combat the replication crisis: a case study from controlled-rearing studies of newborn chicks. Infant Behav. Dev. **57**, 101329 (2019)

Is Free Energy an Organizational Principle in Spiking Neural Networks?

Jose A. Fernandez-Leon[1,3,5]($\boxtimes$) (iD), Marcelo Arlego[2,3,5] (iD), and Gerardo G. Acosta[4,5] (iD)

[1] CIFICEN (UNCPBA-CICPBA-CONICET) & INTIA (UNCPBA-CICPBA), 7000 Tandil, Argentina
jafernandez@intia.exa.unicen.edu.ar
[2] Instituto de Física La Plata (UNLP-CONICET), 1900 La Plata, Argentina
[3] Exact Sciences Faculty (UNCPBA), 7000 Tandil, Argentina
[4] INTELYMEC-CIFICEN (UNCPBA, CICPBA, CONICET), Fac. Eng, B7400 Olavarría, Argentina
[5] National Scientific and Technical Research Council (CONICET), Buenos Aires, Argentina

Abstract. An open question in neuroscience is how the brain self-organizes. Despite significant progress in such understanding, this effort is still difficult to address in biological neural networks due to limitations in recording all the involved network components. It is possible however to approach this issue by examining how relatively small bio-inspired networks self-organize its neural activities under different states. From a computational standpoint, one can have access in this way to all variables and parameters of the network. Here we discuss how (non-variational) free energy varies during drastic changes in a spiking network through a sleep-like transition and in the absence of sensing. This non-variational free energy is defined as in its thermodynamic counterpart, where 'energy' refers to a quantity whose mean value is known or estimated from data sampling or model generated. We propose a novel view of how free energy is organized in a cortical-like neural network differently according to the synchronization of the network under external or internal fluctuations. Empirically testable hypotheses are presented in the context of non-sensory free energy modulation.

Keywords: Free energy · Neural network · Brain · Organization · Sleep

1 Introduction: Decoding the Free Energy Concept

The concept of free energy reached broad interest in neuroscience and cognitive research. However, there are different ways to understand free energy as we will see in this section before discussing free energy as a dynamical, organizational principle of the brain. On the one hand, from the statistical inference point of view, free energy is commonly associated with the difference between sampled data and the expected information from an internal generative model [1, 2]. Free energy in this context can be understood through the (variational) Free Energy Principle (FEP), which inspires one of the most comprehensive frameworks to study cognition and complex adaptive systems (c.f., [1, 3]). In

L. Cañamero et al. (Eds.): SAB 2022, LNAI 13499, pp. 79–90, 2022.
https://doi.org/10.1007/978-3-031-16770-6_7

dynamical systems terms, the FEP is commonly associated with how (biological) systems maintain their internal order through non-equilibrium steady states by restricting themselves to a limited number of states [4]. One of the most salient proposals of the FEP is that organisms actively sample sensory evidence, which is aligned with their predictions to minimize, through continuous actions, the difference between the organism's model of the world and current sensing [5]. This variational density is defined based on a probabilistic model that generates predicted observations from the system's hypothesized causes [1]. For this probabilistic model, the variational term relates to an ansatz depending on parameters that are 'varied' to achieve the maximum agreement between this model and the true distribution that generates the observations. Variational methods of this kind form a central part of Bayesian inference [4]. Through action in the FEP, then variational free energy can be suppressed by increasing the accuracy of sensory data (i.e., selectively sampling data predicted by the internal representation). Nevertheless, this is not necessarily always the case. What brings active inference to contrast with other accounts (e.g., Hohwy's [6] prediction error minimization) is that action plays an essential role in the predictive process, as opposed to a mere passive inference of sensory data. The regulation of free energy consequently can be understood as an adaptive process involving actions under the FEP.

On the other hand, the non-variational free energy (i.e., non-variational refers to a measure from known or estimated values given sampled data) has its genesis in physics, as described below. In equilibrium thermodynamics, the Helmholtz's free energy has a precise definition [7, 8] referring to the difference between the internal mean energy (E) minus the product of the entropy (H) and the temperature (T) of a system (see Supplemental Information). Briefly, T plays the role of a 'hyperparameter' that controls the trade-off between these opposing tendencies: minimizing mean E and maximizing H [8]. In this line, Boltzmann, Helmholtz, and others showed that thermodynamics is a by-product of statistical physics [8], with the Boltzmann distribution as the cornerstone. Jaynes [9], in turn, reduced statistical physics to information theory. From Jaynes' point of view, the basic element for measuring F is not mean energy E but entropy H. Consequently, given a partial knowledge about a system (e.g., the average value of the energy E measured from the observer perspective) the underlying probability distribution (the one that generates E mean) maximizes the entropy. This distribution refers to Boltzmann's [9] and emerges from the principle of maximum entropy (*MaxEnt*). The Boltzmann distribution provides the least informative ansatz (i.e., minimal assumptions) given a partial knowledge of the system. The *MaxEnt* principle can be applied to inference problems where there is incomplete information of a system [10]. Considering these views, the non-variational free energy can be defined as in its thermodynamic counterpart, where 'energy' E refers to a quantity whose mean value is known or estimated from data sampling or model generated, and 'temperature' T is a hyperparameter. This point of view supports the so-called energy-based techniques in statistical inference [10]. It is important to emphasize here that these methods are completely non-variational and are the basis of our work in the following sections.

The analysis of entropy and non-variational free energy in the above context have enabled hypotheses on the brain's organizational principles, which is beneficial for differentiating healthy vs non-functional brain dynamics and to propose treatments for some brain's disorders [11]. To exemplify, it has been used to identify dynamic patterns of EEG activity to differentiate conscious from unconscious brain's states. In this empirically based work [11], network synchronization patterns were evaluated by calculating entropy changes in EEG time series. For this, a synchronization order parameter was taken as probability distribution by assuming a linear dependence between them. In another study [12], the concept of non-variational free energy was used based on a network of randomly coupled Izhikevich's neurons [13] and spike-timing-dependent plasticity (STDP) [14]. The authors analyzed the dynamics of the transition between wakefulness-like (characterized by frequencies in the γ-gamma band) and sleep-like (δ-delta band) states. The mean energy E of the network was defined from a generalized Hopfield's model [15]. The Shannon's entropy H was calculated in this case using the estimated probability distribution of spikes generated from the simulations. With these elements, the free energy H (where the hyperparameter T is set to 1) was proposed (see Supplemental Information).

Considering these perspectives and studies, this position paper makes a differentiation arguing that the non-variational free energy refers to reactive regulations in a self-organizing, cortical-like neural network in terms of its synaptic weights through spike-timing-dependent plasticity. The concept of self-organization in this work therefore would refer from now on to topological (structural) self-organization. We can assume thus that not the 'same' free energy is minimized variationally or non-variationally. Instead, we can argue that there are different but related levels of free energy regulation, one taking part at the organism level (i.e., variational, and predictive) and another acting at a low level (i.e., non-variational and at synaptic-neuronal level). The first case has been extensively discussed and analyzed by Friston and colleagues. Here we discuss the latter view from the non-variational standpoint of free energy. This position paper is based on a previous model [12] and this manuscript is a more general view on the topic. Readers are strongly encouraged to read the first paper for details on the implemented neural network model before reading this one.

2   Free Energy in the Absence of External Sensing

Friston's FEP refers to thermodynamics for biological formulations in adaptive systems. First, in an Ashbian sense [16], a system is selectively adaptive to its environment to preclude phase transitions and stay away from thermodynamic equilibrium. Second, homeostatically, a system behaves adaptively when it changes its relationship with the environment to maintain 'essential' (physiological) variables within certain bounds. Under this view, the FEP adaptivity refers directly to homeostatic viability [1], where adaptive (living) systems fall within a relatively narrow region of all possible states in their phase space. However, living systems may encounter wide ranges of environmental conditions and physiological stressors that will make homeostasis challenging to maintain [17] (see other conceptions of homeostasis involving learning and anticipation in [18]). In its minimal formulation, this restoration of homeostasis seems doable by the organism's subsystems and mechanisms making ancillary regulations rather than made directly at the organism level (e.g., through mechanisms of sensory inference) to which these subsystems belong. Biological systems can also minimize free energy through internal feedback depending on their internal states, which could be seen as implying a reactive control for regulations [17].

Relating these discussions with the FEP, however, makes a conundrum. The homeostatic modulation of variational free energy seems mostly (if not only) pursued by predictive mechanisms rather than by a reactive control system inside the organism's nervous system (c.f., [18]). Despite the significant value of these works, it is still unclear then how free energy changes depending on the system's state in the absence of sensing. This issue is observed during the awake-sleep transition in a neural network, mainly when environmental sensing and conscious state is drastically reduced. Note here that the premise in our discussion is that all perception nearly stops during sleep because it has been suggested the brain is shut-off from the external world during sleep [19, 20]) (c.f., dreaming/asleep involving conscious experiences [21, p. 39]). Furthermore, in [11] it is proposed that entropy is associated with the number of configurations of connected brain networks, where some refer to the free energy available in conscious (e.g., awake) and unconscious (e.g., sleep) states. Based on energy dissipation in the synchronization among cell networks and dissipative structures, authors in [11] hypothesized that energy dissipation is a simple general principle for brain organization.

With these formulations articulated, the next step is to deploy arguments to answer the following question: what characteristics must simple neural systems (or even simple neural self-organizing systems) possess to reduce free energy in the absence of sense? The next section discusses this point in detail.

3   Non-variational Free Energy in a Spiking Neural Network

How can we identify regulations of free energy in a non-variational manner in a cortical-like neural network? One way to understand this phenomenon is considering the effect of external input (i.e., a thalamic input) having an impact on neural activities in a network. This effect could involve dissipative effects on neural activities induced by such input (see the concept of a resonator in [12]). It is then conceivable that the bigger (e.g., in terms of frequency and amplitude) the thalamic input is, the more abrupt the changes in the network frequency across neurons will be, which would end up changing the network rhythmicity. The effect of the induced change would reflect the tendency of neurons to synchronize and desynchronize under the influence of either external or internal fluctuations affecting neuronal ensembles differently in each network state (e.g., one representing an awake- vs sleep-like state). In other words, such neurostimulation could alter synchronous activities' patterns concerning the network's global frequency [22, 23].

After these considerations, we can get similar observations as those presented in the previous section regarding free energy. The modulation of (non-variational) free energy indicates that when the changes in synchrony between neural networks occur due to an induced frequency (i.e., as during induced gamma or delta rhythm [12]), the larger the dissipation becomes across the network, which makes a change in the global free energy. This phenomenon emphasizes the importance of the variability in synchrony patterns during an awake-like state and reflects the expected low variability in a restive-like state. At a high level of description, the tendency mentioned above increases dissipation, increasing the probability of neural connections becoming active and engaging differently in other network states.

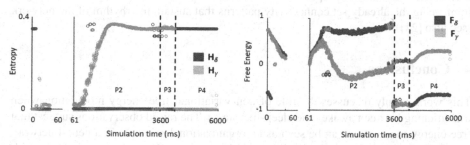

Fig. 1. Time course of the network entropy (H) and free energy (F) indicating state-dependent variations. **(Left)** The H of each network rhythm is shown across the simulation time, with Pi indicating the simulation phase. Phase P1 represents the initial organization of the network. P2 is where a predominant γ (gamma), an awake-like rhythm is observed. A thalamic rhythm is induced at phase P3, and P4 represent the phase where a predominant δ (delta), sleep-like rhythm is predominant. **(Right)** The value of F for both rhythms are shown for the simulated network. See Supplemental Information. Adapted from [12] with permission from Elsevier.

To further discuss this issue, we can say that spiking, self-organizing neural networks can show changes in free energy during the transition from the awake-to-sleep state and vice versa, depending on the global frequency of the network [12]. The definition of non-variational free energy here is then based on the relative difference between the energy and entropy of the network (see Supplemental Information) from the initial distribution (prior to activity-dependent plasticity) to the nonequilibrium steady-state distribution (after plasticity). In more detail, based on a physically plausible, environmentally iso-lated neuronal network that self-organizes its synchronized neural activities after induc-ing a thalamic input, in [12] it was shown that the reduction of non-variational free energy depends sensitively upon thalamic input at a slow, rhythmic Poisson (e.g., delta) frequency due to spike-timing-dependent plasticity. We can think that the entraining slow activity with thalamic input induces a frequency change from gamma (awake-like) to a delta (sleep-like) mode of activity, which can be characterized through modula-tion of the network's energy and entropy (non-variational free energy) of the ensuing dynamics (Fig. 1; see Supplemental Information). This relatively simple circular pro-cess enables stability by changing the network rhythm by means of synaptic plasticity affecting how the neurons fire. The self-organizing response to low and high thalamic drive also showed characteristic differences in the spectrum of frequency content due to spike-timing-dependent plasticity [12]. In other words, the induced input was sufficient to create a global dynamic change in a spiking network.

Such input definition increases variability in neural excitability during the network's sleep-like rhythm, enabling changes to an awake-like rhythm. From a higher-level per-spective, this phenomenon is two-fold: (a) it indicates that an increase in the fluctuations in the spiking neural activity enhances more the entropic term than energy and helps reduce the free energy (see Supplemental Information); (b) the stimulation alters the patterns of synchronous activity, which can be related with brain research (see also [22,

23]). Overall, our observations suggest that the tendency to increase the entropy of spikes increases the probability for neural connections to become active. It can be hypothesized then that it is an intrinsic property of an isolated neural network, perhaps maintaining or reinforcing the already set connectivity patterns that sustain the rhythm of the network (see also [24]).

4 Conclusions

This work mainly discusses the role of non-variational free energy modulation when transitioning between awake- and sleep-like states. The raised observations suggest that free energy modulation can be seen as an organizational principle in a neural network even when sensations are drastically minimized during sleep-like processes, providing empirically testable hypotheses. The non-variational view of free energy helps to understand how modulation is possible through self-organization, where our view of the energy-entropy relationship is directly measurable (see [12]). The observations here support the idea that there are changes in the organization of the network and associated variables conveying localized modulation of free energy in a non-variational, ancillary manner. The introduced perspective is especially interesting for experimental neuroscientists trying to connect network states with that at the synaptic level.

The emphasis of our discussions is that the two approaches to free energy have a different nature. The FEP is based on the variational free energy, which measures the similarity between distributions of beliefs (expectations) from evidence, based on KL divergence from information theory. On the other hand, the concept of non-variational free energy is based on the *MaxEnt* principle. The latter approach is expressed through the balance between opposing tendencies: minimizing an 'energy' distributed in a few degrees of freedom (high certainty) and maximizing entropy (high uncertainty). Although both perspectives propose ways in which the brain generates internal representations of the external world, in this work we presented our thoughts on understanding free energy regulation in line with the later perspective, in the framework of a concrete model approach [12]. This work also conveys the idea that non-variational free energy modulation can occur in the absence of perception as observed during the sleep transition.

There are some further questions to address: can the notion of non-variational free energy be used in the context of the FEP? While there are some kernels of truth in the account of (variational) free energy minimization as we presented in this work (e.g., the KL divergence has a non-zero value, and the FEP is not falsifiable in the Popperian sense), it seems that there are some fundamental observations that need more explanations, where we have presented literature to base our account upon (e.g., [17, 18, 25]). Amongst them, it is worth noting that based on Helmholtz's work [26] on unconscious inference, Friston's variational free energy evaluates observations and a probability density over their hidden causes. Regarding falsification, the FEP is a framework, not a theory; in this sense, it is not falsifiable, which is not a problem. Additionally, measuring (non-variational) free energy at equilibrium would not solve it if it were a problem.

The introduced perspective is of relevance for the community since it complements the current view of the FEP involving a different aspect of the free energy regulation in self-organizing systems, which is a central topic [12, 27–30]. However, more work needs to be done on analyzing the relationship between the modulation of free energy as presented here but focusing on conscious and unconscious brain states (see [11]). The discussion on free energy should be also extended on how neural networks in the brain organize information in non-cortical brain areas, where neural activities are not defined by sensory or motoric input and there is a specific way in which the neurons are connected (see for example [31]). In this, biologically plausible models and experimental data should be analyzed in future systematic studies to push further the relationship between the variational and non-variational free-energy modulation.

5 Supplemental Information

Free Energy, Energy and Entropy from the Non-variational Standpoint. We want to characterize briefly here the relationship between these variables during two states of interest (i.e., during wake- and sleep-like activity of a self-organizing, realistic spiking neural network) in the absence of sensory perceptions (see [12]). A biologically plausible, environmentally isolated [13, 14] network has the capacity of reaching two different states: (1) one associated with an awake-like state (i.e., showing overall rhythmicity of spikes at gamma (γ) frequency); (2) one associated with a sleep-like state (i.e., showing delta (δ) rhythm). Assuming further that we have a way to induce a change in network' state, we could entrain slow activity via thalamic input [13, 14] which could induce a transition from gamma (γ awake-like state) to a delta (δ sleep-like state) mode of activity of the network. This change of the network's state can be characterized through modulation of free energy as the difference between the net-work's energy and entropy of the ensuing dynamics (i.e., non-variational free energy modulation, or non-variational free energy in brief from now on). Despite, alternative expressions of free energy were proposed regarding what its minimization entails ([32]), we can consider $F = E - H$ as an expression for free energy, representing E energy and H entropy. These concepts were defined elsewhere (see [12]), but here we summarize them for the sake of clarity.

Commonly spiking network's self-organization has an energy change associated with it. That change at network level can be originated from the network's energy $\Delta \overline{E}$ given its self-organization, or as a free energy change ΔF from low-level components of the network (i.e., neural and synaptic interactions). Furthermore, based on Jaynes' point of view [9], an information theory model based free energy could be proposed to address the energy-entropy variation $\Delta F = \Delta \overline{E} - T \cdot \Delta H$. The entropy change is ΔH accompanying a reaction measuring how a change in energy affects the orderliness of the system. With this in mind, we can derive a non-variational free energy for an ensemble of spiking neurons. As the free energy is a well-defined quantity, we need to be precise in defining energy in terms of spiking activity of the network and entropy in terms of the ordines of these spikes. We will consider from now on a convenient representation of E, derived from the Hopfield's [15] energy model adapted to an Izhikevich's spiking neural network. Both the energy and the entropy of the spiking network depends on the membrane voltage and membrane recovery providing negative feedback to the former one. The more energy is observed at the spiking network, the higher the probability of action potentials, for very low energy, the lower the probability. Overall, we computed the probability of being in a particular network state (e.g., γ and δ state) based on the detected rhythm of the network in each time step (see [12] for further details).

Let us assume first that we define a network of neurons as described in [13, 14]. Due to the balance between synaptic excitation and inhibition, the neural network reaches stability after self-organization (e.g., after sufficient elapsed time enabling all parameters on the network to stabilize). We assume that the network has a non-symmetric topology. Because there is no constraint asserting that the synaptic weights are symmetric and guaranteeing that the energy function decreases monotonically while following the activation rules, our model network may exhibit some periodic behavior (i.e., network rhythms) that characterize the network's states (i.e., an awake-like γ state and a sleep-like δ state). As Hopfield proposed [15], we can evaluate that the network activity is confined to relatively small parts of the phase space and does not impair the network's ability to destabilize. There is then a relationship between the energy level and the oscillation frequency of the network, reaching a stable energy level during frequency after an initial rhythm, and δ sleep-like state.

The term H in this case indicates then that the system's entropy is a function of the probability P of its state. The overall observation is that the self-organization of the network shows a lower H at γ compared to δ. We can consider that $P_\gamma > P_\delta$ only if the network self-organizes and reaches a dynamical equilibrium at γ, where the intuitive example is homeostasis (i.e., the network maintains a specific global frequency). It is worth noting that these probabilities are not evaluated over an outcome or event space that covers slow and fast activity (i.e., based upon the probability of being in a γ or δ mode of dynamics). However, the probabilities are based on the system's states. Our observations imply that to pass from one macrostate (e.g., γ) to another less probable macrostate (e.g., δ), we should increase H (e.g., through inducing a thalamic frequency I). Consequently, the non-variational free energy change associated with a reaction to, for example, a rhythmic thalamic input I would tell us whether the reaction will occur under the specified conditions (e.g., in the presence or absence of a change in energy) (see [12]). For a reaction to occur spontaneously (i.e., without the addition of energy), ΔF at the specified condition must be negative given that ΔH is higher than $\Delta \bar{E}$; otherwise, ΔF must be positive when ΔH is reduced.

In Jaynes' free energy point of view, temperature acts as a hyperparameter of the model that regulates the trade-off between two opposing tendencies: energy minimization and entropy maximization. As such, temperature is model dependent and following this idea we set it to $T = 1$ [12]. Hence, two elements are playing the most crucial role in our model to determine the spontaneity of a reaction (i.e., the sign of ΔF), the reaction that is based on energy $\bar{E}$ ($\Delta H < \Delta \bar{E}$), and the one based on entropy change ($\Delta H > \Delta \bar{E}$). A careful examination of that relationship allows us to make the following predictions: if the reaction is rooted in releasing neural firing with increasing $\bar{E}$, and the entropy H increases (high disorder), the free energy change ΔF is positive, and the reaction is nonspontaneous (i.e., energy externally induced). On the other hand, if a reaction is energy-based but decreasing, and the entropy change ΔH is negative (lower disorder), the free energy change ΔF is always negative (spontaneous).

Our train of thoughts up to this point indicates a difference in mean energy $\bar{E}$ and entropy H that depends on the network's state. We can say that our view of the energy-entropy relationship is directly measurable based on the spiking activity of neural populations (at least in artificial spiking neurons). However, now let us consider the following situation. As there is entropy associated with these γ an δ rhythms, we can see that the frequency of an induced input (e.g., one that induces change in the network as for example thalamic input; see [12]) will affect the entropy of the network. After a few operations, we can get the following relationship for the energy and entropy measured at γ and δ rhythms of the network: $F_\gamma = \overline{E}_\gamma - H_\gamma > \overline{E}_\delta - H_\delta = F_\delta$. Figure 1 describes the modulation of the non-variational free energy for each frequency of interest across the states of the network, where P1 is an initial phase of self-organization with δ the dominant frequency; P2 a phase where the γ is predominantly high; P3 a short phase of self-organization after inducing the thalamic perturbation; P4 a phase where the δ is high. Note the equation indicates that F_γ is higher than F_δ, mostly during δ rhythm (Fig. 1, P4 phase). Also, the free energy F_δ is only higher during γ rhythm than during δ rhythm (Fig. 1, P2 phase). Because the inequality between the free energy at δ and γ frequency is a central point of this paper, we should ask what is assumed here about the individual terms that justify this inequality? The overall assumption is that we are analyzing a transition from δ to γ state in our experiment, and we have $P_\gamma > P_\delta$. . Furthermore, considering all the possible states of a pair of neurons and being these neurons synaptically connected to some degree during both stable network states (i.e., γ and δ rhythms), we expect then a higher probability of connectivity during γ than δ rhythm. It is important nothing that a larger entropy of P_γ than P_δ does not directly imply that for all neural pair there is a relationship as $P_\gamma > P_\delta$. In fact, the first thought is that P_γ and P_δ can be different, and thus there will be some neural pairs showing $P_\gamma > P_\delta$, and others with $P_\gamma < P_\delta$. We can solve this tension just by considering the dynamical evolution of the network in isolation over time as reported originally in [14]. We can also consider an intrinsic tendency of the network model to move towards a low entropy state associated to γ, and in turn, making the more ordered entropy level associated to δ less probable. Consequently, the relationship between probabilities resembles better the overall tendency of the network's state.

Our discussion till this point indicates that F_δ is different from zero value (i.e., $F_\delta > 0$, F_δ exist during δ rhythm (Fig. 1, P4 phase); c.f. to sensory surprise disappearance during sleep [25]). This difference happens because both $\overline{E}_\delta$ and H_δ are commonly non-zero in an active spiking neural network. It is worth noting that our definition of $\overline{E}$ is based on neurons' spiking activity instead of one based on the change of state after sensations (c.f. [25]). $\overline{E}$ is still present in the network even during a restive state because our definition does not depend on sensing the environment. Instead, it depends on the network intrinsic dynamics, which is biologically relevant when explaining neural activities during restive states. In this respect, as we previously discussed, multiple simultaneous rhythms could be present at any moment, with γ as the more probable frequency. The maximization of the free energy F_δ (due to high $\overline{E}$ and low H_δ) may be invested in some rearrangement of the neural network. Contrarily, we can assume that H_γ is higher than $\overline{E}$ for which F_γ could be negative. During predominant δ rhythm, F_δ could become negative, indicating that H_δ became higher than $\overline{E}$.

Differentiation Between Variational vs Non-variational Free Energy.

Although variational free energy can also be decomposed into the difference between energy and entropy, Friston's FEP and such differences are not the same concepts. The variational free energy (Friston's FEP) is a functional probability distribution encoded by the systemic states and not the probability distribution. The variational free energy is based on the Kullback–Leibler (KL) divergence between two probability densities, representing information divergence, information gain, cross or relative entropy as a non-commutative measure between two probability distributions [32]. In this context, the variational free energy can be negative. It can be written then as the sum of the negative log evidence (which can get negative) and a KL-divergence between recognition density and true posterior or as a sum of the negative accuracy. The expected marginal log-likeli-hood can become negative if the predictions are exact and complex, the KL-divergence between the recognition density and the prior. Regarding optimization, the fact that the KL-divergence is always optimized to a non-zero value is not exactly a problem that needs to be solved (unless one refers to the Hard Problem [33–35]).

We can think of non-variational free energy as self-governed regulations that adjust and engage homeostatic actions to counteract disturbances. In its minimal formulation, this restoration of homeostasis seems doable by the organism's components rather than by behavioral actions made by the organism itself. Ancillary regulations may successfully minimize encountered free energy only after a homeostatic set point has been reached (see [36]). Contrarily, the FEP assumes sequences of actions that minimize the expected free energy due to action, which is crucial for organisms [37]. One might conceive then that FEP-like control could only possibly occur in organisms having predictive forms of nervous systems that forecast the consequences of their actions [38]. More specifically, to select action policies that minimize uncertainty associated with an action-outcome, the organism must be capable of thinking about different courses of action and their outcomes in the safety of their imagination (c.f., [39]). Nevertheless, based on our current understanding, the capacity to disengage from the present and imagine different possible futures is beyond the cognitive capabilities of isolated, local small neural networks.

Non-variational Free Energy and Local Sleep. We have little knowledge on how the effect of homeostasis is continuously spread over an increasing volume of neurons [36]. It is then unclear how these small regulations affect the non-variational free energy regulation. This lack of understanding can be found in the so-called 'local sleep' phenomenon commonly associated with (global) sleep homeostasis. In brief, local sleep refers to periods when populations of neurons in an awake-brain display sleep-like activity while other neurons continue to show wake-like activity [40, 41]. During sleep, activity in the cortex is mainly internal [42], resulting from slow oscillations or other endogenous rhythms [20]. A probability density of sensory input affecting the brain's state cannot be directly quantified given sensory data. Such a measure during the drastic reduction of perception during sleep is unclear (see discussions on similar difficulties in [43, 44]).

References

1. MacKay, D.J.: Information Theory, Inference and Learning Algorithms. Cambridge (2003)
2. Sims, A.: A problem of scope for the free energy principle as a theory of cognition. Philos. Psychol. **7**, 967–980 (2016)

3. Buckley, C.L., Kim, C.S., McGregor, S., Seth, A.K.: The free energy principle for action and perception: a mathematical review. J. Math. Psychol. **81**, 55–79 (2017)
4. Friston, K., Kilner, J., Harrison, L.: A free energy principle for the brain. J. Physiol. Paris. **100**(1–3), 70–87 (2006)
5. Hohwy, J.: Prediction error minimization in the brain. The Routledge handbook of the computational mind, pp. 159–72 (2018)
6. Kiefer, A., Hohwy, J.: Representation in the prediction error minimization framework. In: The Routledge Companion to Philosophy of Psychology, pp. 384–409. Routledge (2019)
7. Callen, H.B.: Thermodynamics and an Introduction to Thermostatistics. Wiley (1991)
8. Pathria, R.K., Beale, P.D.: Statistical Mechanics. Academic Press (2011)
9. Jaynes, E.T.: Information theory and statistical mechanics. Phys. Rev. **106**(4), 620 (1957)
10. Mehta, P., Bukov, M., Wang, C.H., Day, A.G., Richardson, C., et al.: A high-bias, low-variance introduction to machine learning for physicists. Phys. Rep. **810**, 1–24 (2019)
11. Perez Velazquez, J.L., Mateos, D.M., Guevara, E.R.: On a simple general principle of brain organization. Front. Neurosci. **13**, 1106 (2019)
12. Fernandez-Leon, J.A., Acosta, G.: A heuristic perspective on non-variational free energy modulation at the sleep-like edge. Biosystems **208**, 104466 (2021)
13. Izhikevich, E.M.: Simple model of spiking neurons. IEEE Trans. Neural Networks **14**(6), 1569–1572 (2003)
14. Izhikevich, E.M.: Polychronization: computation with spikes. Neural Comput. **18**(2), 245–282 (2006)
15. Hopfield, J.J.: Neural networks and physical systems with emergent collective computational capabilities. Proc. Natl. Acad. Sci. USA **79**, 2554 (1982)
16. Ashby, R.: Principles of the self-organising system. ECO **6**, 102–126 (2004)
17. Kiverstein, J., Sims, M.: Is free-energy minimisation the mark of the cognitive? Biol. Philos. **36**(2), 1–27 (2021). https://doi.org/10.1007/s10539-021-09788-0
18. Davis, K.: Adaptive homeostasis. Mol Aspects Med. **49**, 1–7 (2016)
19. Steriade, M.: The corticothalamic system in sleep. Front Biosci. **8**(4), d878–d899 (2003)
20. Steriade M. Neuronal substrates of sleep and epilepsy. Cambridge University Press (2003)
21. Seth, A.: Being You: A New Science of Consciousness. Penguin, Dutton (2021)
22. Latchoumane, C.F., Jackson, L., Sendi, M.S., Tehrani, K.F., Mortensen, L.J., et al.: Chronic electrical stimulation promotes the excitability and plasticity of ESC-derived neurons following glutamate-induced inhibition in vitro. Sci. Rep. **8**(1), 1–6 (2018)
23. Hu, M., et al.: Electrical stimulation enhances neuronal cell activity mediated by Schwann cell derived exosomes. Sci. Rep. **9**(1), 1–2 (2019)
24. Vincent, J.L., Patel, G.H., Fox, M.D., Snyder, A.Z., Baker, J.T., et al.: Intrinsic functional architecture in the anaesthetized monkey brain. Nature **447**(7140), 83–86 (2007)
25. Hobson, J.A., Friston, K.J.: Waking and dreaming consciousness: neurobiological and functional considerations. Prog. Neurobiol. **98**(1), 82–98 (2012)
26. Helmholtz, H.: Concerning the perceptions in general. Visual Perception: Essential Readings, pp. 24–44 [1866: In Treatise on physiological optics (J. Southall, Trans., 3rd ed., Vol. III). New York: Dover] (2021)
27. Evans, D.J.: A non-equilibrium free energy theorem for deterministic systems. Mol. Phys. **101**(10), 1551–1554 (2003)
28. Benjamin, L., Thomas, P.J., Fellous, J.M.: A renewed vision for biological cybernetics. Biol. Cybern. **114**, 1–2 (2020)
29. Friston, K.J., Daunizeau, J., Kilner, J., Kiebel, S.J.: Action and behavior: a free-energy formulation. Biol. Cybern. **102**(3), 227–260 (2010)
30. Parr, T., Friston, K.J.: Generalised free energy and active inference. Biol. Cybern. **113**(5), 495–513 (2019)

31. Gardner, R.J., et al.: Toroidal topology of population activity in grid cells. Nature **13**, 1–6 (2022)

32. Friston, K.: The free-energy principle: a unified brain theory? Nat. Rev. Neurosci. **11**(2), 127–138 (2010)

33. Chalmers, D.: Facing up to the problem of consciousness. Consc. Stud. **2**, 200–219 (1995)

34. Solms, M.: The hard problem of consciousness and the free energy principle. Front. Psychol. **9**, 2714 (2019)

35. Solms, M., Friston, K.: How and why consciousness arises: some considerations from physics and physiology. J. Conscious. Stud. **25**(5–6), 202–238 (2018)

36. Kim, B., et al.: Differential modulation of global and local neural oscillations in REM sleep by homeostatic sleep regulation. Proc. Natl. Acad. Sci. **114**(9), E1727–E1736 (2017)

37. Friston, K., Levin, M., Sengupta, B., Pezzulo, G.: Knowing one's place: a free-energy approach to pattern regulation. J. R. Soc. Interface **12**(105), 20141383 (2015)

38. Corcoran, A.W., Pezzulo, G., Hohwy, J.: From allostatic agents to counterfactual cognisers: active inference, biological regulation, and the origins of cognition. Biol. Philos. **35**(3), 1–45 (2020). https://doi.org/10.1007/s10539-020-09746-2

39. Dennett, D.: Darwin's Dangerous Idea. Evolution and the Meaning of Life. Simon & Schuster, New York (1995)

40. Tononi, G., Cirelli, C.: Sleep function and synaptic homeostasis. Sleep Med. Rev. **10**(1), 49–62 (2006)

41. Tononi, G., Cirelli, C.: Perchance to prune. Sci. Am. **309**(2), 34–39 (2013)

42. Braun, A.R.: Regional cerebral blood flow throughout the sleep-wake cycle. An H2 (15) O PET study. Brain J. Neurol. **120**(7), 1173–97 (1997)

43. Colombo, M., Wright, C.: First principles in the life sciences: the free-energy principle, organicism, and mechanism. Synthese **198**(14), 3463–3488 (2018). https://doi.org/10.1007/s11229-018-01932-w

44. Wright, J.J., Bourke, P.D.: The growth of cognition: Free energy minimization and the embryogenesis of cortical computation. Phys. Life Rev. **36**, 83–99 (2021)

Create Efficient and Complex Reservoir Computing Architectures with ReservoirPy

Nathan Trouvain[1,2,3] , Nicolas Rougier[1,2,3] , and Xavier Hinaut[1,2,3(✉)]

[1] INRIA Bordeaux Sud-Ouest, Talence, France
xavier.hinaut@inria.fr
[2] LaBRI, Bordeaux INP, CNRS, UMR 5800, Talence, France
[3] Institut des Maladies Neurodégénératives, Université de Bordeaux,
CNRS, UMR 5293, Bordeaux, France

Abstract. Reservoir Computing (RC) is a type of recurrent neural network (RNNs) where learning is restricted to the output weights. RCs are often considered as temporal Support Vector Machines (SVMs) for the way they project inputs onto dynamic non-linear high-dimensional representations. This paradigm, mainly represented by Echo State Networks (ESNs), has been successfully applied on a wide variety of tasks, from time series forecasting to sequence generation. They offer de facto a fast, simple yet efficient way to train RNNs.

We present in this paper a library that facilitates the creation of RC architectures, from simplest to most complex, based on the Python scientific stack (NumPy, Scipy). This library offers memory and time efficient implementations for both online and offline training paradigms, such as FORCE learning or parallel ridge regression. The flexibility of the API allows to quickly design ESNs including re-usable and customizable components. It enables to build models such as DeepESNs as well as other advanced architectures with complex connectivity between multiple reservoirs with feedback loops. Extensive documentation and tutorials both for newcomers and experts are provided through GitHub and ReadTheDocs websites.

The paper introduces the main concepts supporting the library, illustrated with code examples covering popular RC techniques from the literature. We argue that such flexible dedicated library will ease the creation of more advanced architectures while guarantying their correct implementation and reproducibility across the RC community.

Keywords: Reservoir computing · Echo state network · Recurrent neural networks · Python · Online learning · Offline learning · Toolbox

1 Introduction

Within the field of Recurrent Neural Networks (RNNs), Reservoir Computing (RC) is an interesting paradigm of timeseries and sequence processing. Most of

Supported by Inria.

RC techniques rely on a *reservoir*, a pool of randomly – and recurrently – connected neurons, in charge of projecting data into a high dimensional space able to encode temporal information. This reservoir is connected to an output layer called *readout* whose role is to extract information from the reservoir activity. In a more formal way, the readout neurons act as a linear layer which can be used to perform regression or classification on high dimensional representations of any timeseries processed by the reservoir. As opposed to more popular Deep Learning strategies, Reservoir Computing techniques do not require gradient error backpropagation algorithm to work. The only trained connections being the readout connections, a simple linear regression can be computed between the activations of the reservoir and the desired target values to obtain a functional model.

Reservoir Computing is mostly known through its two first and most widely used instances: Echo State Networks (ESNs) [10] and Liquid State Machines (LSMs) [11], their spiking neural networks counterpart. Although existing since the beginning of the 2000s, RC techniques are less well-known compared to other RNN-based Deep Learning architectures like Long Short-Term Memory networks (LSTMs). In the meantime, they have been successfully applied to various tasks and problems (some are listed in this review by [21]) and even demonstrates state of the art performances for tasks such as chaotic timeseries forecasting [25] or sound processing [23]. It was shown that ESNs needed less data than LSTMs to obtain good performances while being trained in much less time (e.g. see [23]).

Several code implementations of RC, in particular for ESNs, can be found online, but these implementations are often isolated scripts written in Python or Matlab. They often provide reusable objects intended to allow reproduction of specific results and techniques, but do not offer any way to re-use, re-combine or extend their code. Whereas Deep Learning architectures have thrived, supported by complete, user-friendly toolboxes enabling such flexibility and re-usability, RC may remain an underground technique without this kind of off the shelf, ready to use and yet permissive programming frameworks and libraries. Libraries like *Oger* were successful attempts of creating a rather complete RC tool. However, *Oger* was originally written in Python 2 (whose support have ended in 2020) and its maintenance has not been continued.

ReservoirPy provides an implementation only relying on general scientific libraries like *Numpy* and *Scipy*, in order to be more versatile than specific frameworks (e.g. *TensorFlow*, *PyTorch*) and provide more flexibility when building custom architectures. On the one hand, *TensorFlow* and *PyTorch* were mostly developed for gradient descent based learning algorithms, and most of their features are useless, if not cumbersome, to develop RC techniques. For instance, they are usually optimized to perform several epochs of training on batches of independent samples, or to differentiate any kind of operations happening under their scope, which is not often useful for RC. On the other hand, libraries such as *Scikit-Learn* [13] are geared towards static data processing and do not integrate much timeseries processing or online learning tools. Most importantly, we designed ReservoirPy as a highly flexible tool offering the possibility to design several kinds of RC architectures while promoting reusable components. Indeed, numerous Reservoir Computing extensions and derivatives have been developed (see [19] for a recent review): they generally include modified learning methods and architectures and some of them allow for the composition of several reservoirs (decoupled-ESNs [26], tree ESNs [6], deep reservoirs [5], hierarchical-task reservoirs [14], and more exotic architectures like Reservoir-of-Reservoirs (RoR) [3] or self-supervised pairs of reservoirs [2]).

In this paper, we detail the backbone of ReservoirPy, its major components and how to combine them to design complex architectures, with different learning rules and feedback loops. We then introduce the library usage with a simple example of timeseries forecasting using online and offline trained ESNs. In Appendices[1], we give more details about more advanced features and minimal implementations of advanced or exotic RC architectures, such as Deep ESNs or Extreme Learning Machines (ELMs) [9], as a proof of concept of ReservoirPy capacities. Finally, we present future features and conclude about the potential of ReservoirPy on the RC community.

2 Flexible Reservoir Computing

Most RC techniques rely on interconnected and interchangeable building blocks: an ESN can be defined as a network connecting a reservoir of neurons to a layer of readout neurons. Inside an ESN, a reservoir can be connected to several independent readouts, and to several input sources. In more complex architectures, like DeepESNs [5] or Hierarchical ESNs [14,22], reservoirs can be layered, and readouts inserted between them, with feedback connections possibly connecting all these blocks in different ways. Some architectures might also use other additional blocks and operators than reservoirs and readouts.

Our tool enables such flexibility using 4 components.

2.1 Functional Nodes

The minimal component is the `Node`. A Node is a Python class that can be equipped with several functions and parameters in order to operate on a timeseries.

All Nodes are recurrent operators, meaning that they at least carry two elements: (1) an internal state vector x_t storing their last output, accessible anytime through the `state()` method, and (2) a generic *forward* function defined as $forward(x_t, u_t) = x_{t+1}$. This function takes as input a single timestep of input data u_t and the current value of the Node's internal state x_t, and outputs an updated value x_{t+1} for this state. A new Node can either be created by passing a forward function and its parameters as argument to the Node class constructor, or by defining a new specialized class that inherits from the Node class.

---

[1] Appendices are available at https://github.com/reservoirpy/publications/tree/main/2022-SAB.

An initialization function may also be added, to allow for the dynamic initialization of the Node's parameters as well as the inference of input and internal state vectors dimensions directly from data. Hence, the minimal creation of a new Node requires the declaration of two functions and an optional dictionary mapping parameters and hyperparameters names to their values, without enforcing any inheritance from the class itself.

For instance, our `Reservoir` Node implementation of a reservoir is a subclass of Node holding several parameters and hyperparameters, among which:

- a matrix $\mathbf{W}$, defining the connection weights between the reservoir neurons,
- a matrix $\mathbf{W}_{in}$ defining the connection weights between the input neurons and the reservoir neurons,
- a coefficient lr, called *leak rate*, which defines the time constant of the reservoir neurons.
- a function f, used as an activation function for the reservoir neurons, usually the hyperbolic tangent applied element-wise on the activation vector.

These parameters are used in the Reservoir *forward* function definition:

$$\text{forward}(x_t, u_t) = (1 - lr)x_t + lr f(\mathbf{W}x_t + \mathbf{W}_{in}u_t)$$
$$= x_{t+1}$$

(1)

Nodes *forward* function can be triggered by calling the Node on a single data point like a Python function. Since Nodes are mainly designed to process timeseries or sequential data, it is also possible to use a *forward* function on several points of a timeseries, updating its Node internal state several times and gathering temporal information. This can be done using the `run()` method of a Node.

```python
import numpy as np
from reservoirpy.nodes import Reservoir

# A Reservoir with 100 neurons and lr=0.1
res = Reservoir(units=100, lr=0.1) # Activation is tanh by default.

u = np.array([[1.0, 0.0]]) # 1 timestep of 2D data.
U = np.array([[1.0, 0.0],  # 2 timesteps of 2D data.
              [0.0, 1.0]])
s1 = res(u) # Update reservoir state on 1 timestep.
s = res.state() # Current state of the reservoir.

# Update reservoir state on a sequence of 3 timesteps.
S = res.run(U)

# Parameters can be accessed as attributes.
print(res.lr, res.Win)
```

In the code above, as the `Reservoir` class is already implemented as a subclass of Node within the library, internal code machinery like Reservoir's *forward* function is hidden. Only necessary hyperparameters, like the number of neurons inside the reservoir, were given to the Reservoir constructor. All other parameters were initialized when the Node was first used, i.e. when `s1 = res(u)` was executed. This allows the Node to infer the shape of all other parameters like the input matrix $\mathbf{W}_{in}$ based on data dimension and to build them using initialization functions.

2.2 Learning Rules

The second major component of the library are the learning rules. A learning rule can be declared as a function that takes sequences of data as arguments and updates the Node parameters. Once learning rules functions have been loaded into a Node, it is possible to use the same mechanisms described in the previous section about *forward* function definition. There is two main ways of using them:

Offline Learning. A learning rule is said to be *offline* if the parameters estimation of the learned model is performed only once, on a single corpus of data, and cannot be modified later. This is for instance the case for the L2-regularized linear regression, also called *ridge regression* or Tikhonov regression, widely used in Reservoir Computing to train ESNs, and implemented by our library in the `Ridge` Node. Nodes equipped with offline learning rules can be trained using the `fit()` method.

```
import numpy as np
from reservoirpy.nodes import Ridge

readout = Ridge()

# Update parameters of the Node.
readout.fit(X_train, y_train)
```

Additionally, offline learning can be performed incrementally or using batches of data to pre-compute some parts of the learning process. A `partial_fit()` method can be defined in order to perform such operations on chunks of the dataset.

Online Learning. *Online* learning rules describe continuous learning processes, during which the learned parameters are updated as soon as new data is fed to the model. This learning procedure is more biologically relevant since the model does not learn its parameters in one single step but rather in small successive steps, trying to improve its predictions to minimize a cost function. Taking inspiration from this idea of progressive training, Nodes carrying an online learning rule can update their parameters using a method named `train()`. The `FORCE` Node is an example of Node trained using the online learning rule described by [20].

```
import numpy as np
from reservoirpy.nodes import FORCE

readout = FORCE()

# Update parameters of the Node once.
s0 = readout.train(one_x, one_y)

# Update parameters of the Node
# on a sequence (several times in a row)
S = readout.train(X_train, Y_train)
```

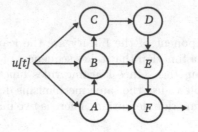

Fig. 1. An advanced example of Model graph, involving 6 interconnected Nodes.

Note that the `train()` method can be called on single timesteps of data, triggering a single step of learning. Calling this methods returns an array holding the output of the Node *forward* function, before learning was applied. This method can also be called on sequences of data. In such case, the Node parameters evolve at each timestep of data in the sequence, and the method call will return the sequence of responses obtained from each training step.

2.3   Models as Computational Graphs

While Nodes offer a way to quickly define reusable operations and estimators, *Models* allow to compose these operations and create complex architectures involving several Nodes in interaction. We define Models as a simple mean of managing computational graphs, without any heavy pre-existing framework.

Models are subclasses of Node, and therefore expose the same interface: function-like calls, `run`, `fit` and the `train` method of a Model triggers one-timestep update of all Nodes in the Model, sequential update of all Nodes in the Model, fitting of all offline learner Nodes and training of all online learner Nodes, respectively.

Models are created by linking Nodes using the ">>" Python operator. The *forward* function of a Model created by linking a Node A to a Node B will be defined as the composition $f_{Model} = f_B \circ f_A$ of A and B forward functions. However, Nodes involved in a Model do not store any reference to other Nodes in the Model. That is, Nodes can be shared between different Models without requiring to copy or to reinitialize them. This feature provides a flexible way of defining Reservoir Computing architectures involving several readouts or several pathways, allowing to train Nodes using a Model and to run them using another.

```
model1 = nodeA >> nodeB  # A Model with two Nodes.

# Another Model. nodeA state and parameters are
# shared with model1.
model2 = nodeA >> nodeC

# The result of nodeB(nodeA(u)):
s = model1(u)
```

Since Models are a Node subclass, they can also be linked to other Nodes, allowing to chain the linking operator. Models can also be merged using the

"&" Python operator. Merging a Model A and a Model B will create a third model containing an unique version of all the Nodes present in A and B, along with the union of all their connections. This allows to design architectures with several pathways, as shown in the code below, defining the graph of Nodes in Fig. 1. Note the usage of Input() and Output() Nodes in order to clearly define the input and output of the graph. These Nodes have no effect on the Model behavior other than forcing Nodes A, B and C to receive inputs from the input source, and F to be the final output of the Model. Note also that many-to-one and one-to-many connections can be declared by connecting Nodes to lists of Nodes and vice-versa.

```
from reservoirpy.nodes import Input, Output

path1 = A >> F
path2 = B >> E

# One-to-many connection using a list
path3 = Input() >> [nodeA, nodeB, nodeC]

# Chain of connections
path4 = A >> B >> C >> D >> E >> F >> Output()

# Merge all pathways to create Fig. 1 graph:
model = path1 & path2 & path3 & path4
```

One limitation of the Model object is the necessity for the declared computational graph to be a directed acyclic graph of Nodes. If this condition is not met, Nodes cannot be topologically sorted and operation order within the Model *forward* function is undefined. Nevertheless, this condition can be skirted using feedback connections between Nodes in the graph as explained in 2.4.

Once a Model has been defined, it can be either fitted offline or trained online using the same methods as for a Node. Models training procedure is identified using "duck-typing". If all trainable Nodes (e.g. all readout Nodes such as Ridge or FORCE) in the Model exposes an offline learning interface, then the Model is considered to be an offline learner. Similarly, if all trainable Nodes are online learners, then the Model is considered to be an online learner. For now, mixing different learning procedure is not an allowed behavior, although it can be achieved by splitting the Model into different pathways with different learning rules.

2.4 Feedback Loops

RC models might require time-delayed connection between different components of neural networks or computational models. Usually, these connections are used to connect readout layer of neurons to reservoir neurons in a feedback loop, in order to tame reservoir neurons activities using the output signal of the network.

Our library differentiates itself from most other RC tools by providing a rather simple and flexible interface to define such delayed connections, using a similar operation than the Model definition in 2.3. A feedback connection between two Nodes can be defined using the "<<" Python operator. This operation must be performed on the receiver Node, and will create a copy of the Node storing the feedback link. This mechanism is different from the linking mechanism used to define Models. Feedback connections are stored in the form of a reference to the signal sender within the signal receiver. This implies that feedback connections can only be defined once on a receiver Node, instead of being decoupled from the Node object like regular connections stored in a Model.

```
nodeA = nodeA << nodeB # Copying nodeA.
nodeA <<= nodeB # Using in place modification.
```

Feedback connections may need an initialization step. Reservoirs, for instance, receive the feedback signal through neuronal connections whose weights are stored in a $\mathbf{W}_{fb}$ matrix. Feedback connections initialization functions can be created and loaded into Nodes to tackle these situations. Plus, feedback signal may come from any type of Node, including Models. It is therefore possible to design complex feedback graphs to transform the feedback signal before it reaches the receiver Node, or to get feedback from several Nodes gathered in a Model at once.

Once a feedback connection has been defined, a feedback receiver Node can retrieve the current feedback signal sent by the connected Node using the method `feedback()`. This method will fetch the state of the feedback sender Node, or the state of the outputs Nodes of the feedback sender Model. When running or training a Model over a sequence of data, and if the feedback sender and receiver Nodes are part of the Model, then feedback will be sent through the connection while respecting a one timestep delay between the sender and the receiver. For instance, if a reservoir and a readout are connected to form a Model, and if the reservoir receives feedback from the readout, then the reservoir will receive at t inputs u_t and feedback signal y_{t-1}, y being the state (or output) of the readout.

In addition to setup regular feedback connections as defined in RC, feedback connections mechanism can be hijacked to build teacher Nodes or reward Nodes, and help building architectures based on online learning such as the model from (see [2]), or help implementing reward-modulated online learning rule like the 3-factor Hebbian learning rule proposed by [8] (ongoing work). These reward or teaching Nodes can be used to provide a connected Node with some target values for training at runtime, even if these targets values are not available *before* runtime, e.g. if these values are computed by some part of a Model and used to train some other part.

3   Getting Started: ESN for Timeseries Forecasting with ReservoirPy

This section introduces how to use ReservoirPy to define, train and run Echo State Networks (ESN) for some classic literature benchmarks. Since ESN is among the most used techniques of Reservoir Computing, ReservoirPy introduces special optimizations to increase their performances and leverage larger corpus of data. Reservoirs and readouts objects also provide users with many options to precisely tune and adapt their behavior to different needs. For example, it is possible to switch the `Reservoir` *forward* function between two different definitions, the first one applying leaky integration to neurons states after applying the activation function, like in [5] or [10], the second one before like in [2] or [4]. Other tunable parameters include spectral radius of the recurrent matrix $\mathbf{W}$, input and feedback scaling, random weights distribution, leaking rate, additive noise in the input, internal states and feedback, and many more. On top of these included features, users may also define their own Nodes and Models using the interface described in 2

3.1 Step 1: Choose a Timeseries for One Timestep Ahead Prediction

ReservoirPy contains 7 timeseries generators, and this number is steadily increased with each new release. Currently available timeseries generators are listed in sec:datasets.

For this tutorial, we draw 2000 points of the well-known Mackey-Glass timeseries, used in many RC benchmarks. We then split this timeseries in order to create two series shifted in time by one timestep. The goal of our task will thus be to predict u_{t+1} knowing u_t.

```
from reservoirpy.datasets import mackey_glass

# tau=17 series is chaotic
X = mackey_glass(2000, tau=17)

test_len = 500 # Split for training/testing.
X_train, y_train, X_test, y_test = ...
```

3.2 Step 2: Define Your ESN

An ESN can be defined as a simple Model with two Nodes: a *reservoir*, connected to a *readout*. We will create two Models for this tutorial: an ESN geared with an offline learning rule, and an ESN equiped with an online learning rule. Both can share the same reservoir. Inside the 100 neurons reservoir, spectral radius of matrix $\mathbf{W}$ is set to 0.9, input scaling of $\mathbf{W}_{in}$ to 0.1, leaking rate to 0.3, and a Gaussian noise with a gain of 0.01 is added to the inputs. These hyperparameters may be suboptimal, and are just provided for the sake of example. We also set the offline readout regularization parameter to 10^{-6} (also called *ridge*).

```
from reservoirpy.nodes import Reservoir, Ridge, FORCE

reservoir = Reservoir(100, sr=0.9, lr=0.3,
                      input_scaling=0.1,
                      noise_in=0.01)

off_readout = Ridge(ridge=1e-6) # Offline readout
on_readout  = FORCE()           # Online readout

esn_off = reservoir >> off_readout # Offline ESN
esn_on  = reservoir >> on_readout  # Online ESN
```

3.3   Step 3.1: Train the Offline Model

The offline learner ESN can be trained using the `fit()` method of the Model. Because this method call will also be the first use of our ESN on our dataset, `fit()` will also trigger all initialization functions available in the Nodes, building random parameters matrices using the previously defined spectral radius and input scaling for instance. These functions will also infer the input and output dimension of all Nodes in the Model, i.e. an input dimension of 1 and an output dimension of 1 as the input of our Model is the 1-dimensional Mackey-Glass timeseries and the output is a 1-dimensional forecast of this timeseries.

```
esn_off.fit(X_train, y_train)
```

3.4   Step 3.2: Train the Online Model

Whereas offline learning can only be performed once *via* the `fit()` method, online learning may happen several times in the life cycle of a Model. Hence, the `train()` method can be invoked several times in a row to sequentially train the online learner ESN. For the sake of example, let's create a simple for-loop updating the Model's parameters several time on only one timestep of data at a time.

```
Y = []
for x, y in zip(X_train, y_train):
    # Nodes and Models only accept 2D arrays
    # as parameters, so reshaping is important.
    y_hat = esn_on.train(x.reshape(1, -1),
                         y.reshape(1, -1)
    Y.append(y_hat)
```

Models can also be trained in one line of code be providing the `train()` method with a sequence of inputs and targets values.

```
Y = esn_on.train(X_train, y_train)
```

3.5   Step 4: Evaluate the Model

Once trained, Models or Nodes can be run to outputs predictions. ReservoirPy exposes some common metrics in the `obersvables` module to evaluate this kind of tasks, such as Root-Mean Square Error (RMSE).

```
from reservoirpy.observables import rmse

y_pred_off = esn_offline.run(X_test)
y_pred_on  = esn_online.run(X_test)

print("RMSE offline: ", rmse(y_test, y_pred_off))
>>> RMSE offline: ...
print("RMSE online: ", rmse(y_test, y_pred_on))
>>> RMSE offline: ...
```

4 Discussion

ReservoirPy is a Python library for Reservoir Computing architectures, from ESNs to deep ESNs, providing users with online and offline learning rules, complete feedback loop support, and a powerful syntax to quickly develop any kind of model using reusable building blocks. We demonstrated its ability to handle exotic architectures of reservoirs where learning could be performed in unusual ways. Such architectures provide new ideas "to think how learning could be performed", which is particularly interesting in computational neuroscience were people try to understand how different learning and memory mechanisms interact in the brain [1]. Some of these works studied how a couple of reservoirs could learn to train one another to find chunks in a sequence [2] or how to model working memory in reservoirs [12,18]. More generally, we are aiming at replication and implementation of additional tools emerging from literature, like new learning rules such as Intrinsic Plasticity (unsupervised training of reservoir units) [15] or the three-factor Hebbian learning rule from [8], and new results on non-linear vector autoregressive machines equivalence with reservoirs from [7]. Other ongoing and future work will also focus on improving general performance and usability of the tool and add spiking version of reservoirs. We thus plan on integrating parallel computation procedures to any kind of model, and study the possibility to perform some computations on graphical processing units (GPU) to speed up linear algebra operations for large sized reservoirs.

ReservoirPy has been built without strongly enforcing design principles from other classical libraries (e.g. *TensorFlow* or *Scikit-Learn*). This choice has been motivated by the will to offer a high degree of flexibility, tailored to RC techniques. Such flexibility and design choice allow for rapid and efficient prototyping of original reservoir architectures. We believe this is an important step towards the development of a new family of more complex reservoir architectures, such as Deep Learning ones (e.g. Transformers [24]). Indeed, future trends in machine learning are probably in-between Reservoir Computing and Deep Learning approaches where parts of advanced models are kept untrained [16,17].

ReservoirPy is a community oriented project: we provide tutorials and extensive documentation. We welcome any feedback or contribution, from improvement of the code base to implementation of new tools, or publication of new examples and use cases.

References

1. Alexandre, F., Hinaut, X., Rougier, N., Viéville, T.: Higher cognitive functions in bio-inspired artificial intelligence. ERCIM News **125** (2021)
2. Asabuki, T., Hiratani, N., Fukai, T.: Interactive reservoir computing for chunking information streams. PLoS Comput. Biol. **14**(10), e1006400 (2018)
3. Dale, M.: Neuroevolution of hierarchical reservoir computers. In: Proceedings of the Genetic and Evolutionary Computation Conference, pp. 410–417 (2018)
4. Enel, P., Procyk, E., Quilodran, R., Dominey, P.: Reservoir computing properties of neural dynamics in prefrontal cortex. PLoS Comput. Biol. **12**(6), e1004967 (2016)

5. Gallicchio, C., Micheli, A., Pedrelli, L.: Deep reservoir computing: a critical experimental analysis. Neurocomputing **268**, 87–99 (2017)
6. Gallicchio, C., Micheli, A.: Tree echo state networks. Neurocomputing **101**, 319–337 (2013)
7. Gauthier, D.J., Bollt, E., Griffith, A., Barbosa, W.A.S.: Next generation reservoir computing. Nat. Commun. **12**(1), 5564 (2021)
8. Hoerzer, G.M., Legenstein, R., Maass, W.: Emergence of complex computational structures from chaotic neural networks through reward-modulated Hebbian learning. Cereb. Cortex **24**(3), 677–690 (2014)
9. Huang, G.B., Wang, D.H., Lan, Y.: Extreme learning machines: a survey. Int. J. Mach. Learn. Cyber. **2**(2), 107–122 (2011)
10. Jaeger, H.: The "echo state" approach to analysing and training recurrent neural networks. German National Research Center for Information Technology GMD Technical Report 148, 34, Bonn, Germany (2001)
11. Maass, W., Natschläger, T., Markram, H.: Real-time computing without stable states: a new framework for neural computation based on perturbations. Neural Comput. **14**(11), 2531–2560 (2002)
12. Pascanu, R., Jaeger, H.: A neurodynamical model for working memory. Neural Netw. **24**(2), 199–207 (2011)
13. Pedregosa, F., et al.: Scikit-learn: machine learning in Python. J. Mach. Learn. Res. **12**, 2825–2830 (2011)
14. Pedrelli, L., Hinaut, X.: Hierarchical-task reservoir for online semantic analysis from continuous speech. IEEE TNNLS 1–10 (2021)
15. Schrauwen, B., Wardermann, M., Verstraeten, D., Steil, J.J., Stroobandt, D.: Improving reservoirs using intrinsic plasticity. Neurocomputing **71**(7), 1159–1171 (2008)
16. Shen, S., Baevski, A., Morcos, A.S., Keutzer, K., Auli, M., Kiela, D.: Reservoir transformers. arXiv preprint arXiv:2012.15045 (2020)
17. Shrivastava, H., Garg, A., Cao, Y., Zhang, Y., Sainath, T.: Echo state speech recognition. In: ICASSP, pp. 5669–5673. IEEE (2021)
18. Strock, A., Hinaut, X., Rougier, N.P.: A robust model of gated working memory. Neural Comput. **32**(1), 153–181 (2020)
19. Sun, C., Song, M., Hong, S., Li, H.: A review of designs and applications of echo state networks. arXiv preprint arXiv:2012.02974 (2020)
20. Sussillo, D., Abbott, L.F.: Generating coherent patterns of activity from chaotic neural networks. Neuron **63**(4), 544–557 (2009)
21. Tanaka, G., et al.: Recent advances in physical reservoir computing: a review. Neural Netw. **115**, 100–123 (2019)
22. Triefenbach, F., Jalalvand, A., Schrauwen, B., Martens, J.: Phoneme recognition with large hierarchical reservoirs. In: NIPS, pp. 2307–2315 (2010)
23. Trouvain, N., Hinaut, X.: Canary song decoder: transduction and implicit segmentation with ESNs and LTSMs. In: Farkaš, I., Masulli, P., Otte, S., Wermter, S. (eds.) ICANN 2021. LNCS, vol. 12895, pp. 71–82. Springer, Cham (2021). https://doi.org/10.1007/978-3-030-86383-8_6
24. Vaswani, A., et al.: Attention is all you need. In: NIPS, pp. 5998–6008 (2017)
25. Vlachas, P.R., et al.: Backpropagation algorithms and Reservoir Computing in Recurrent Neural Networks for the forecasting of complex spatiotemporal dynamics. Neural Netw. **126**, 191–217 (2020)
26. Xue, Y., Yang, L., Haykin, S.: Decoupled echo state networks with lateral inhibition. Neural Netw. **20**(3), 365–376 (2007)

Adaptive Inhibition for Optimal Energy Consumption by Animals, Robots and Neurocomputers

Trond A. Tjøstheim[iD], Birger Johansson[iD], and Christian Balkenius[✉][iD]

Lund University Cognitive Science, Lund, Sweden
{trond_arild.tjostheim,birger.johansson,christian.balkenius}@lucs.lu.se

Abstract. In contrast to artificial systems, animals must forage for food. In biology, the availability of energy is typically both precarious and highly variable. Most importantly, the very structure of organisms is dependent on the continuous metabolism of nutrients into ATP, and its use in maintaining homeostasis. This means that energy is at the centre of all biological processes, including cognition. So far, in computational neuroscience and artificial intelligence, this issue has been overlooked. In simulations of cognitive processes, whether at the neural level, or the level of larger brain systems, the constant and ample supply of energy is implicitly assumed. However, studies from the biological sciences indicate that much of the brain's processes are in place to maintain allostasis, both of the brain itself and of the organism as a whole. This also relates to the fact that different neural populations have different energy needs. Many artificial systems, including robots and laptop computers, have circuitry in place to measure energy consumption. However, this information is rarely used in controlling the details of cognitive processing to minimize energy consumption. In this work, we make use of some of this circuitry and explicitly connect it to the processing requirements of different cognitive subsystems and show first how a cognitive model can learn the relation between cognitive 'effort', the quality of the computations and energy consumption, and second how an adaptive inhibitory mechanism can learn to only use the amount of energy minimally needed for a particular task. We argue that energy conservation is an important goal of central inhibitory mechanisms, in addition to its role in attentional and behavioral selection.

Keywords: Adaptive inhibition · Energy consumption · Robots

We explore how adaptive inhibition can lead to reduced energy consumption for a cognitive system.

This work was partially supported by the Wallenberg AI, Autonomous Systems and Software Program - Humanities and Society (WASP-HS) funded by the Marianne and Marcus Wallenberg Foundation and the Marcus and Amalia Wallenberg Foundation.

L. Cañamero et al. (Eds.): SAB 2022, LNAI 13499, pp. 103–114, 2022.
https://doi.org/10.1007/978-3-031-16770-6_9

We report an experiment where the actual power consumption of a computer is first estimated through a learning process and then controlled by an active inhibitory system that monitors the contribution of each cognitive process to the goals of the system (or organism) and only uses as mush as is necessary in every case.

1   Introduction

Current machine learning algorithms are extremely energy costly, with large scale models requiring very large amounts of energy to train. This can be compared with the efficiency of biological systems, including the human brain, which yields versatile and robust classifying and behavioural performance with only a few Watts of energy [12]. Given the present outlook on global energy availability, and the environmental costs of energy production, minimizing energy costs of computation is desirable.

Optimality in computation can carry excessive costs in behavioural contexts; for a behaving robot system, sensory resolution can be reduced, navigation pathways may be approximate. By "coarse–graining" computation, significant energy savings can be possible. Current machine learning models can approach human classifying capabilities in some domains [26], but these capabilities come with very high energy costs, as mentioned above. Biological systems rarely spend excessive energy; that is, energy expenditure tends to become calibrated and matched to predicted energy gains or – savings [9]. Similarly, animals can have preferences with regards to food, but will make do with what they can find if food is scarce. In many cases, optimality is not desired as the cost is too high, instead an organism, or robot, should strive for sufficiently good processing to fulfil its task.

One way to approach this is to consider rewards in terms of energy. This is certainly true for animals, but also makes sense for artificial organisms since energy can usually be related to cost in a straight forward manner. This suggests that cognitive processing could be framed in a reinforcement framework where rewards and punishments are expressed as energy gains or costs.

In the brain, dopamine is associated with a plethora of functions in the central nervous system, but is often associated with reinforcement learning [14,30], where those behaviours that tend to yield rewards are increasingly triggered at the presentation of a salient signal [17].

Researchers have been debating whether dopamine is directly associated with reward, referred to as liking, or whether it functions as a signal of unexpected reward, i.e. as reward prediction error, and that this signal is used to facilitate learning [31]. There are also indications that dopamine is involved with perception via incentive salience that is associated with wanting [6,7].

Dopamine appears also to be involved with motivation, the facilitation or energizing of behaviour. Matsumoto and Hikosaka [19] found that when exposing monkeys to both rewarding as well as aversive stimuli, recordings of dopaminergic neurons in areas near basal ganglia became active in response to both kinds of events. Hence dopamine is not only used in connections with reward, but also with negatively valued events.

Where dopamine mediates triggering of allostatic seeking behaviour, the opioids appear to mediate the biological substrate for consummate value, in particular the value of food. Allostasis here denotes processes that work to bring the organism towards homeostasis, for example finding and eating food to restore energy levels. There are three types of opioid receptors, called mu, kappa, and delta [24]. The mu opioid receptor is mainly inhibitive and expressed subcortically; the kappa opioid receptor is implicated in reward from fatty food, and in satiation, and appears to oppose mu receptor activity. The delta opioid receptor is implicated in rewards from fatty food, like the kappa receptor. Similarly to the mu opioid receptor, it appears to have a mainly inhibitive effect, but is expressed more broadly in cortex rather than subcortical areas [24]. According to these authors, opioid receptors are primarily disinhibitive, tending to reduce activity of inhibitive GABAergic interneurons.

As mentioned above mu and delta receptors have an inhibitory effect on neurons, while kappa receptors oppose this inhibitory effect [24]. Typical physiological effects of opioids include suppressed breathing, drowsiness, as well as constipation [21]. Hence mu and delta stimulation can reduce activity of smooth muscle, both in the respiratory system, and in the gut. Opioids also reduce arousal.

In a recent review, [25] propose that mu receptors can contribute not only to liking mechanisms in the basal ganglia, but also to networks involved in higher level decision making. The authors mention that such areas as orbitofrontal cortex, basal ganglia, the amygdala, anterior cingulate cortex, and prefrontal cortex are now found to be dense in mu receptors. The authors propose that subjective value of reward may be increased also by these receptors reducing aversive arousal.

In summary, the dopaminergic system appears to mediate allostatic approach to required resources, while the opioid system may viewed as responding to energy gain through consumption of energy rich foods such as sugars and fat. The opioid system may in some way also may mediate energy saving by lowering arousal, and tuning down energy costly inhibitive interneurons.

1.1   Specific and Non-specific Inhibition in Animals

For neural circuits, the mutual inhibition motif entails that all participating neurons inhibit each others. The result is that all but the few most stimulated neurons become active. This motif is involved in selecting percepts [3, 8, 32] as well as in the process of choice [15], and the release of behaviour.

In the context of behavioural control, Gray and McNaughton [16] theorize that approach – and avoidance behaviour can be simultaneously activated e.g. in the case of novel stimuli the threat of which cannot be determined. In the presence of such stimuli, an animal may respond by freezing in a sort of forward "scanning" pose. According to the authors, this is likely due to a mutual inhibition of the two behaviours. Since the potential threat or gain is uncertain, however, no clear winner emerges, leaving the animal frozen between escape and exploration.

Similarly, Frank et al. [13] propose that the hyper-direct pathway from the cortex to the subthalamic nucleus of the basal ganglia can act as a non-specific behavioural stopping mechanism. Given that behavioural activation happens by means of disinhibition of a single behaviour by specific inhibition of the reticular nucleus of the thalamus via the globus pallidus interna, the hyperdirect pathway in effect turns off all disinhibition, shutting down behavioural selection. In this case, we can see how specific and non-specific inhibition can interact to elicit or shut down behaviour.

In the context of attention, Posner et al. [23] show how visual attentional focus can be moved around without getting stuck at some particular saccade targets. In this case, previous saccade targets are specifically inhibited for some time. This ensures that eyes cannot directly move back to where they came form, but must continue to a different location first. Although inhibition in these cases act on externally visible processes such as behavioral choice or attention, inhibition may also have a role in regulating the processing levels of internal processes to limit the unnecessary use of energy. This is the internal equivalent to not spending energy on a task that is not likely to lead to a reward. In fact, there is a simple relation between energy consumed for a cognitive task and the energy contained in a possible reward caused by that cognitive process. The reward must be higher than the effort spent on the task. In the next section we formalize this notion in terms of modules or subsystems of a cognitive system.

1.2   The Quality of Cognitive Processes

We define the quality of the output of a module m as $Q_m(E)$ as a function of the energy E used by the module. The quality is in the range 0 to 1 where 0 means a completely useless result and 1 means an optimal or perfect output relative to some performance criterion. For example, for a vision module, a quality of 1 could mean maximal resolution, while a quality of 0.5 would reduce the resolution by half. There are four important types of quality functions (Fig. 1):

Linear. For a linear function, the output quality is proportional to the energy used. Typically the output is capped at 1, which means that the function is only linear up to a certain point.

Faster than Linear. This includes polynomial and exponential functions. For both these cases the quality increases more the more energy is used, meaning that some fixed additional quality cost less the more energy has already been spent.

Slower than Linear. Slower than linear growth includes logarithmic functions, and other functions of similar shape, that indicate diminishing returns from additional energy use.

Threshold. A threshold function is an extreme form of slower than linear growth. For a threshold function, the output quality jumps from 0 to its maximum value once a specific amount of energy has been used.

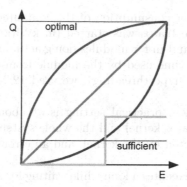

Fig. 1. Some different types of quality functions that describe the relation between quality, Q and energy use, E. The red line denotes a logarithmic–like increase of quality per unit energy used. The green line denotes a linear increase in quality per unit energy. The blue line denotes a exponential–like increase of quality per unit energy. The orange line shows a step increase in quality at a particular energy use. The black horizontal line denotes the threshold of sufficient quality. See text for further explanation. (Color figure online)

Combining Quality Functions. For most practical problems the quality of the complete computation is a function of the quality functions of the individual modules. We define a quality combination as an increasing function of each individual quality

$$C(Q_1 \ldots Q_n) \geq 0 \tag{1}$$

$$\forall i : \frac{\partial C(Q_1 \ldots Q_n)}{\partial Q_i} \geq 0 \tag{2}$$

The reward *Rew* obtained by the system is assumed to be the amount of energy received for a particular processing quality. Reward is thus a (potentially stochastic) function of combined quality $Rew(C)$.

2   Energy Measurements in a Physical System

To investigate energy use as a function of processing, we performed an experiment with our neural simulation platform Ikaros [4] running on an Apple Mac Mini with a 3.2 GHz 6-Core Intel Core i7 processor. To measure the actual power consumption a Shelley Plug (Allterco Robotics Ltd.) was used. The Ikaros framework was used for the implementation of the code for power measurement and energy calculations. We choose to measure actual energy use in a physical system rather than to use simulations to obtain a more realistic view on how such as system should operate.

To obtain an accurate estimation of the power consumption of each module running in Ikaros, we designed two Ikaros modules. The first, called EnergyMeasure, communicates with the Shelley Plug over WiFi and has two outputs that indicate the current power consumption of the computer (in W) and the accumulated energy use since Ikaros was started (in kWh). The second module is called Burner and is a stand-in for modules doing actual work. A parameter sets the amount of processor time used by the module from 0 to 100%. Since there are 12 processors (using hyperthreading), we used 12 Burner modules for the tests.

In practice, the highest practical setting is at about 95%, since a higher setting will starve the Ikaros kernel and the whole system will start to lag. This condition is readily detected by the kernel, and an error message is produced if this occurs.

Each burner module executes a loop while waiting for its time quota to expire. Within this loop a counter is increased to count the number of cycles executed. The first ten iterations are used to estimate the nominal number of cycles in the loop. For subsequent iterations, a throttling output is set to the current cycles, divided by the nominal number of cycles. This is used to indicate throttling of CPU performance which is sent to a dedicated output of the module. The throttle estimation is reset if and when the time quota is changed. The throttle output is useful to indicate when throttling is going on, but can only be trusted in manual mode when the quota of each module is set manually to make sure that there is no throttling initially.

The profiling system of the Ikaros kernel was modified to measure processor use for all modules, and to automatically add a power output that reports the usage of that module. This output is initially in the range 0–1 where 1 corresponds to 100% use of the allotted time. However, after calibration, this value is multiplied with a power factor to obtain a measure of the actual power used in W.

Processor time used is obviously not the only factor that influences energy use, but for the current system, other factor such as "switches" are negligible. Also note that there is no access to the file system once Ikaros has started.

To map from processor time to power use, we used a calibration procedure. Twelve Burner–modules were run together with the EnergyMeasure module. The EnergyMeasure module measured the total power use of the computer, P.

Each Burner module is set to randomly change how much CPU time it uses during each iteration. The power output of each Burner module i, P_i is recorded for each iteration together with the measured power use.

The power use of the computer is assumed to be described by the equation

$$P(t) = P_c(t) + c \sum_i P_i(t) \tag{3}$$

Here, c is a coefficient that maps percent processor use to the effect P_i, $P_c(t)$ is the power used by the rest of the computer.

We want to find the coefficient c that minimizes

$$\left\| P(t) - P_c(t) + c \sum_i P_i(t) \right\| \tag{4}$$

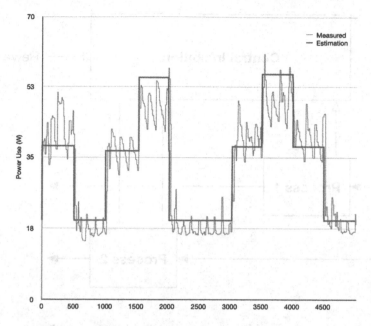

Fig. 2. The measured (blue) and estimated (red) power consumption in a situation where only two Ikaros-modules are used at different levels. Measurement were used during 5000 iteration at 100 ms per iteration. (Color figure online)

This is a straight forward regression problem that can be solved by a combination of math-modules in Ikaros. Once the coefficient c has been estimated, it allows each module in Ikaros to indicate its actual energy use on one of its output.

Figure 2 shows the estimated and actual energy use after calibration for the simple case of two modules that operate at different levels. As can be seen, the estimation if fairly accurate on average.

3   Adaptive Inhibition

Once the energy consumed by each module can be estimated, it can be used by a central inhibition module that control the processing in each module. In this section we outline the design of such a module that can learn the relation between energy use in each module and the expected reward.

Figure 3 shows the overall structure of the system. A central inhibitory modules collects rewards from the environment, measured in kWh. It also receives inputs from each of the modules, or processes, in the overall system. These inputs indicates the amount of power used by each process at any time. The task for the central inhibitory system is to learn the optimal level of inhibition, that is suppression of processing of each module, that will give the maximum reward when the energy used is subtracted.

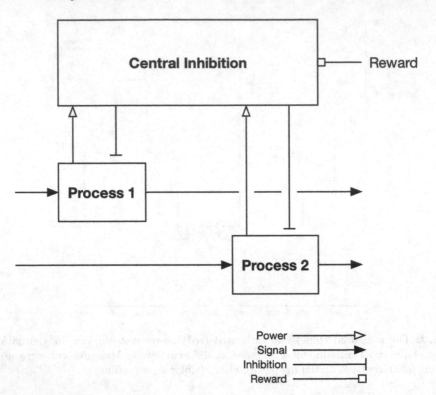

Fig. 3. The inhibition model for a system with two processes. Each process reports its current power use to the central inhibitory system that determines the amount of inhibition that is optimal to obtain the maximal reward over time.

This problem can be formulated as a reinforcement learning problem where the inhibitory output of the central inhibition system can be seen as the 'action' while the state input is the task at hand. For a single task, the central inhibitory system needs to find the inhibition vector I_i that maximizes

$$\sum_{t=0}^{\infty} \left(Rew(t) - \sum_i (1 - I_i) P_i(t) \right) \tag{5}$$

where P_i is the power used by each of the modules at time t, I_i is the inhibition of each module or process, and Rew is the reward. For $I_i = 0$ there is no inhibition and the process operates at its maximum level. For $I_i = 1$ is completely suppressed.

A central inhibitory system of this kind has earlier been described by Balkenius and Morén as a way to learn task switching in different context [5]. A central idea in this work was that inhibition is the results of unfulfilled expectations. When reward is lower than expected, behaviors are inhibited in the current context.

The view presented here, that inhibition relates to energy conservation, adds to this picture. Namely that, any external reward can not be used on its own without taking into account the energy needed to obtain that reward. Central inhibition is thus not only a result of a reward that is lower than expected, but also of the energy used to obtain the reward.

4 Discussion

We have described how a central inhibition system can help an organism or a robot to reduce its energy use, while still performing tasks at a sufficient level. We presented a framework where energy can be measured and related to the quality of cognitive processing, and to the reward received. A central notion is that, processing as well as reward should be measured as energy.

Simulating energy consumption in addition to neuronal activity must necessarily increase the computational load of a simulation cycle. This means that the number of computations (addition, multiplication etc.) involved in completing an iteration of simulation will increase, everything else being equal, if energy dynamics is added to existing computations of action potentials or neural activity. Though this can be interesting and informative, the point of this work is to use energy both as a measure to regulate which kinds of algorithms are run, but also to show how such a measure can potentially ground (rather than abstractly represent) value for artificial cognitive systems. As we have attempted to show above, there are indications that energy grounds value also for biological systems. Although metabolic energy in the form of ATP is not the same as electrical energy in terms of current and voltage, they can be held to be equivalent in the context discussed here.

When energy use by cognitive processes is grounded in consumption of electricity, it becomes directly applicable to battery operated robotic systems. This means that energy drain by motors, as well as physical circuitry for current control can be integrated with the software that controls both cognitive and physical behaviour. In effect, energy dynamics and availability can then be used to both prioritize behaviour (e.g. carry out a task, or go to the charging station), and to influence the resolution of cognitive processes like perception and decision making. Concretely, this may manifest as the robot down–regulating visual acuity, or making "fast and frugal" choices. The application cost of such abilities is the potential for errors, analogous to human errors: sloppiness and poor judgement. The upside, in addition to extended and more robust operation, is that robotic behaviour may become more recognizable and predictable by humans, in the sense that a potentially more gradual deterioration of operational quality can happen. This is in contrast with the typically abrupt and unpredictable stopping that tends to happen in traditional systems when the battery runs out.

In most, if not all, multi-celled organisms sleep is required to maintain homeostasis [27]. The day/night cycle is thus an apparently fundamental part of life. During rest periods, organisms down-regulate arousal, and metabolic processes shift from powering physical activity to replenishing energy reserves, repair, and synthesis of tissues [18]. This means that overall energy expenditure of an organism is typically lower during rest and sleep periods, than when it is fully awake and active. Such differentiation is relevant also to robotic systems, particularly ones that are meant to be "always on". However, even if a robot is not completely turned off, large energy savings may be had by adding support for resting periods. Combining behavioural inactivity with algorithms that are minimally energy costly, but with reduced responsiveness, reduced resolution, and reduced processing speed, may thus make robotic systems more energy thrifty. By differentiating awake low arousal from sleep, it could be possible to further reduce energy demands.

In biological nervous systems, neuronal populations that carry signals from sensors are regulated by inhibitive neurons that e.g. maintain dynamic range [33], or carry out gating functions to direct signals along different pathways [34]. In mammalian brains, the noradrenergic system, including the locus coeruleus, contributes to the regulation of noise and signal gain [2]. In the context of energy consumption, this is interesting in relation with decision making. For very salient stimuli, or for stimuli with clear differences in terms of value, discrimination and decision making can happen automatically and effortlessly [28]. However, when choices are not obvious, and stimuli are similar, it may be necessary to upregulate neural gain, or contrast, for the system to come to a conclusion and make a decision. This upregulation increases energy costs, and is usually associated with feelings of effort [11].

In traditional computers, transistors are used to mediate discrete up or down states [29]. This kind of circuitry is designed to be highly resistant to noise, and hence is reliable in the sense that a computer program can typically be expected to produce the exact same result no matter how many times it is run. The price of this reliability is a high energy cost, which is typically used to maintain a sufficient voltage difference between the up and down states [29]. Though the reliability has proved to be useful, since it indeed underlies the modern information economy, biological systems indicate that appropriately designed software can be made tolerant of errors [1]. This tolerance can relax energy requirements and provide substantial savings in energetic costs; savings may be converted to extended run–time between charging, or smaller and lighter batteries.

In contrast to computers, biological brains are dependent on noise. Noise contributes both to maintaining a minimum activity level which is necessary for neurons to be healthy [10], but also as a signal source that can be shaped via e.g. sculpting inhibition [20, 22].

Although we here mainly have addressed energy consumption of internal processes, similar ideas could be applied to external motor systems as well. A robot could use a central inhibition system to learn to only use the minimal energy necessary to perform a particular task. This could lead to artificial systems that optimize their energy use at all levels, just like biological systems.

References

1. Arora, A., Gouda, M.G.: Closure and convergence: a foundation of fault-tolerant computing. IEEE Trans. Softw. Eng. **19**, 1015–1027 (1993)
2. Aston-Jones, G., Cohen, J.D.: Adaptive gain and the role of the locus coeruleus-norepinephrine system in optimal performance. J. Comp. Neurol. **493**, 99–110 (2005)
3. Baca, S.M., Marin-Burgin, A., Wagenaar, D.A., Kristan, W.B.: Widespread inhibition proportional to excitation controls the gain of a leech behavioral circuit. Neuron **57**, 276–289 (2008)
4. Balkenius, C., Johansson, B., Tjøstheim, T.A.: Ikaros: a framework for controlling robots with system-level brain models. Int. J. Adv. Robot. Syst. **17** (2020)
5. Balkenius, C., Morén, J.: A computational model of context processing. In: 6th International Conference on the Simulation of Adaptive Behaviour. Citeseer (2000)
6. Berridge, K.C.: The debate over dopamine's role in reward: the case for incentive salience. Psychopharmacology **191**, 391–431 (2006). https://doi.org/10.1007/s00213-006-0578-x
7. Berridge, K.C., Robinson, T.E.: What is the role of dopamine in reward: hedonic impact, reward learning, or incentive salience? Brain Res. Rev. **28**, 309–369 (1998)
8. Blakemore, C., Carpenter, R.H.S., Georgeson, M.A.: Lateral inhibition between orientation detectors in the human visual system. Nature **228**, 37–39 (1970)
9. Charnov, E.L.: Optimal foraging, the marginal value theorem. Theor. Popul. Biol. **9**(2), 129–36 (1976)
10. Choi, D.W.: Glutamate neurotoxicity in cortical cell culture is calcium dependent. Neurosci. Lett. **58**, 293–297 (1985)
11. Cole, B.J., Robbins, T.W.: Forebrain norepinephrine: role in controlled information processing in the rat. Neuropsychopharmacol. Off. Publ. Ame. Coll. Neuropsychopharmacol. **7**(2), 129–42 (1992)
12. Cox, D.D., Dean, T.L.: Neural networks and neuroscience-inspired computer vision. Curr. Biol. **24**, R921–R929 (2014)
13. Frank, M.J.: Hold your horses: a dynamic computational role for the subthalamic nucleus in decision making. Neural Netw. Off. J. Int. Neural Netw. Soc. **19**(8), 1120–1136 (2006)
14. Glimcher, P.W.: Understanding dopamine and reinforcement learning: the dopamine reward prediction error hypothesis. Proc. Natl. Acad. Sci. **108**(Supplement 3), 15647–15654 (2011)
15. Gold, J.I., Shadlen, M.N.: The neural basis of decision making. Ann. Rev. Neurosci. **30**, 535–574 (2007)
16. Gray, J., McNaughton, N.: The Neuropsychology of Anxiety. Oxford University Press, New York (2000)
17. Holroyd, C.B., Coles, M.G.H.: The neural basis of human error processing: reinforcement learning, dopamine, and the error-related negativity. Psychol. Rev. **109**(4), 679–709 (2002)
18. Horne, J.A.: Sleep function, with particular reference to sleep deprivation. Ann. Clin. Res. **17**(5), 199–208 (1985)
19. Matsumoto, M., Hikosaka, O.: Two types of dopamine neuron distinctly convey positive and negative motivational signals. Nature **459**, 837–841 (2009)
20. Merchant, H., Naselaris, T., Georgopoulos, A.P.: Dynamic sculpting of directional tuning in the primate motor cortex during three-dimensional reaching. J. Neurosci. **28**, 9164–9172 (2008)

21. Merrer, J.L., Becker, J.A.J., Befort, K., Kieffer, B.L.: Reward processing by the opioid system in the brain. Physiol. Rev. **89**(4), 1379–1412 (2009)
22. Pertermann, M., Mückschel, M., Adelhöfer, N., Ziemssen, T., Beste, C.: On the interrelation of 1/f neural noise and norepinephrine system activity during motor response inhibition. J. Neurophysiol. **121**(5), 1633–1643 (2019)
23. Posner, M.I., Rafal, R.D., Choate, L.S., Vaughan, J.: Inhibition of return: neural basis and function. Cogn. Neuropsychol. **2**, 211–228 (1985)
24. Satoh, M., Minami, M.: Molecular pharmacology of the opioid receptors. Pharmacol. Ther. **68**(3), 343–364 (1995)
25. van Steenbergen, H., Eikemo, M., Leknes, S.: The role of the opioid system in decision making and cognitive control: a review. Cogn. Affect. Behav. Neurosci. **19**(3), 435–458 (2019). https://doi.org/10.3758/s13415-019-00710-6
26. Taigman, Y., Yang, M., Ranzato, M., Wolf, L.: DeepFace: closing the gap to human-level performance in face verification. In: 2014 IEEE Conference on Computer Vision and Pattern Recognition, pp. 1701–1708 (2014)
27. Tononi, G., Cirelli, C.: Sleep and the price of plasticity: from synaptic and cellular homeostasis to memory consolidation and integration. Neuron **81**, 12–34 (2014)
28. Towal, R.B., Mormann, M.M., Koch, C.: Simultaneous modeling of visual saliency and value computation improves predictions of economic choice. Proc. Natl. Acad. Sci. **110**, E3858–E3867 (2013)
29. Tsividis, Y.: Operation and Modeling of the MOS Transistor. McGraw-Hill, Inc. (1987)
30. Watkins, C.J., Dayan, P.: Q-learning. Mach. Learn. **8**(3), 279–292 (1992). https://doi.org/10.1007/BF00992698
31. Wise, R.A.: Dopamine, learning and motivation. Nat. Rev. Neurosci. **5**, 483–494 (2004)
32. Xiong, W., Chen, W.R.: Dynamic gating of spike propagation in the mitral cell lateral dendrites. Neuron **34**, 115–126 (2002)
33. Xue, M., Atallah, B.V., Scanziani, M.: Equalizing excitation-inhibition ratios across visual cortical neurons. Nature **511**, 596–600 (2014)
34. Yang, G.R., Murray, J.D., Wang, X.J.: A dendritic disinhibitory circuit mechanism for pathway-specific gating. Nat. Commun. **7**, 1–14 (2016)

Adapting to Environment Changes Through Neuromodulation of Reinforcement Learning

Jinwei Xing[1($\boxtimes$)], Xinyun Zou[1], Praveen K. Pilly[2], Nicholas A. Ketz[2], and Jeffrey L. Krichmar[1]

[1] University of California, Irvine, CA 92697, USA
{jinweix1,xinyunz5,jkrichma}@uci.edu
[2] HRL Laboratories, LLC, Malibu, CA 90265, USA
{pkpilly,naketz}@hrl.com

Abstract. Reinforcement learning (RL) enables agents to learn actions that can give maximum reward in an interactive environment. The environment is normally described as a predefined Markov Decision Process (MDP) which is assumed to remain unchanged throughout the life of RL agents. However, RL faces challenges when the environment changes. First, the agent needs to be able to detect the environment change rapidly when it occurs. Second, the agent needs to retain the knowledge learned before the environmental change. When facing an environment that was interacted with before, the learned knowledge should be recalled and utilized. To overcome these two challenges, we developed a biologically-inspired neuromodulation system that enables RL agents to quickly detect and adapt to environment changes. Our neuromodulation system is inspired by the effects of the cholinergic (ACh) and noradrenergic (NE) neuromodulatory systems on tracking uncertainties in the environment. We conducted experiments in the Gridworld environment and on a simulated MuJoCo robot to demonstrate the efficacy of our approach.

Keywords: Neuromodulation · Reinforcement learning · Uncertainty

1 Introduction

Reinforcement learning is a type of learning technique that enables agents to select the appropriate actions in an environment to maximize cumulative reward. In recent years, by combining RL with deep neural networks, deep RL has achieved success in a wide range of applications such as games [1,2], robot control [3,4] and mobile autonomous driving [5,6]. Despite these successes, RL still faces challenges when applied to more practical scenarios such as dynamic environments that contain uncertainty.

In this work, we investigate how an RL agent can cope with uncertainty in dynamic environments. There are two challenges for the agent. First, the agent

© The Author(s), under exclusive license to Springer Nature Switzerland AG 2022
L. Cañamero et al. (Eds.): SAB 2022, LNAI 13499, pp. 115–126, 2022.
https://doi.org/10.1007/978-3-031-16770-6_10

needs to detect the environment change rapidly. Without rapid detection, the knowledge learned before the change could be tainted by the different reward feedback received by the agent after the change. Furthermore, not recognizing the change could result in performance drops. Second, the agent needs to remember the knowledge learned under each environment setting. This requires the agent to not only detect the environment change but also identify whether the changed environment has been interacted with before. When facing a familiar environment setting, the agent needs to recall the knowledge and avoid learning from scratch again.

To address the challenges above, we take inspiration from humans and animals. Decision making is a core competency for humans and animals to survive in the environment. In the past several decades, neuroscience research in decision making tasks support the idea that the brain uses a form of reinforcement learning to shape decision making [7–10]. However, humans and animals face a similar problem of adapting to environment changes as the real world is normally uncertain. We suggest that brain's neuromodulatory system plays an important role in coping with this uncertainty.

In prior work, we investigated how neuromodulated neural networks could rapidly adapt to goal changes in classification tasks [12]. It was based on a Bayesian model of neuromodulation to track the uncertainty of interactions with the environment [11] in which the cholinergic (ACh) system tracked expected uncertainty (i.e., the known degree of unreliability of predictive relationships in the environment) and the noradrenergic (NE) system tracked unexpected uncertainty (i.e., large changes in the environment that violate prior expectations). In addition, the NE system caused a rapid adaptation to goal changes by triggering a 'network reset' [16,17]. The present work extends this goal-driven perception model to RL agents, which must recognize changes to their reward function and adapt appropriately.

Inspired by the neuromodulation system described above, we developed a reinforcement learning system in which ACh system tracks the expected uncertainty of the current reward function while NE system tracks the unexpected uncertainty which could increase when prior actions no longer produce rewards. These two systems allow the agent to detect task changes rapidly and identify whether a task is novel or not and thus decide whether and which knowledge should be recalled. We show how this approach can improve the performance of RL agents in a Gridworld environment and a MuJoCo walking robot.

2   Problem

In this work, we focus on the problem of how to enable reinforcement learning agents to rapidly adapt to changes in the environment. We first introduce the basic setting of reinforcement learning and then explain the form of environmental changes used in the present work.

2.1   Reinforcement Learning

In reinforcement learning, agents learn to take actions to maximize their cumulative rewards in the environment. The environment is typically stated in the form of a Markov Decision Process (MDP), which is expressed in terms of the tuple (S, A, T, R) where S is the state space, A is the action space, T is the state transition function and R is the reward function. At each time step t in the MDP, the agent takes an action a_t in the environment based on current state s_t and receives a reward r_{t+1} following R and next state s_{t+1} following T. The state transition and reward feedback follows:

$$s_{t+1} = T(s_t, a_t) \tag{1}$$

$$r_t = R(s_t, a_t) \tag{2}$$

The goal of RL agent is to find a policy $\pi(s)$ to select actions that maximize the discounted cumulative future reward $r_t + \gamma r_{t+1} + \gamma^2 r_{t+2} + ...$, where γ is the discount factor ranging from 0 to 1.

2.2   Environment Changes

In this work, we focus on how to adapt when feedback from the environment changes the reward function R while other elements including state space S, action space A and state transition function T remain unchanged. Here we define a task as a MDP:

$$Task_i = <S, A, T, R_i> \tag{3}$$

where i is the identity of the task. All tasks share the same $<S, A, T>$ while each task has its own R_i. The environment change could be demonstrated as task switching in a task sequence. As noted below, we define the environment to be composed of a sequence of tasks.

$$Env = [Task_1, Task_2, Task_3, ...Task_N] \tag{4}$$

where N is the number of tasks in the sequence. Note that $Task_i$ and $Task_j$ may share the same reward function, in which case $R_i = R_j$. This means a given task can occur multiple times in the sequence, and so the agent needs to learn the task and re-utilize the learned knowledge when exposed to the task again.

3   Method

We developed a bio-inspired neuromodulatory system to track the uncertainty of the environment which facilitates rapid adaptation to environment changes. Similar to the model in [12], our system is composed of ACh and NE neuromodulatory systems. We introduce their underlying equations below.

3.1   ACh and NE Neuromodulation

In our system, the ACh system has K ACh neurons where K is the number of tasks the agent has detected and initialized as 1. As more tasks are detected by our neuromodulatory system, the value of K increases accordingly. We use a vector to represent the activity of ACh neurons, where ACh_i represents the uncertainty of $Task_i$. The higher ACh_i is, the more certain that the current task is $Task_i$. A task change is detected when the maximum ACh value is below a threshold ch_{change}.

$$Task\_Change = \begin{cases} True & \text{if } \max(ACh) < ch_{change} \\ False & \text{otherwise} \end{cases} \tag{5}$$

Once a task change is detected, the agent needs to judge whether the new task is a task that has been learned before and thus previous knowledge should be recalled or the new task is novel and needs to be learned from scratch. We call this step a "task match". A task match should happen when the agent has low uncertainty on one task and high uncertainty on all other tasks, as described below.

$$P_i = \frac{exp(\beta * ACh_i)}{\sum_j^K exp(\beta * ACh_j)} \tag{6}$$

$$Task\_Match_i = \begin{cases} True & \text{if } P_i > p_{match} \\ False & \text{otherwise} \end{cases} \tag{7}$$

where P_i represents the certainty that the new task is $Task_i$. Once P_i goes above the threshold of p_{match}, the system matches the new task with $Task_i$ and $Task\_Match_i$ is set as True. The softmax function in Eq. 6 allows the agent to take the complete ACh system into consideration in task match.

In addition to the task change detection and task match based on ACh system, we use the NE system to decide whether a new task is novel. The NE system consists of one NE neuron whose activity represents the unexpected uncertainty on the environment. The activity of the NE neuron increases when a task change is detected by the ACh system while the new task cannot be matched with previous tasks. When the activity of the NE neuron goes above a hyperparameter threshold $ne_{threshold}$, the new task is believed to be novel.

$$Task\_Novel = \begin{cases} True & \text{if } NE > ne_{threshold} \\ False & \text{otherwise} \end{cases} \tag{8}$$

3.2   Update of ACh and NE System

Since the only difference between tasks is the reward function R, the uncertainty about the environment and the update of our neuromodulatory system are based on the difference between the reward feedback expected by the agent and the actual reward, which is called reward prediction error in this work. To produce the reward expectation, the agent learns a reward predictor $\tilde{R}_i$ to approximate R_i for each $Task_i$. For a set of $<s, a, r>$, the reward prediction error is defined as the difference between the predicted reward $\tilde{R}_i(s, a)$ and the true reward r is

$$RPE_i = \tilde{R}_i(s, a) - r \tag{9}$$

The expected uncertainty (ACh neuron activity) increases when the reward prediction error is high and decreases when the reward prediction error is low. To simulate this, we use RPE_{mean} and RPE_{std} to track the running mean and standard deviation, respectively, of the reward prediction error and update the ACh system as follows:

$$Expected_i = \begin{cases} True & \text{if } abs(RPE_i - RPE_{mean}) < k * RPE_{std} \\ False & \text{otherwise} \end{cases} \tag{10}$$

$$ACh_i = \begin{cases} min(ch_{max}, ACh_i * ch_{expected}) & \text{if } Expected_i \\ max(ch_{min}, ACh_i * ch_{unexpected}) & \text{otherwise} \end{cases} \tag{11}$$

where $Expected_i$ represents whether the reward for $Task_i$ is expected by the agent. If so, ACh_i will increase. Otherwise, it will decrease. The hyperparameter k in Eq. 10 controls the strictness of $Expected_i$. $ch_{expected}$ and $ch_{unexpected}$ are scaling factors used to increase or decrease ACh neuron activities while ch_{max} and ch_{min} represents their maximum and minimum values.

The NE system tracks the unexpected uncertainty of the environment and can be used to detect novel tasks that have not been observed before. It is updated when a task change is detected and increases when the task match is incorrect. If the current task is matched with an old task, then the unexpected uncertainty is resolved and the NE neuron is reset.

$$NE = \begin{cases} min(ne_{max}, NE * ne_{unmatched}) & \text{if not any } Task\_Match \\ ne_{init} & \text{otherwise} \end{cases} \tag{12}$$

where $ne_{unmatched}$ is a hyperparameter bigger than 1 that is used to increase the NE neuron activity. ne_{max} and ne_{init} represent the maximum and initial values of the NE neuron.

3.3   The Complete System

The complete system of our work includes an agent conducting reinforcement learning and a neuromodulatory system that helps it track the uncertainty of the environment and adapt to environment changes. The agent needs to remember the knowledge learned in each task. When a task is encountered again, the agent needs to conduct a task match based on the neuromodulatory system and reactivate the knowledge once it is matched to avoid learning from scratch again. In this work, the knowledge includes the RL policy and reward predictor that the agent learns for each task. We describe the complete system with the pseudocode below.

Algorithm 1: Reinforcement Learning with Neuromodulatory System

Input: $ch_{init}, ch_{max}, ch_{min}, ch_{expected}, ch_{unexpected}, \beta, k, ne_{max}, ne_{init}, ne_{threshold}$
$ne_{unmatched}, max\_step$

Init: $task \leftarrow 1, ACh_1 \leftarrow ch_{init}, NE \leftarrow ne_{init}, task\_change \leftarrow False, step \leftarrow 0, K \leftarrow 1$

1 **while** $step < max\_step$ **do**
2   Agent selects action and receives feedback from the environment
3     $step \leftarrow step + 1$
4   **if** *not Task_Change* **then**
5   Agent stores experiences for RL training
6   Compute the reward predictor error RPE_{task} // Equation 9
7   Update ACh system   // Equations 10,11
8   Update *Task_Change* based on ACh system   // Equation 5
9   **if** *not Task_Change* **then**
10   Update RPE_{mean} and RPE_{std}
11   Train the RL agent
12   Train the reward predictor
13   **else**
14   Save the learned knowledge for *task*
15   **else**
16   **for** $i \leftarrow 1$ **to** K **do**
17   Compute $Task\_Match_i$ // Equation 6, 7
18   **if** $Task\_Match_i = True$ **then**
19                $task \leftarrow i$
20                $Task\_Change \leftarrow False$
21   reactivate the saved knowledge for task i
22   reset neuromodulation system
23   Update NE system   // Equation 12
24   Compute $Task\_Novel$ // Equation 8
25   **if** $Task\_Novel = True$ **then**
26            $K \leftarrow K+1$
27            $task \leftarrow K$
28            $Task\_Change \leftarrow False$
29   create a new policy and reward predictor for the novel task
30   reset neuromodulation system

---

4   Experiments

We conduct two experiments to demonstrate the efficacy of our neuromodulatory system for RL applications: 1. Gridworld (Fig. 1) and 2. bipedal walking with a MuJoCo robot (Fig. 2).

The first experiment is based on a Gridworld Environment [13]. In this grid-based environment, there are four objects with unique colors where the red color represents the agent while the green, blue and yellow colors represent objects that can be picked up. The agent needs to navigate in the grid world and pick up the correct object. Based on the target object to pick up, we define three tasks named as pickup-green, pickup-blue and pickup-yellow. The agent receives non-zero reward only when picking up an object. The reward is 1 if the agent picks up the correct object and is −1 if the wrong object is picked up.

The second experiment is conducted on a MuJoCo simulated bipedal walker robot. DeepMind control suite [18] contains three walker-based tasks including walker-stand, walker-walk and walker-run. In the walker-stand task, the reward is a combination of terms encouraging an upright torso and some minimal torso height. The walker-walk and walker-run tasks include a component encouraging forward velocity. We list the hyperparameters in two experiments in Table 1.

Table 1. Hyperparameters of ACh and NE neuromodulatory systems.

Hyperparameters	GridWorld	Worker robot
ch_{init}	0.5	0.5
ch_{max}	1.0	1.0
ch_{min}	0.1	0.1
ch_{change}	0.2	0.2
$ch_{expected}$	1.1	1.1
$ch_{unexpected}$	0.9	0.9
p_{match}	0.5	0.5
β	2	2
ne_{max}	1.0	1.0
ne_{init}	0.1	0.1
$ne_{unmatched}$	1.05	1.05
$ne_{threshold}$	0.9	0.9

In our experiments, the environment change is demonstrated as a task switch. For Gridworld, we set the task sequence for the experiment of Gridworld as [pickup-green, pickup-blue, pickup-yellow, pickup-green, pickup-blue, pickup-yellow]. For the MuJoCo robot, we set the task sequence for the walker as [walker-stand, walker-walk, walker-run, walker-stand, walker-walk, walker-run]. The task switch in each sequence requires the agent to quickly detect environment changes while the recurrence of tasks requires the agent to achieve successful task match and re-utilize learned knowledge.

Our neuromodulatory system is compatible with different types of reinforcement learning algorithms and settings. In the Gridworld experiments, the agent has a discrete action space and we use the Proximal Policy Optimization (PPO) algorithm [15], which is an on-policy RL method. In the MuJoCo walker robot experiment, the agent has a continuous action space and we use the Twin Delayed Deep Deterministic policy gradient (TD3) [14], which is an off-policy RL method.

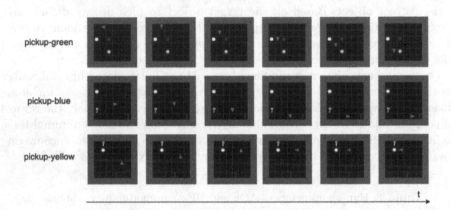

Fig. 1. Gridworld environment. Examples of three tasks (pickup-green, pickup-blue and pickup-yellow) in Gridworld environment. In each task, the agent moves towards the object with a specified color. (Color figure online)

Fig. 2. MuJoCo environment. Examples of three tasks (stand, walk and run) of MuJoCo walker robot. The agent has unique behavior in each task.

5 Results

5.1 Reinforcement Learning Performance

In both experiments, the addition of our neuromodulatory system improved performance. To demonstrate the efficacy of our method, we conducted an ablation study by disabling the NE system or disabling both the ACh and the NE system. Since the NE system depends on the ACh system, we avoided the setting of disabling the ACh while keeping the NE system. We compared the performance of the RL agent with and without ablations (Fig. 3). The better performance on novel tasks when neuromodulation was included due to the agent detecting environment changes quickly and avoiding detrimental knowledge transfer between tasks. Meanwhile, the immediate high score on recurring tasks demonstrates that the neuromodulatory system allows the agent to recognize previously observed tasks and utilize prior knowledge. In the ablation experiments, when the NE system is disabled, the agent cannot correctly identify whether a new task after task change is novel or not. As a result, all new tasks were simply recognized as novel tasks and the agent conducted learning from scratch every time a task change was detected. When the ACh system is also removed, the agent cannot detect task changes and conduct normal RL training throughout the whole task sequence. As a result, the agent would have only one task policy and the knowledge learned in the previous task will all be transferred to the next one. Its influence on the reward performance depends on the similarities of tasks in the task sequence. For example, the knowledge transfer in Gridworld is negative since the correct object to pick up in the last task will be wrong in the next task. As for tasks on walker robot, knowledge transfer could be more positive since learning to run could benefit from the knowledge of how to walk. However, in both two experiments, the RL agent with our neuromodulatory system achieved the best performance.

Besides the general RL performance, we're also interested in the benefits of our neuromodulatory system in fast performance recovery. In the experiments above, each task occurs multiple times in the task sequence and the agent gradually improves performance via learning when interacting with each task. Although task changes regularly following the task sequence, an intelligent agent should quickly recover the performance when encountering the same task again. As a result, we compute the average time steps needed to recover 90% of the performance when facing a task that has been learned before. As shown in Table 2, our neuromodulatory system allows the agent to achieve much faster performance recovery compared to the ablated agents.

5.2 Activity of Neuromodulatory System

We examined the activity of the ACh and NE systems in these two experiments. As shown in Fig. 4, our ACh system is able to track the uncertainty on each task and always show high certainty on the correct task. This allows the agent to efficiently identify the correct task identity and adapt to task switches.

Table 2. Average time steps needed to achieve 90% performance recovery of each task of our method and ablated studies. The results are averaged over 6 runs.

	Time steps of performance recovery		
	Ours	No NE	No NE, No ACh
pickup-green	**150.3**	45060.5	59753.3
pickup-blue	**130.7**	25510.7	69535.2
pickup-yellow	**143.3**	29428.7	87605.6
walker-stand	**796.0**	311000.0	354500.0
walker-walk	**1843.0**	411500.0	598000.0
walker-run	**1542.2**	501000.0	585333.3

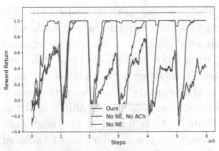
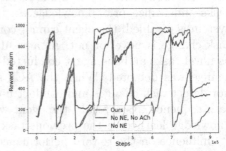

(a) RL Performance on Gridworld   (b) RL Performance on walker Robot

Fig. 3. Results of reinforcement learning performance with and without the neuromodulatory system. The bar on top of the figure represents the task sequence. The task sequence in Gridworld experiment is [pickup-green, pickup-blue, pickup-yellow, pickup-green, pickup-blue, pickup-yellow] and the task sequence in walker robot experiment is ['walker-stand', 'walker-walk', 'walker-run', 'walker-stand', 'walker-walk', 'walker-run', 'walker-stand', 'walker-walk', 'walker-run']. (Color figure online)

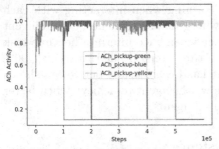
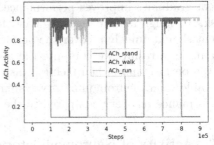

(a) ACh activity for the Gridworld experiment.   (b) ACh activity for the walker robot experiment.

Fig. 4. Dynamics of the activity of the ACh system in the two experiments. The bar on top of the figure represents the task sequence.

As shown in Fig. 5, our NE system shows high activity for the first and second task switches since the second and third tasks are novel. The activity of the NE system also increased for other task switches but didn't reach the threshold because those switched tasks had been encountered before by the agent and were not novel. This demonstrates that our NE system can track the unexpected uncertainty of the environment which allows the agent to distinguish between novel and familiar tasks. This capability helps the agent to better adapt to environment changes.

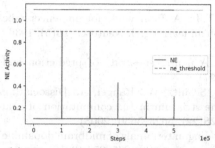 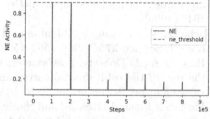

(a) NE activity for the Gridworld experiment.   (b) NE activity for the walker robot experiment

Fig. 5. Dynamics of the activity of the NE system in the two experiments. The bar on top of the figure represents the task sequence.

6 Conclusion

We developed a system inspired by neuromodulation to track the uncertainty of the environment and help reinforcement learning agents to quickly adapt to environment changes. We demonstrated the efficacy of the neuromodulatory system in two reinforcement learning experiments; namely, a Gridworld environment and a simulated walker robot. We believe these results provide insights into how intelligent agents survive in uncertain environments and also enable the deployment of artificial agents in complicated real-world applications.

Acknowledgements. This material is partially based upon work supported by the United States Air Force and DARPA under Contract No. FA8750-18-C-0103. Any opinions, findings and conclusions or recommendations expressed in this material are those of the author(s) and do not necessarily reflect the views of the United States Air Force and DARPA. Authors are also thankful to computing resources provided by CHASE-CI under NSF Grant CNS-1730158.

References

1. Silver, D., et al.: Mastering the game of Go with deep neural networks and tree search. Nature **529**(7587), 484–489 (2016)

2. Mnih, V., et al.: Human-level control through deep reinforcement learning. Nature **518**(7540), 529–533 (2015)
3. Akkaya, I., et al.: Solving Rubik's cube with a robot hand. arXiv preprint arXiv:1910.07113 (2019)
4. Lillicrap, T.P., et al.: Continuous control with deep reinforcement learning. arXiv preprint arXiv:1509.02971 (2015)
5. Kahn, G., Abbeel, P., Levine, S.: BADGR: an autonomous self-supervised learning-based navigation system. IEEE Robot. Autom. Lett. **6**(2), 1312–1319 (2021)
6. Xing, J., Zou, X., Krichmar, J.L.: Neuromodulated patience for robot and self-driving vehicle navigation. In: 2020 International Joint Conference on Neural Networks (IJCNN), pp. 1–8. IEEE, July 2020
7. Montague, P.R., Dayan, P., Sejnowski, T.J.: A framework for mesencephalic dopamine systems based on predictive Hebbian learning. J. Neurosci. **16**(5), 1936–1947 (1996)
8. Schultz, W., Dayan, P., Montague, P.R.: A neural substrate of prediction and reward. Science **275**(5306), 1593–1599 (1997)
9. Hare, T.A., O'Doherty, J., Camerer, C.F., Schultz, W., Rangel, A.: Dissociating the role of the orbitofrontal cortex and the striatum in the computation of goal values and prediction errors. J. Neurosci. **28**(22), 5623–5630 (2008)
10. Parker, N.F., et al.: Reward and choice encoding in terminals of midbrain dopamine neurons depends on striatal target. Nat. Neurosci. **19**(6), 845–854 (2016)
11. Angela, J.Y., Dayan, P.: Uncertainty, neuromodulation, and attention. Neuron **46**(4), 681–692 (2005)
12. Zou, X., Kolouri, S., Pilly, P.K., Krichmar, J.L.: Neuromodulated attention and goal-driven perception in uncertain domains. Neural Netw. **125**, 56–69 (2020)
13. Chevalier-Boisvert, M., Willems, L., Pal, S.: Minimalistic gridworld environment for OpenAI Gym. GitHub Repository (2018). https://github.com/maximecb/gym-minigrid
14. Fujimoto, S., Hoof, H., Meger, D.: Addressing function approximation error in actor-critic methods. In: International Conference on Machine Learning, pp. 1587–1596. PMLR, July 2018
15. Schulman, J., Wolski, F., Dhariwal, P., Radford, A., Klimov, O.: Proximal policy optimization algorithms. arXiv preprint arXiv:1707.06347 (2017)
16. Grella, S.L., et al.: Locus coeruleus phasic, but not tonic, activation initiates global remapping in a familiar environment. J. Neurosci. **39**(3), 445–455 (2019)
17. Bouret, S., Sara, S.J.: Network reset: a simplified overarching theory of locus coeruleus noradrenaline function. Trends Neurosci. **28**(11), 574–582 (2005)
18. Tassa, Y., et al.: Deepmind control suite. arXiv preprint arXiv:1801.00690 (2018)

Multi-task Learning with Modular Reinforcement Learning

Jianyong Xue[1,2,3](✉) and Frédéric Alexandre[1,2,3]

[1] Inria Bordeaux Sud-Ouest, 33405 Talence, France
{jianyong.xue,frederic.alexandre}@inria.fr
[2] LaBRI, Université de Bordeaux, Bordeaux INP, CNRS, UMR 5800, Talence, France
[3] Institut des Maladies Neurodégénératives, Université de Bordeaux, CNRS, UMR 5293, Bordeaux, France

Abstract. The ability to learn compositional strategies in multi-task learning and to exert them appropriately is crucial to the development of artificial intelligence. However, there exist several challenges: (i) how to maintain the independence of modules in learning their own sub-tasks; (ii) how to avoid performance degradation in situations where modules' reward scales are incompatible; (iii) how to find the optimal composite policy for the entire set of tasks. In this paper, we introduce a Modular Reinforcement Learning (MRL) framework that coordinates the competition and the cooperation between separate modules. Furthermore, a selective update mechanism enables the learning system to align incomparable reward scales in different modules. Moreover, the learning system follows a "joint policy" to calculate actions' preferences combined with their responsibility for the current task. We evaluate the effectiveness of our approach on a classic food-gathering and predator-avoidance task. Results show that our approach has better performance than previous MRL methods in learning separate strategies for sub-tasks, is robust to modules with incomparable reward scales, and maintains the independence of the learning in each module.

Keywords: Multi-task learning · Modular reinforcement learning · Incomparable reward scale · Compositionality policy · Model-based reinforcement learning

1 Introduction

Multi-task learning is popularly observed in humans and several other intelligent animal species, and the ability to tackle with diverse tasks has gradually increased with the enrichment of skills that are learned from experience. For example, in a wild natural environment, most animals must pursue two tasks simultaneously: look for food and avoid predators. Meanwhile, long-time evolution has allowed animals to generate a more sensitive olfactory system to find food rapidly and to be more alert to predators, as well as to run faster.

© The Author(s), under exclusive license to Springer Nature Switzerland AG 2022
L. Cañamero et al. (Eds.): SAB 2022, LNAI 13499, pp. 127–138, 2022.
https://doi.org/10.1007/978-3-031-16770-6_11

A hallmark of multi-task learning benefits from the reusage of similar patterns underlying a set of regularities across tasks, in order to improve performance on any other single task [15,18]. Generally, the goal of multi-task learning is to find an optimal solution for solving the entire set of tasks in parallel. However, there exist several challenges: (i) how to maintain the independence of modules in learning their own sub-tasks; (ii) how to avoid performance degradation in situations where modules' reward scales are incompatible; (iii) how to find the optimal composite policy for the entire set of tasks.

These challenges have inspired the emergence of modular reinforcement learning (MRL) approaches, which decompose a multi-task problem into a collection of concurrently running RL modules, each of which learns a separate policy (or sub-policy) to solve a portion of the original problem [6,13]. Accordingly, these joint modules implicitly form a complex composite RL problem, thus the goal is to find the optimal policy for it [16]. Considering the performance degradation in the composability of modules that have incomparable reward scales, [13] introduced a special module named "command arbitrator", and proposed the architecture Arbi-Q to reformulate the MRL. Specifically, the arbitrator's policy assigns modular preferences given the observation of the state, then the selected module's preferred action will be used to interact with the environment. After each interaction, the state-abstraction function in the selected module transforms the world observation into a module-specific subset of the world states, in which modules are associated with the world that they operated in and not coupled to other modules or to an arbitrator.

Nevertheless, the Arbi-Q model has the following limitations: (i) all the modules need to be evaluated at each time-step without considering prior knowledge of modular selection, which slows down the learning process and the decision-making; (ii) learning system's action preference always comes from one single module, which may lead to dictatorship in decision-making; (iii) function approximation needs to be improved for complex continuous tasks (or the complex hybrid of discrete and continuous tasks).

Focused on these limitations, in this article, we adopt the idea of multiple model-based reinforcement learning from [3] and present a new MRL architecture named "Inverse Arbi-Q" to coordinate the competition and the cooperation between separate modules. A selective update mechanism enables the learning system to align incomparable reward scales in different modules. Furthermore, the learning system follows a "joint policy" to calculate actions' preferences combined with their responsibility for the current task.

2   Related Work

Growing evidence from behavioral and biological neuroscience notes that most animals' brain parses ongoing behavior into discrete, bound segments [5]. Specifically, internal models in separated areas of the cerebellum are responsible for given tasks via a competitive and cooperative way [1,14]. In cases when a new task appears, multiple models learn it through competition, but only one or a small part of them will be recruited for this task [3]. Meanwhile, human behaviors are hierarchically organized: actions cohere into sub-task sequences, which fit together to achieve overall task goals [2,8].

In order to scale up the RL to address multiple goals at once, an intuitive approach is to train RL modules to handle each of the sub-goals, then the learned policies for each module will be reused according to their distribution in the given multi-goal scenario. However, these component policies are usually sub-optimal in the context of the composite tasks. Focusing on this problem, [16] replace the Q-learning rule within each module with a SARSA(0) learning rule, and propose a model of GM-Sarsa(0) for finding approximate solutions to multiple-goal RL problems. In order to better coordinate competitions between modules, the mixture of experts architecture from [7,11] introduced a learning system that is composed of a list of "experts" network, plus a gating network that determines which of the experts should be responsible for the training case. However, this modular architecture relies heavily on the performance of the gating network.

An alternative family of approaches [3,10,12] employs a state predictor within each expert (or module), which enables the environmental dynamics to be predictable. The controllers associated with these experts are decided by the prediction error: the one that has the smallest prediction error will be recruited at any particular moment. Nevertheless, models based on this idea mainly emphasize the competition between modules to choose one single expert that is the most suitable for a specific task (or sub-task), but the cooperation between modules as a compositional strategy for composable complex tasks is relatively lacking. As an improvement, [3] propose a model of multiple model-based reinforcement learning (MMBRL). In the MMBRL, a complex task is decomposed into multiple modules, particularly, the computation of "responsibility" for each modules was introduced to represent their responsibility distribution in a given task. However, the parallel update strategy degrades its performance when modules has incomparable reward scales, and the composite policy will be far from optimal as the complexity of the learning problem increases.

Generally, the original MRL supports not only the decomposition of complex tasks into modules, but also the composability of separately learned modules as new strategies for tasks that were never solved before [4,13]. Focusing on the optimality of the composite strategy for the entire task and the independence of learning in separate modules, [12] introduced the specific concept of "modular reward", which comes from the actual reward after each interaction plus a bonus for passing the task on a proper module. Specifically, this bonus is calculated from the modular value function and the temporal difference in the module gating signal. In situations where the tasks are required to perform the sub-tasks concurrently, [4] propose an hierarchical RL approach to learn both compound and composable policies within the same learning process, by which exploiting the off-policy data generated by the compound policy. The results show that the experience collected with the compound policy permits not only to solve the complex task but also to obtain useful composable policies that successfully perform in their corresponding sub-tasks.

Aiming at modules that have conflicting goals and misaligned reward scales, [6] presented the framework GRACIAS that assigns fine-grained importance to different modules and enables composable decision making based on modern deep RL methods. More precisely, arbitrator learns the relative importance of each module in a given state, combined with action-value of the individual modules to calculate the joint action preferences. However, since the number of modules in this architecture is preset in advance, which will gradually limit its performance when the complexity of the task continues to increase. Moreover, when the arbitrator is trained with little prior knowledge, the performance will be initially far from optimal.

In the present work, the idea of Inverse Arbi-Q model is trying to address all the major concerns mentioned above. First, it's different from [7] where experts are determined by a gating network. Instead, modules in the present architecture learn their own behavioral policy and solve their own sub-tasks by competition. Second, it's also different from [13] where the action selection follows a "joint policy". Here action preferences come from the combination of all MBRL modules, rather than from one single preferred module. Furthermore, different from [3] where not all modules are involved in the update procedure after each interaction, instead, only the most related module will be targeted for amelioration. Moreover, the update of parameters in the selected module is gated by a dynamic signal, the "responsibility signal" [3,12], which comes from the gaussian softmax function of prediction error in each module and determines how much the module is responsible for the current situation, rather than only according to a fixed parameter of learning rate as in [4,13] as we will explain in Sect. 5.1.

3 Preliminaries

3.1 Reinforcement Learning

Reinforcement Learning (RL) paradigm focuses on learning an optimal policy π^* that enables the agent to gain the maximum accumulated rewards from future steps [17]. At each time step t, the agent stays in state $s_t \in S$ and follows the current policy $\pi(a|s)$ to execute an action $a_t \in A$; as a result, it receives an immediate feedback r_{t+1} from the environment and transitions stochastically to the next state $s_{t+1} \in S$. Note that performing this policy requires either knowing the underlying state transition model $P(s_{t+1}|s_t, a_t)$ and reward function $R(s_t, a_t)$, or estimating the state value $V(s_t)$ through rewards received in trajectories.

Based on differences in learning optimal policy, RL approaches could be divided into two categories: (a) model-free RL, which focuses on learning a policy or value function, and (b) model-based RL, which aims at learning a dynamic model and a reward function. In the model-free RL approaches, policy learning only focuses on interaction trajectories, and their parameters are mainly updated by the TD-error between state-values within two (or several) steps. Obviously, it requires a large amount of samples to achieve good performance, and typically only learns a single task at a time; also it usually suffers from high sample complexity.

However, in the model-based RL system, a dynamic model is used to make predictions of the probabilities of transition to the next state s_{t+1}, and of a reward function to provide the expected values r', given the current state s_t and the action a_t selected by the current policy $\pi(a|s)$. Model-based reinforcement learning algorithms are generally regarded as being more sample efficient [9]. However, to achieve good sample efficiency, model-based RL algorithms conventionally use relatively simple function approximators, which fails to generalize well in complex tasks, or with probabilistic dynamics models in complicated and high-dimensional domains.

3.2   Modular Reinforcement Learning

The Modular Reinforcement Learning (MRL) framework is composed of several concurrently running RL modules, each of which learns a specific policy to solve a simpler sub-problem of the main RL problem. In particular, each module has access to the observation of the environment and shares a common action space [16]. During each interaction, all modules are required to execute the same action, while observing the state transition and a reward signal specific to the module [13]. The goal of MRL is to learn the optimal policy for the entire problem, in order to maximize the accumulative global reward in the long run.

Furthermore, action selection in MRL follows a "joint policy", in which action preferences come from the combination of all (or partially related) RL controllers in each module. At each time step, the candidate actions are evaluated by the weighted summation of their value expectations of future rewards from the RL controller in each module.

$$Q(s,a) = \sum_{i=1}^{n} Q_i(s,a)w_i \tag{1}$$

where the weight w_i assigned to each module indicates the responsibility of the module in the current task.

4   The Inverse Arbi-Q Architecture

The basic idea of the Inverse Arbi-Q architecture lies in the learning system that decomposes a multi-task learning problem into a collection of RL modules, each of which learns a separate strategy for a specific sub-task concurrently. Figure 1 presents the overall organization of Inverse Arbi-Q architecture, which is composed of a list of n model-based RL (MBRL) modules. Each of MBRL modules shares a common inputs (state space and action space) and has an identical structure that consists of three components: the reward predictor, the RL controller and the state predictor, which provide the elementary realization of the module for learning its own behavioral policy and its own designated sub-task.

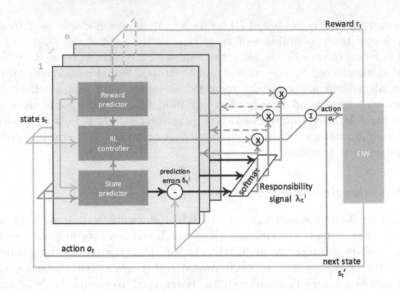

Fig. 1. Schematic diagram of Inverse Arbi-Q architecture.

5   Implementation

In this section, we explain the details for the implementation of Inverse Arbi-Q architecture. Subsection 5.1 introduces the state predictor and the calculation of responsibility signal for each module. Subsection 5.2 is about the reward predictor, we used a specific "modular reward" [12] for rewarding the module that is more suitable for the current sub-task, which encourages the architecture to be more concentrated to update to modules that better fit the current task. In Subsects. 5.3 and 5.4, we are more focused on the state-value function and the state-action function in the RL controller, as well as the action selection based on these two functions. Additionally, in order to make decisions more coherent, we adopted eligibility traces for each state, which are also introduced in this subsection.

5.1   State Predictor

The dynamic function $F_i(s_{t+1}, s_t, a_t)$ in the state predictor of module i gives the probability distribution of the newly observed state s_{t+1} based on the previous state s_t and the action a_t performed by the agent at step t.

$$F_i(s_{t+1}, s_t, a_t : \theta_i) = P_i(s_{t+1}|s_t, a_t : \theta) \tag{2}$$

where $s_t \in \{1, \ldots, N\}$ and $a_t \in \{1, \ldots, M\}$ are discrete states and actions, $i \in \{1, \ldots, n\}$ is the index of modules. Specifically, this dynamic function is realized through a neural network with three fully-connected layers, where the vector of parameters θ represents the weights of the network. This network was trained by a collection of pairs of inputs (s_t, a_t) and their corresponding output labels s'_{t+1} from trajectories $\tau = \{s_0, a_0, \dots, s_{T-2}, a_{T-2}, s_{T-1}\}$ of length T [9]. The initial parameters in this neural network were set as a small random value with uniform distribution between 0.0 and 1.0. With the newly observed state s_{t+1}, the state prediction error δ^i_{st} of module i is calculated as follows:

$$\delta^i_{st} = F_i(j, s_t, a_t : \theta_i) - c(j, s_{t+1}), j \in \{1, \dots, N\} \tag{3}$$

$$c(j, s_{t+1}) = \begin{cases} 1 & j = s_{t+1}, \\ 0 & otherwise. \end{cases} \tag{4}$$

Along with state prediction errors in each module, the responsibility signal λ^i_t of each module is formulated as the gaussian softmax function,

$$\lambda^i_t = \frac{\hat{\lambda}^i_t e^{-\frac{1}{2\sigma^2}\delta^{i~2}_{st}}}{\sum_{j=1}^{n} \hat{\lambda}^i_t e^{-\frac{1}{2\sigma^2}\delta^{j~2}_{st}}} \tag{5}$$

$$\hat{\lambda}^i_t = \frac{\lambda^i_{t-1}{}^\rho}{\sum_{j=1}^{n} \lambda^j_{t-1}{}^\rho} \tag{6}$$

where the responsibility predictor $\hat{\lambda}^i_t$ represents the prior information about module selection, which is used to maintain the temporal continuity of the selected module [3]. Parameter ρ $(0 < \rho < 1)$ controls the effects of past module selections on current decision-making. Parameter vector θ is updated as follows:

$$\theta_i = \theta_i + \alpha\lambda^i_t\delta^i_{st}\frac{\partial F_i(s_{t+1}, s_t, a_t : \theta_i)}{\partial \theta_i} \tag{7}$$

where $0 < \alpha < 1$ is the learning rate.

5.2   Reward Predictor

The reward function $R_i(r', s_t, a_t)$ provides an expected reward r'_t based on the previous state s_t and the action a_t selected at step t. Traditionally, parameters in the reward predictor are updated by the reward prediction error, which comes from the error between reward prediction r'_t and actually received immediate reward r_t after each interaction.

As described in the previous section, the responsibility signal represents how responsible the modules are for the current situation; the temporal difference of the responsibility signals between two steps could be used to reflect whether the current module is more sensitive than the previously selected one. Based on this idea, we utilize a "modular reward" [12], which comes from the immediately received reward and an extra bonus for rewarding the module that better fits the current sub-task. Specifically, this bonus is calculated from the conduct of modular value function and the temporal difference in the responsibility signal, which encourage the learning system to be more focused on the modules they are responsible for, and lead to the optimality of the composite strategy for the entire task. Basically, the modular reward is calculated as:

$$\hat{r}_t^i = r_t + (\lambda_{t+1}^i - \lambda_t^i) V^i(s_{t+1}) \tag{8}$$

and we have the reward prediction error δ_{rt}^i as follows:

$$\delta_{rt}^i = \hat{r}_t^i - R_i(r', s_t, a_t) \tag{9}$$

Weighted by the responsibility signal and the learning rate, parameters in the reward predictor will be updated as follows:

$$R_i(r', s_t, a_t) = R_i(r', s_t, a_t) + \alpha \lambda_t^i \delta_{rt}^i \tag{10}$$

5.3   RL Controller

The RL controller in module i provides two functions: the state-value function $V^i(s_t)$ and the state-action-value function $Q^i(s_t, a_t)$. The value function $V^i(s_t)$ gives the reward expectation of state s_t at step t and the state-action-value function $Q^i(s_t, a_t)$ provides the reward expectation of action a_t in state s_t. Technically, the goal of reinforcement learning is to improve the policy so that a maximal accumulative reward will be obtained in the long run [17]. The basic strategy of reinforcement learning is to use this value function to estimate the state value under the current policy, and then to improve the policy based on the value function. We define the value function of the state $s(t)$ under the current policy π as:

$$V_\pi^i(s_t) = E_\pi \left[\sum_{k=0}^{\infty} \gamma^k r(t+k) \right]$$
$$= E_\pi(R_{t+1} + \gamma V_\pi^i(s_{t+1}) | s_t) \tag{11}$$

where γ is the discount factor that controls the effects of future rewards. Traditionally, $R_{t+1} + \gamma V_\pi^i(s_{t+1})$ is also called the "target value" of state s_t. Combined with the state transition function $F_i(s_{t+1}, s_t, a_t)$ and the reward function $R_i(r', s_t, a_t)$, we have the full Bellman equation [17] of value function:

$$V_\pi^i(s_t) = \sum_{a_t \in A} \pi_t^i(a_t | s_t) [R_i(r_t', s_t, a_t) + \gamma \sum_{s_{t+1} \in S} F_i(s_{t+1}, s_t, a_t : \theta_i) V_\pi^i(s_{t+1})] \tag{12}$$

In order to make decisions in each step more coherent with previous ones, we recorded the eligibility traces $e_t^i s$ for each state s, which are updated as:

$$e_t^i(s) = \begin{cases} \eta \gamma e_{t-1}^i(s) & \text{if } s \neq s_t \\ \eta \gamma e_{t-1}^i(s) + 1 & \text{if } s = s_t \end{cases} \tag{13}$$

The temporal-difference (TD) error δ_{vt}^i comes from the deviation between the target value and the evaluated value:

$$\delta_{vt}^i = \hat{r}_t^i + \gamma V^i(s_{t+1}) - V^i(s_t) \tag{14}$$

where $\hat{r}_t^i$ is the modular reward and the state value $V^i(s_t)$ will be updated with responsibility signal as:

$$V^i(s_t) = V^i(s_t) + \alpha \lambda_t^i \delta_{vt}^i e_t^i(s) \tag{15}$$

5.4   Action Selection

At each step, the action preferences follow a "joint policy", in which state-action values derive from the combination of RL controllers in each module. Specifically, action is decided based on the weighted summation of its value expectation $Q^i(s_t, a_t)$ of future rewards in each module at state s_t. For each candidate action $a_j \in A, (j = 1, \ldots, M)$, their values are calculated as:

$$Q(s_t, a_j) = \sum_{i=1}^{n} \lambda_t^i [R_i(r', s_t, a_j) + \gamma \sum_{j \in X} F_i(s_j, s_t, a_j : \theta_i) V(s_j)] \tag{16}$$

where X is the set of possible states that the agent observes after taking action a_j in state s. In a greedy policy, the action that has the largest value will be selected:

$$a_t = \arg\max_{a_j \in A} Q(s_t, a_j) \tag{17}$$

Furthermore, we use a softmax function to explore the action space in a stochastic way, where the action a_t is selected by

$$P_i(a_t|s_t) = \frac{e^{\beta Q(s_t, a_t)}}{\sum_{k=1}^{M} e^{\beta Q(s_t, a_k)}} \tag{18}$$

where β is set as $trials/500$ and controls the stochasticity of action selection.

6   Simulation

6.1   Settings

In order to investigate the effectiveness of Inverse Arbi-Q architecture, we use a food-gathering and predator-avoidance task derived from [13,16]. In this carrot-rabbit-predator task, the environment is designed as a 5×5 grid world (as shown in Fig. 2. The blue rectangle, purple triangle and green circle represent the rabbit, the predator, and the carrot respectively. Specifically, the rabbit searches carrots with one of eight possible one step actions: {north (N), east (E), south (S), west (W), northeast (NE), southeast (SE), northwest (NW), southwest (SW)} while avoiding being caught by the predator. When the rabbit moves in the location of any of the carrots, it receives a reward of 1.0 and a new carrot will be allocated to an otherwise position. In each step where the rabbit does not find any carrot, it gets a reward of -0.1 to represent increasing hunger. Meanwhile, the predator moves one step directly toward the rabbit while the rabbit moves two steps. If the rabbit avoids the predator, it will receive a reward of 0.5, and a reward of -1.0 if it is caught by the predator, which also means the termination of this trial. In this environment, the observation state of the rabbit and the predator are their absolute coordinates respectively.

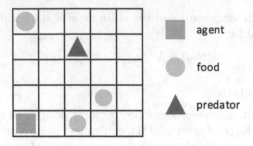

Fig. 2. The food-gathering and predator-avoidance world. (Color figure online)

6.2 Results

At the begining, we'd like to compare the performance of Inverse Arbi-Q with previous MRL approaches. Figure 3(a) shows the average number of steps during 5000 trial epochs in 20 simulation runs. It can be seen that the Inverse Arbi-Q model works significantly better than Arbi-* approaches (Arbi-Q, Arbi-MBRL and Arbi-SARSA(0)) and GM-MBRL.

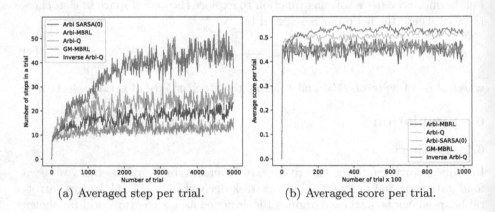

(a) Averaged step per trial.   (b) Averaged score per trial.

Fig. 3. Performance comparison with other MRL approaches.

Furthermore, we utilize another performance metric of "score" from [13] to compare Inverse Arbi-Q with different models. Specifically, the calculation of a score follows this method: for each time that the rabbit finds a carrot, the score is defined as 1.0, however, if it was caught by the predator, the score is 0.0, in situations that the rabbit avoids the predator while no carrot was eaten, the score is set as 0.5. Figure 3(b) shows the scores between Inverse Arbi-Q with other approaches. We can find that Inverse Arbi-Q receives more scores that other models.

Moreover, we'd like to know the performance of Inver Arbi-Q with incomparable reward scales. Here we increase the avoidance reward by 10 times to observe the performance of Inverse Arbi-Q in the incomparable rewards. As shown in Fig. 4, Inverse Arbi-Q is robust across different incomparable reward scales.

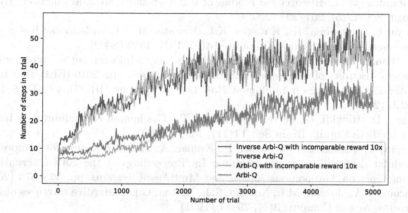

Fig. 4. Performance of Inverse Arbi-Q with incomparable reward scales.

7 Conclusions and Future Work

In summary, we present the simple yet effective architecture Inverse Arbi-Q to scale up the RL to learn compositional strategies and to exert them appropriately in multi-task learning. Particularly, the responsibility signal, the outcome of a gaussian softmax function of prediction error in each module, was used to represent module's responsibility distribution in a given task, as well as to gate the learning for each of them. Furthermore, action preferences are calculated by a "joint policy", which comes from the combination of state-action values in each module multiplied by corresponding responsibility signal. Moreover, the selective update mechanism enables the learning system to align incomparable reward scales between different modules.

Our ultimate goal with modular reinforcement learning is to facilitate the integration of multiple modules into a developmental way, in order to learn compositional strategies, as well as to generate appropriate behaviors according to the specific contexts. Nevertheless, a number of questions stands out as important targets for the next stage of research, such as: (i) the improvement of planning strategy or the proactive way in the evaluation of modular reward; (ii) enabling module selection and responsibility calculation in high dimensionality situations; (iii) the design of bidirectional (top-down and bottom-up) solutions for task decomposition and compositionality. Inspirations from continual learning and meta-learning approaches will be a promising direction for learning tremendous tasks effectively without creating additional modules.

References

1. Bernard, J.A.: Don't forget the little brain: a framework for incorporating the cerebellum into the understanding of cognitive aging. Neurosci. Biobehav. Rev. **137**, 104639 (2022)
2. Botvinick, M.M.: Hierarchical models of behavior and prefrontal function. Trends Cogn. Sci. **12**(5), 201–208 (2008)
3. Doya, K., Samejima, K., Katagiri, K.I., Kawato, M.: Multiple model-based reinforcement learning. Neural Comput. **14**(6), 1347–1369 (2002)
4. Esteban, D., Rozo, L., Caldwell, D.G.: Hierarchical reinforcement learning for concurrent discovery of compound and composable policies. In: 2019 IEEE/RSJ International Conference on Intelligent Robots and Systems (IROS), pp. 1818–1825. IEEE (2019)
5. Gatti, D., Rinaldi, L., Ferreri, L., Vecchi, T.: The human cerebellum as a hub of the predictive brain. Brain Sci. **11**(11), 1492 (2021)
6. Gupta, V., Anand, D., Paruchuri, P., Kumar, A.: Action selection for composable modular deep reinforcement learning. In: Proceedings of the 20th International Conference on Autonomous Agents and MultiAgent Systems, pp. 565–573 (2021)
7. Jacobs, R.A., Jordan, M.I., Nowlan, S.J., Hinton, G.E.: Adaptive mixtures of local experts. Neural Comput. **3**(1), 79–87 (1991)
8. Logan, G.D., Crump, M.J.: Hierarchical control of cognitive processes: the case for skilled typewriting. In: Psychology of Learning and Motivation, vol. 54, pp. 1–27. Elsevier (2011)
9. Nagabandi, A., Kahn, G., Fearing, R.S., Levine, S.: Neural network dynamics for model-based deep reinforcement learning with model-free fine-tuning. In: 2018 IEEE International Conference on Robotics and Automation (ICRA), pp. 7559–7566. IEEE (2018)
10. Narendra, K.S., Balakrishnan, J., Ciliz, M.K.: Adaptation and learning using multiple models, switching, and tuning. IEEE Control Syst. Mag. **15**(3), 37–51 (1995)
11. Nowlan, S.J., Hinton, G.E.: Evaluation of adaptive mixtures of competing experts. In: NIPS, vol. 3, pp. 774–780 (1990)
12. Samejima, K., Doya, K., Kawato, M.: Inter-module credit assignment in modular reinforcement learning. Neural Netw. **16**(7), 985–994 (2003)
13. Simpkins, C., Isbell, C.: Composable modular reinforcement learning. In: Proceedings of the AAAI Conference on Artificial Intelligence, vol. 33, pp. 4975–4982 (2019)
14. Smith, B.J., Read, S.J.: Modeling incentive salience in Pavlovian learning more parsimoniously using a multiple attribute model. Cogn. Affect. Behav. Neurosci. **22**, 244–257 (2021). https://doi.org/10.3758/s13415-021-00953-2
15. Sodhani, S., Zhang, A., Pineau, J.: Multi-task reinforcement learning with context-based representations. In: International Conference on Machine Learning, pp. 9767–9779. PMLR (2021)
16. Sprague, N., Ballard, D.: Multiple-goal reinforcement learning with modular Sarsa(0) (2003)
17. Sutton, R.S., Barto, A.G.: Reinforcement Learning: An Introduction. MIT Press, Cambridge (2018)
18. Wang, J.X., et al.: Learning to reinforcement learn. arXiv preprint arXiv:1611.05763 (2016)

Bio-inspired Vision and Navigation

Same/Different Concept: An Embodied Spiking Neural Model in a Learning Context

André Cyr[1]([✉]) [iD] and Frédéric Thériault[2] [iD]

[1] School of Psychology, University of Ottawa, Ottawa, Canada
andre.cyr1@videotron.ca
[2] Department of Computer Science, Cégep du Vieux Montréal, Montreal, Canada

Abstract. Understanding abstract concept is a major topic in cognitive science. This complex phenomenon is studied under different approaches, but remains unexplained at the cellular level in a full sensorimotor to behavior model. In this study, an artificial spiking neural circuit is proposed to simulate the same/different (S/D) relational concept through the context of a simple discriminative visual learning task. This computational method is used as a brain controller for virtual and physical robots, reflecting the embodied perspective of the present model. Specifically, with an operant conditioning procedure, the robot learns to associate a correct left/right action from a two items side-by-side image and a positive reinforcer. Following the learning phase, a transfer test is performed and the robot succeeds with pairs of novel stimuli. As novelty, this learning process involving the S/D concept is entirely based on spike timing, synaptic changes and a sensorimotor robot model. This work could serve as a prototype toward the inclusion of other types of relational concepts, possibly sharing similar functional neural circuits.

Keywords: Relational concepts · Learning process · Spiking neural networks · Neurorobotics · Same-different

1 Introduction

Abstract concepts are a hallmark of the general intelligence phenomenon. The manipulation of abstract concepts through learning is thought to be a dynamical neural process providing an adapted response to novel stimuli, based on past experiences. In psychology, a concept represents the construction of relational categories that link objects, features or facts. As such, different types of concepts could be considered, depending on whether they are related to physical or abstract objects (perceptual, associative, relational) [39]. A concept acquisition is validated by its generalization property, a prediction of the specific relational rule with the presentation of novel stimuli.

Studying abstract concepts is mainly based on experimental data and no precise sensory to motor neural circuit is currently known in animals. However,

L. Cañamero et al. (Eds.): SAB 2022, LNAI 13499, pp. 141–152, 2022.
https://doi.org/10.1007/978-3-031-16770-6_12

the neurorobotics field [24] may provide an alternative approach in simulating this cognitive process. The present paper proposes to simulate an abstract concept, manipulated from a learning context and using an artificial spiking neural network (SNN) embodied as a brain-controller for virtual and physical robots.

To achieve this goal, the same/different (S/D) concept was chosen as a canonical example. It consists in the ability to categorize things based on their similarities or differences. As such, a two-items visual learning task [6] was used as experimental context, built from compound images of simple colored shapes. In the past, side-by-side sample comparison and matching-to-sample (MTS) [33] or non-matching-to-sample (NMTS) protocols were tested with the S/D concept [22,31,35]. It was shown with bees that despite their tiny brain, these invertebrates exhibit the capacity of categorization [41] and can learn different concepts [2,7,11,20,21] when used in their decision-making processes [40]. Since relatively few neurons seem sufficient to manipulate different type of concepts, it was conceivable to build an artificial solution that simulates it.

Currently, few embodied models of abstract concept manipulation from learning context were introduced [8,13]. This study focused at suggesting a precise neural design from the spike and synaptic levels to the behavior. This SNN simulate an abstract concept manipulation through a learning procedure and aims to represent a generic model for the expansion or the inclusion of other type of abstract concepts. Finally, a main issue was to embody this bio-inspired cognitive framework in virtual and physical robot, dealing with minimal yet realistic sensorimotor processes and physical world constraints.

The relevant functional elements of this SNN are: memory buffers, comparator micro-circuits and plastic synapses. These components were sufficient to discriminate stimuli and categorize them. More precisely, the detection of the S/D abstract concept among other object features and its capability to influence the action is guided from a dichotomic visual choice and a given reinforcer. Thus, this article does not focus on the emergence of the abstract concept neural network, which may happen during a developmental phase in natural organisms. Nevertheless, this SNN mimics functional outcomes of detecting basic visual object features to complex abstract S/D concept levels.

Spiking neural models [1] are mathematical tools commonly used in bio-inspired artificial intelligence [10]. SNNs possess sufficient similar properties of their natural counterpart to predict and reproduce experimental data [19,23,32]. A strength of using SNN is that it includes the representation of time at the level of spike events, a crucial factor in the investigation of dynamical cognitive phenomena occurring in real world experiments. Learning is also a key feature of SNN, allowing synaptic changes between neurons from several mechanisms, such as the temporal spikes order in spike-timing-dependent plasticity (STDP) rules [4,9,28]. Amongst different STDP rules, some includes a third factor [16] or reinforcer (STDP-R, positive or negative) as a synaptic changing condition [5,17,25,29], more or less simulating the natural dopamine/octopamine role with its increase sensitivity in the reward system [3,30].

Results obtained from the virtual and physical simulations succeeded in showing the manipulation of the S/D abstract concept, and they are entirely explained with an embodied SNN framework. This was contextualized with an operant conditioning procedure from a dichotomic action and by a two side-by-side objects as input during both the learning phase and the transfer test.

2   Methodology

In this study, SIMCOG [14] software was used, it allowed the elaboration of the SNN as well as the conception of the experimental protocol in a virtual 3D environment. It also contained the necessary tools required for data analysis and to transfer the SNN in a physical robot. The general setup (see Fig. 1) consisted in a stationary robot that exhibits a dichotomic behavioral action response following the presentation of a visual two-items stimulus projected on a block in front of it. If the expressed motor response from the robot is the desired one, an external reward is given. Therefore, the robot learns to associate precise object features, its action and a positive reinforcer, selecting eventually the S/D abstract concept object feature among others and apply the rule with novel stimuli. Precisely, the S/D visual scenario includes repetition of images displayed in front of the robot, which are composed of two side-by-side colored shapes (see Fig. 1). The objective is for the robot to learn the S/D rule, associating the object features (shapes and colors) to a desired action (blink a left or right LED) using an external visual reinforcer (arbitrarily set to a purple color).

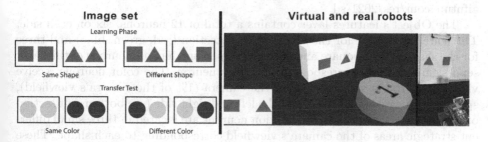

Fig. 1. On the left: compound visual images displayed in front of the robot. On the right: virtual world representing the image with two side-by-side shapes, the robot and its viewfield. The two gray spheres on top of the robot correspond to the left and right LEDs (possible actions). On the far right: physical robot facing a similar input. (Color figure online)

2.1   Protocol

The simulation starts new trials every 500 cycles. Each trial starts with a random compound image. The image set for the learning phase includes red triangles and squares. After the robot perceives the image from its camera, it expresses a behavioral motor response, blinking its left or right LED for one cycle. At first, the actions are random and few trials are necessary to ensure that the SNN reaches its learning threshold. At the end of each trial, a purple colored circle acting as reward is displayed to the robot if the desired behavior was expressed. The chosen associative rule was defined arbitrarily to reward the left LED action for the "same" feature (ex: both stimuli were of the same shape) and right LED for "different". This could be reversed without consequence, as well as having color variations in the learning phase and shape variations for the transfer test. After the learning phase, a transfer test was activated, which consisted in displaying other sets of images composed of novel color and shape features (right of Fig. 1). More precisely, blue and green circles were used.

2.2 Neural Architecture

The SNN architecture (see Fig. 2) that was used in the discriminative S/D task is composed of three main layers (see Fig. 3). The Object's features layer includes retina-like neurons connected to the camera. On each side, the Object's features layer contains color and shape detection hard-coded neurons as well as a reward (unique color) detection neuron. Each of those neurons forwards signal to the Memory layer, which holds information for the Concept layer. In the latter, neurons are organized in three hierarchical/serial levels that integrate and compare the specific perceptual features. Those neurons also embed a facultative and independent learning process in their synapses (STDP function). This neural design strategy allows response plasticity from extracted object features. All neural and synaptic parameters are available as supplementary materials http://aifuture.com/res/2021-sd.

The Object's features layer contains a total of 12 neurons, six on each side. Three are responsible for the object color detection (red, green, blue) and three for the shape (circle, square and triangle). Upon spiking, all neurons of this layer send signals to their corresponding memory neuron. The color neurons receive visual data from a small section of the camera (1% of the camera's viewfield), specifically located at the center of the left and right side (see bottom left section of Fig. 2). On each side, shape detection neurons are located in three small different strategic areas of the camera's viewfield corresponding to each shape. These simplified sensory regions are sufficient, with few additional inhibitory synapses, to discriminate each of the three possible shapes regardless of their color. Once a memory neuron spikes, it fires regularly from a recurrent synapse. It also sends signals with a delay to the RandomDecision neuron, which triggers a randomized action when no other actions were made before. Thus, every image shown in a trial generates an action. Finally, member neurons of this layer forward signals to specific concept neurons.

The Concept layer is divided in three different hierarchical/serial levels of neural integration and comparison: primary, secondary and tertiary. The primary level consists in integrating and comparing object features coming from both sides of the retina. For example, to detect whether the two perceived objects are squares (SquareSame), the corresponding concept neuron must receive signals from the retina left side (Mem1-LeftSquare) as well as the right side (Mem1-RightSquare). To know whether the colors are different when comparing a green object and a blue one, these neurons (GreenDifferent or BlueDifferent neurons) must receive from a Mem1-Green neuron (left or right) as well as from the other side's Mem1-Blue neuron. Each concept neuron has a long absolute refractory period, preventing the constant initiation of actions. In the Concept layer, there are also two other levels of neurons: secondary and tertiary. Two concept neurons of the secondary level integrate color features (ex: GreenSame) and two others integrate shape features (ex: CircleDifferent). Hence, those four neurons are more general than the concept neurons of the primary level since they combine colors together and shapes together. In the example of two objects being red, the RedSame neuron would spike, as well as the secondary level SameColor neuron. This allows the categorization by feature types (ex: coloring, shape). Finally, the two neurons of the tertiary level are even more general, by merging secondary level neurons as global Same and Different neurons.

   With this neural structure, object features are totally extracted in all dimensions available (shape and color). The information is gathered from an automatic passive process. At this point, all actions remain randomized, since the synapses between the concept neurons and action neurons (PredLeft/PredRight) send insufficient signal to reach the threshold of the predictor neurons. Thus, they not influencing the resulting action. However, each synapse in the Concept layer contains an STDP-R function. Whenever an action (randomized or predicted) triggers a reward, the synaptic weight between relevant concept neurons and the

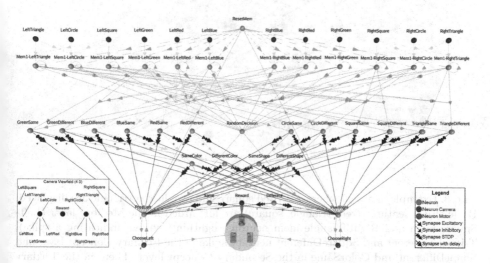

Fig. 2. Complete neural architecture. plastic synapses (darker and with three arrowheads symbol) are located between the concept layer neurons and predictor neurons. To enhance clarity of the figure, all static synapses were faded. The bottom left section shows the viewfield of the camera and the black dots represent the visual neural sensing areas (receptive fields).

predictor neuron increases (1000% for the primary layer, 500% for the secondary and 250% for the tertiary). Once the synaptic weight is sufficiently strong to generate spikes, then, on the next trial with the same context, this neural circuit will bypass the randomized behavior.

In the primary Concept layer (ex: RedSame), synapses increase their weight after one successful trial. Hence, the next similar trial will trigger an action predicting the reward. In the secondary Concept layer (ex: ColorSame), synapses need two successful trials to have their synaptic weight strong enough to generate spikes. Finally, the tertiary Concept layer synapses (ex: Same) need four successful trials to trigger an action. Since the delays are shorter in the tertiary Concept layer, these neurons will generate an action before the secondary and primary layers. The same mechanism applies between the secondary and primary layers. At any time, whenever a false association arises after a synaptic weight increase, it goes back to its initial value. Finally, after an action, the ResetMemory neuron is triggered and all the neurons from the Memory layer are inhibited, stopping the recurrent spikes of the memory neurons. This action allows to forget the previous image and prepares it for the next trial.

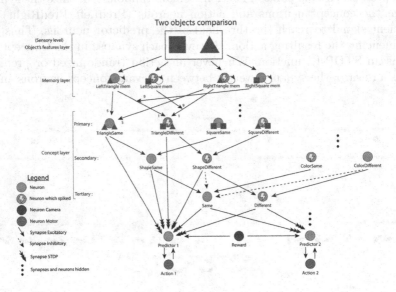

Fig. 3. Example of a trial where a left red square and a right red triangle are displayed. Basic object features (red, triangle, square) are forwarded in the Memory layer (Left-Square mem and RightTriangle mem neurons, lightning symbol indicating a spike). TriangleDifferent and SquareDifferent neurons spike in the Primary Concept layer and ShapeDifferent and ColorSame in the Secondary Concept layer. Then, in the Tertiary Concept layer, the Different neuron spikes. After choosing an action, if a reward follows, learning occurs through STDP. (Color figure online)

Neural Dynamic. The general mathematics behind neural behaviors are detailed and available in supplementary materials. A main property of a spiking neuron consists in the variation of its membrane potential. In the SIMCOG model, these variations are set between 0 and 100, 0 representing the hyperpolarization state and 100 the spike emission. Each neuron contains other parameters (threshold, resting potential, after-spike and absolute refractory period (ARP)). Longer ARPs were used to prevent some neurons from spiking too soon after their response, allowing enough time to properly complete the sensory-motor-reward loop. Neurons from the primary Concept layer have fixed ARPs set to 120 cycles. Neurons from the secondary and tertiary Concept layer differ by being set to a subthreshold value with an ARP set to 150 cycles. Upon reaching its threshold, a neuron spikes and emits postsynaptic potentials (PSP).

Variability of synaptic delays are defined to allow enough time to gather all object features as well as S/D concepts before triggering an action. Prior to learning, synaptic delays were also organized from longer to smaller to match S/D hierarchical neural responses. Synapses between Concept layer neurons and predictor neurons include an STDP-R learning function, which consists in a synaptic weight variation, depending on the neural direction and spike timing. If a pre-spike arises before a post-spike in a defined time window, then the synaptic weight increases (and inversely). In this simulation, a reward was also a necessary condition to strengthen the synaptic weight.

2.3 Physical Environment

To validate the SNN model under real world constraints and noisy conditions (imprecise input values and delays), such as timing of events and object perception, the experiment was evaluated using a GoPiGo 3 physical robot (see right part of Fig. 1). This robot, powered by a Raspberry Pi 4 board, contains a PiCamera for the visual perception as well as two LEDs for its dichotomic instance of motor actions. The SNN used in the virtual environment was transferred without any core alteration and succeeded in resolving the discriminative S/D visual task with the learning phase and the transfer test.

3 Results

The experiment was divided in two distinct parts. In the virtual simulation (see Fig. 4), the learning phase had a duration of 4500 cycles and executed a total of 18 trials. Each of these trials showed a random image from learning image sets (left part of Fig. 1). Second, the four images (right part of Fig. 1) of the transfer test were sequentially displayed in loop until the end. The learning phase included shape variations, all of them in red. Novel stimuli were used in the transfer test, composed of circle shapes and two possible color variations.

As seen in Fig. 4, after the presentation of an image (see the five examples on top of figure), the robot first takes a randomized decision (graph A), followed by an action (graphs D and E). Once the robot has learnt an association, predictor

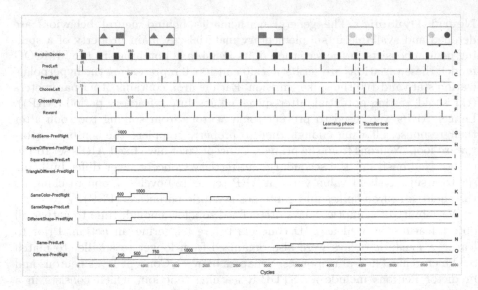

Fig. 4. The first 4500 cycles correspond to the learning phase, followed by the transfer test phase. While the learning phase varies only in terms of shapes (triangle and squares), the transfer test phase shows other colors on a circle shape.

neurons spike before the randomized decision (graphs B and C). Whenever the desired action was made depending on the displayed image and the rewarding rule, an external reward was applied (graph F). STDP coefficient multiplicators (STDP-CM) of the synaptic weight between primary level neurons of the Concept layer and their predictor are shown in graphs G to J. Secondary level STDP-CM are displayed in graphs K to M. Graphs N and O represent STDP-CM of the tertiary level. As shown in the figure, primary layer STDP-CM reach their full synaptic weight variation in one trial (increased by 1000%). The secondary layer reaches their full weight variation in two trials and the tertiary layer in four trials. Among the 36 synapses including the STDP-CM rule, only those that varied are shown and the others were hidden.

The image of the third trial (starting at cycle 500) consisted of a left red triangle and a right red square. As seen in graph E, after the perception of these objects, the robot randomly chose the ChooseRight action, which was followed by a reward since the two shapes are different. This allowed the relevant STDP-CM to increase (graphs G, H, J, K, M and O). As seen in graphs G, H and J, STDP-CM of the primary Concept layer reached their full synaptic weight variation after a single reward. The following trial displayed the same image (not shown). Contrarily to the previous trial, the action came from a predictor neuron (PredRight, spiked at cycle 827), which spiked before the random decision neuron (RandomDecision, that spiked at cycle 845). In the previous trial, the ChooseLeft action was triggered by the RandomDecision neuron, which spiked (cycle 70) before the left predictor neuron (PredLeft, cycle 86). From cycle 4500, the learning phase was completed and the robot made the expected action. As a remark, since the tertiary STDP-CM are at their full variation, tertiary neurons sufficiently influence predictor neurons before the secondary and primary neurons of the Concept layer.

In the transfer test, all trials end with the correct action, since the learning rule (same-left/different-right) does not change and the tertiary STDP-CM remain at their maximum synaptic weight. Despite novel features, the SNN applied the same learning rule (generalization). Even if the rule changed at runtime, the synapse plasticity would eventually be tuned to match the new rule (unlearning and relearning processes from STDP), see extra materials for an example. The experiment made with the physical robot (i.e. GoPiGo 3) is available as supplementary materials. It tested the robustness of the architecture and verified that the S/D abstract concept manipulation could match real-time events.

4 Discussion

This study approaches the S/D abstract concept in a learning context from simulating the natural phenomenon with an original embodied neurorobotics framework. As such, an SNN was proposed to learn the association between visual object features and dichotomic actions based on a rewarding S/D rule under operant conditioning procedures. The validation of the relational concept was shown using a transfer test with novel stimuli.

Similar to animal brains, neural circuits and connections are specific regarding their body structure. Hence, the adopted strategy in the SNN was to precisely design a neural circuit with layers and concept neurons, which are independent of the internal varying learning process. These concept neurons were organized in hierarchical layers and comparator components. This topology (lower to higher concepts abstraction) allows the generalization of the same object feature for new stimuli (ex: novel colors), but also for different features.

What is the exact neural design behind an abstract concept? The specific S/D discrimination behavior literature points toward a possible continuum explanation from animals to humans [34], though experimental protocols could differ significantly. Since invertebrates can discriminate abstract concepts through a learning context, a minimal neural circuit kernel may be sufficient to explain the phenomenon. As a hypothesis, the components of an embodied artificial neural model could include: input stimuli that generate spikes and dynamical synaptic changes in regard of the action and the reward contingencies. Therefore, the functional elements are: a perceptual object feature extraction module, a set of actions, a learning mechanism, concept neurons and a reinforcer system.

Though this embodied SNN is simplistic, it was validated in the physical realm. This offered a higher challenge in terms of imprecise events timing and inputs impurity, adding realistic noise. Even if the robot passively received visual inputs and that its behavior did not change the following incoming visual stimuli (stimulus set), its actions influenced whether it received a reward. Hence, its actions have consequences. The robot learnt from its actions and adapted itself from synaptic weight changes, depending on rewards and contexts.

In biological experiments, the number of trials during the training phase to reach the learning point could depend on the minimal occurrence of inputs, the working memory capacity [12] and the number of features per object. As concurrent learning mechanisms, it has been shown that within few trials, specific elemental associations could be made. As such, two or multi-items stimuli, set-size, temporal parameters or dynamically switching the reinforcer rule in the protocols were parameters investigated to discriminate between the generalization of stimuli features and the true concept [15,18,27,36].

In the presence of novel input stimuli, this SNN still accurately decomposes the object to extract its separate features. Nevertheless, the focus remains biased toward the S/D concept from previous experiences, instead of other lower-level features. The right association between the action, the stimuli and the reward was already strengthened in the learning phase. Thus, the transfer process consists of predicting, in continuity, the adequate response to obtain its reward. In materials, a simulation is available where the rewarding rule changes at real time, unlearning and relearning the new rule.

Asymmetry is a feature of the S/D concept, particularly in the performance that could be explained from more than one neural mechanism [37]. A positive bias towards similarity (enhancing the Same concept), or simulating a neophobic behavior (enhancing the Different concept) [38] could reflect divergence of results. The introduced SNN includes such an asymmetric architecture to express the Same and Different concept. Finally, a robust S/D abstract concept SNN model should sustained several concepts. In this view, spatial concepts such as above/below [26] of complex objects should eventually be explored.

5   Conclusion

This article introduced an embodied SNN that simulates the S/D abstract concept in a learning context. It was explained with spikes timing and synaptic changes, from the stimuli input to the behavior. Using a discriminative visual task of two side-by-side colored shapes images, the robot succeeded in learning the S/D rule from an operant conditioning procedure. Results show that the robot can transfer the learnt rule with novel objects and across different features.

References

1. Ahmed, F., Yusob, B., Hamed, H.N.A.: Computing with spiking neuron networks: a review. Int. J. Adv. Soft Comput. Appl. **6**, 1–21 (2014)
2. Avarguès-Weber, A., Giurfa, M.: Conceptual learning by miniature brains. Proc. R. Soc. B Biol. Sci. **280**(1772), 1–9 (2013)
3. Behrends, A., Scheiner, R.: Octopamine improves learning in newly emerged bees but not in old foragers. J. Exp. Biol. **215**(7), 1076–1083 (2012)

4. Bi, G.Q., Poo, M.M.: Activity-induced synaptic modifications in hippocampal culture: dependence on spike timing, synaptic strength and cell type. J. Neurosci. **18**, 10464–10472 (1998)
5. Bing, Z., Baumann, I., Jiang, Z., Huang, K., Cai, C., Knoll, A.: Supervised learning in SNN via reward-modulated spike-timing-dependent plasticity for a target reaching vehicle. Front. Neurorobot. **13**, 18 (2019)
6. Blaisdell, A.P., Cook, R.G.: Two-itemsame-different concept learning in pigeons. Anim. Learn. Behav. **33**(1), 67–77 (2005)
7. Brown, M.F., Sayde, J.M.: Same/different discrimination by bumblebee colonies. Anim. Cogn. **16**(1), 117–125 (2013)
8. Cangelosi, A., Stramandinoli, F.: A review of abstract concept learning in embodied agents and robots. Philos. Trans. R. Soc. B Biol. Sci. **373**(1752), 20170131 (2018). https://doi.org/10.1098/rstb.2017.0131. http://rstb.royalsocietypublishing.org/content/373/1752/20170131
9. Caporale, N., Dan, Y.: Spike timing-dependent plasticity: a hebbian learning rule. Annu. Rev. Neurosci. **31**, 25–46 (2008)
10. Chance, F.S., Aimone, J.B., Musuvathy, S.S., Smith, M.R., Vineyard, C.M., Wang, F.: Crossing the cleft: communication challenges between neuroscience and artificial intelligence. Front. Comput. Neurosci. **14**, 39 (2020)
11. Chittka, L., Jensen, K.: Animal cognition: concepts from apes to bees. Curr. Biol. **21**(3), 116–119 (2011)
12. Chuderski, A., Chuderska, A.: How working memory capacity constrains the learning of relational concepts. In: Proceedings of the Annual Meeting of the Cognitive Science Society, vol. 35 (2013)
13. Cyr, A., Avarguès-Weber, A., Theriault, F.: Sameness/difference spiking neural circuit as a relational concept precursor model: a bio-inspired robotic implementation. Biol. Inspired Cogn. Archit. **21**, 59–66 (2017)
14. Cyr, A., Boukadoum, M., Poirier, P.: AI-SIMCOG: a simulator for spiking neurons and multiple animat's behaviours. Neural Comput. Appl. **18**(5), 431–446 (2009)
15. Daniel, T.A., Cook, R.G., Katz, J.S.: Temporal dynamics of task switching and abstract-concept learning in pigeons. Front. Psychol. **6**, 1334 (2015)
16. Foncelle, A., et al.: Modulation of spike-timing dependent plasticity: towards the inclusion of a third factor in computational models. Front. Comput. Neurosci. **12**, 49 (2018)
17. Frémaux, N., Gerstner, W.: Neuromodulated spike-timing-dependent plasticity, and theory of three-factor learning rules. Front. Neural Circuits **9**, 85 (2016)
18. Galizio, M., Mathews, M., Prichard, A., Bruce, K.E.: Generalized identity in a successive matching-to-sample procedure in rats: effects of number of exemplars and a masking stimulus. J. Exp. Anal. Behav. **110**(3), 366–379 (2018)
19. Gerstner, W., Kistler, W.: Spiking Neuron Models: Single Neurons, Populations, Plasticity. Cambridge University Press, Cambridge (2002)
20. Giurfa, M.: Cognition with few neurons: higher-order learning in insects. Trends Neurosci. **36**(5), 259–312 (2013)
21. Giurfa, M.: Learning of sameness/difference relationships by honey bees: performance, strategies and ecological context. Curr. Opin. Behav. Sci. **37**, 1–6 (2021)
22. Giurfa, M., Zhang, S., Jenett, A., Menzel, R., Srinivasan, M.V.: The concepts of 'sameness' and 'difference' in an insect. Nature **410**(6831), 930–933 (2001)
23. Izhikevich, E.M.: Simple model of spiking neurons. IEEE Trans. Neural Networks **14**(6), 1569–1572 (2003)
24. Krichmar, J.L.: Neurorobotics-a thriving community and a promising pathway toward intelligent cognitive robots. Front. Neurorobot. **12**, 42 (2018)

25. Kuśmierz, Ł, Isomura, T., Toyoizumi, T.: Learning with three factors: modulating Hebbian plasticity with errors. Curr. Opin. Neurobiol. **46**, 170–177 (2017)
26. Lazareva, O.F., Gould, K., Linert, J., Caillaud, D., Gazes, R.P.: Smaller on the left? Flexible association between space and magnitude in pigeons (Columba livia) and blue jays (Cyanocitta cristata). J. Comp. Psychol. **134**(1), 71 (2019)
27. Lazarowski, L., Goodman, A., Galizio, M., Bruce, K.: Effects of set size on identity and oddity abstract-concept learning in rats. Anim. Cogn. **22**(5), 733–742 (2019). https://doi.org/10.1007/s10071-019-01270-5
28. Markram, H., Lubke, J., Frotscher, M., Sakmann, B.: Regulation of synaptic efficacy by coincidence of postsynaptic APs and EPSEs. Science **275**, 213–215 (1997)
29. Pawlak, V., Wickens, J.R., Kirkwood, A., Kerr, J.N.: Timing is not everything: neuromodulation opens the STDP gate. Front. Synaptic Neurosci. 138 (2010)
30. Schultz, W.: Predictive reward signal of dopamine neurons. J. Neurophysiol. **80**(1), 1–27 (1998)
31. Smirnova, A.A., Obozova, T.A., Zorina, Z.A., Wasserman, E.A.: How do crows and parrots come to spontaneously perceive relations-between-relations? Curr. Opin. Behav. Sci. **37**, 109–117 (2021)
32. Taherkhani, A., Belatreche, A., Li, Y., Cosma, G., Maguire, L.P., McGinnity, T.M.: A review of learning in biologically plausible spiking neural networks. Neural Netw. **122**, 253–272 (2020)
33. Truppa, V., Mortari, E.P., Garofoli, D., Privitera, S., Visalberghi, E.: Same/different concept learning by capuchin monkeys in matching-to-sample tasks. PLoS ONE **6**(8), e23809 (2011)
34. Wasserman, E.A., Young, M.E.: Same-different discrimination: the keel and backbone of thought and reasoning. J. Exp. Psychol. Anim. Behav. Process. **36**(1), 3 (2010)
35. Wright, A.A.: Concept learning and learning strategies. Psychol. Sci. **8**(2), 119–123 (1997)
36. Wright, A.A., Katz, J.S.: Generalization hypothesis of abstract-concept learning: learning strategies and related issues in Macaca mulatta, Cebus apella, and Columba livia. J. Comp. Psychol. **121**(4), 387 (2007)
37. Zentall, T.R.: Sameness may be a natural concept that does not require learning. Curr. Opin. Behav. Sci. **37**, 7–12 (2021)
38. Zentall, T.R., Andrews, D.M., Case, J.P.: Sameness may be a natural concept that does not require learning. Psychol. Sci. **29**(7), 1185–1189 (2018)
39. Zentall, T.R., Wasserman, E.A., Urcuioli, P.J.: Associative concept learning in animals. J. Exp. Anal. Behav. **101**(1), 130–151 (2014)
40. Zhang, S.: Visually guided decision making in foraging honeybees. Front. Neurosci. **6**, 88 (2012)
41. Zhang, S., Srinivasan, M.V., Zhu, H., Wong, J.: Grouping of visual objects by honeybees. J. Exp. Biol. **207**(19), 3289–3298 (2004)

Sparse and Topological Coding for Visual Localization of Autonomous Vehicles

Sylvain Colomer[1,2(✉)], Nicolas Cuperlier[1], Guillaume Bresson[2],
Steve Pechberti[2], and Olivier Romain[1]

[1] Laboratoire ETIS UMR8051, Université Paris Seine, ENSEA, CNRS, Paris, France
sylvain.colomer@ensea.fr

[2] Institut VEDECOM, 23 bis Allée des Marronniers, 78000 Versailles, France
https://www.etis-lab.fr/, https://www.vedecom.fr/

Abstract. Efficient encoding of visual information is essential to the success of vision-based navigation tasks in large-scale environments. To do so, we propose in this article the Sparse Max-Pi neural network (SMP), a novel compute-efficient model of visual localization based on sparse and topological encoding of visual information. Inspired by the spatial cognition of mammals, the model uses a "topologic sparse dictionary" to efficiently compress the visual information of a landmark, allowing rich visual information to be represented with very small codes. This descriptor, inspired by the neurons in the primary visual cortex (V1), are learned using sparse coding, homeostasis and self-organising map mechanisms. Evaluated in cross-validation on the Oxford-car dataset, our experimental results show that the SMP model is competitive with the state of the art. It thus provides comparable or better performance than CoHog and NetVlad, two state-of-the-art VPR models.

Keywords: Visual place recognition · Sparse coding · Autonomous vehicle · Visual cortex · Bio-inspired robotics

1 Introduction

The problem of autonomous navigation on a robotised vehicle requires the simultaneous resolution of a multitude of issues [11]. Indeed, driving a vehicle on an open road requires a lot of techniques and knowledge, even to carry out simple navigation tasks in favorable environments. To name a few, a vehicle must be at the same time able to locate accurately its position, stay in its lane, avoid accidents and respect traffic rules. Consequently, the models of autonomous vehicle are often based on the use of numerous modules, specialized in one or more sub-problems.

Among the different modules traditionally used in navigation, the localization one is particularly important for its central role in the navigation task. Its performance can severely limit the ability of a navigation system to complete a navigation task. To reach the best performance, the module is usually made with powerful sensors such as GNSS or LiDAR. Although highly efficient, these sensors suffer from high cost and significant operating limitations [11]. This leads

L. Cañamero et al. (Eds.): SAB 2022, LNAI 13499, pp. 153–164, 2022.
https://doi.org/10.1007/978-3-031-16770-6_13

to the development of new techniques relying on different modalities, notably the methods of Visual place recognition (VPR) that propose to use visual information as a source of localization, since cameras are rich, inexpensive and low consumption sensors.

In recent years, a lot of VPR models have been proposed in various application fields such as robotics, big data or machine vision. However, despite significant progress in terms of performance and computing time, the methods proposed are still struggling to provide a complete alternative for the localization system of autonomous cars. Although visual space is a very rich source of information, this space is also the object of a strong dynamic which makes its use more complicated, especially when moving to large scales of time and distance. To operate even on a single day, the methods proposed must be robust at the same time to multiple issues like lighting problems, changing weather or variation in human activity. However, obtaining such performance is often accompanied by a high computational cost that limits the use of such a system to small scales of deployment. This implies finding a method for representing visual information that is light enough to limit its computational cost, while maintaining enough information to distinguish locations under varying visual conditions.

Up to now, the only system known which has the ability to build such a representation are biological ones. Indeed, several studies have shown that certain species of mammals are able to perform large-scale trajectories by relying essentially on the vision [4]. This ability is thought to rely on several key structures in mammals brain, notably the hippocampal system (HS) and the visual cortex (VC). HS would thus be involved in the memory processes of animal cognition and would contain a neuronal map of the environment [8]. On the other hand, VC would be responsible for the encoding the visual information upstream to the HS. Thus, several studies suggest that the first layers of the visual cortex use mechanisms similar to sparse coding methods for representing visual information. VC would break down the visual information into elementary patterns a bit like a visual sparse dictionary, except that it would respect a topological arrangement of patterns.

Following a bio-inspired approach, we present in this paper the following contributions:

- We propose the topologic sparse coding (TSC) algorithm, a new method of sparse coding intended for the encoding of visual information for localization. This method allows the construction of a topologic sparse dictionary, i.e. a dictionary of visual features that respects both a constraint of sparsity and of spatial topology. The topology allows, unlike a classical sparse dictionary, to build a structured dictionary where neurons coding for similar features are physically close in the dictionary. As a result, similar images have much closer codes and are therefore much easier to recognise.
- We propose the Sparse Max-Pi (SMP) neural network, a novel model of VPR for autonomous vehicles. This model, based by the LPMP model, allows to build in an unsupervised way a neural representation of the environment. Unlike the original model, the SMP model uses a topological sparse dictionary

to encode information. By this way, the system uses a more compact code to represent landmarks, allowing to strongly divide the memory cost of a place while maintaining equivalent (or slightly better) localization performance.

- We evaluated the SMP model on the OxfordCar dataset in cross-validation and compare its performances with two lead models of VPR: CoHog [12] and NetVLAD [1].

The remaining of this paper is organized as follows: On first, we describe the TSC algorithm and the SMP model. Afterwards, we present the experiments carried out and their results. The last part is left to the conclusions.

2   Related Work: Definition of the Sparse Coding

Sparse Coding (SC) refers to the set of methods that aim to construct a "sparse" representation for a data space, i.e. a representation that can be characterised by its propensity to encode data through the activity of a small number of its components. This representation, called dictionary, has the advantage of efficiently capturing redundant patterns in the data space, allowing to build an efficient code for the data space. To generate a sparse representation, a "sparsity criteria" is defined, whose purpose is to determine towards which definition of sparsity the system should converge. The most common is to use the l0 norm of the sparse code (the code generate by the representation), as defined by the following equation:

$$s = \sum_{m=1}^{M} a_m \phi_m \quad \text{subject to} \quad \min_{a} \|a\|_0 \tag{1}$$

where $s \in \mathbb{R}^n$ is the input vector, a_m is an coefficient of activity, $\|.\|_0$ the L_0 norm and $\phi_m \in \mathbb{R}^N$ is an element of the dictionary Φ called an atom. In this equation, the L_0 norm imposes that the system must converge to a representation using as many atoms as possible to represent a data while retaining its ability to reconstruct all the patterns in the data space. Contrary to other methods such as a PCA, sparse coding builds an overcomplete base of a data space. It allows to better capture the general patterns of the space and to achieve a more efficient representation of the input space.

3   Topological Sparse Coding

The topological sparse coding (TSC) algorithm is a new method of SC intended for the encoding of visual information. Based on the Sparse Hebbian Learning algorithm [7], this method allows to learn from a set of data a "topological sparse dictionary" i.e. a sparse dictionary arranged on a 2D grid like a Kohonen network. Thus, unlike a traditional sparse coding algorithm, the dictionary has two dimensions and respects a topology. Consequently, neurons coding for similar features are physically close in the dictionary, allowing to have similar codes for two close images, which eases their comparison.

TSC was first designed to compress visual information in the same way as the "primary visual cortex", known to be the first stage of visual information encoding in mammals. In particular, it reproduces the functioning and the organisation of the first layer of neurons, composed of "single cells". These neurons, sensitive to specific orientations, are used by the visual cortex to break down visual information into robust elementary patterns [9]. Thus, the use of a sparse coding mechanism enables the construction of neurons with receiver fields similar to simple cells [6]. The addition of the topology allows to reproduce the retinotopic structure of the visual cortex, where neurons sensitive to similar orientations are side by side.

To build a dictionary of size (M, N), TSC uses a large batch of images (in our case, thumbnails of landmarks), pre-processed with a whitening filter [7]. It produces a sparse dictionary by alternating between two processes: an *encoding stage* where the current image is reconstructed with a limited number of atoms, and an *update stage* where the dictionary is modified to improve it reconstruction performance, depending of the encoding result.

Encoding Stage: To encode an image, TSC uses an homeostatic version of the "Matching Pursuit" algorithm. The objective of this algorithm is to recursively find the best combination of atoms and activity in the dictionary that allows a better reconstruction of the input signal. The number of atoms for the reconstruction of the signal is limited by the value N_0, which indirectly controls the level of sparsity of the dictionary. Thus, at an iteration t, the system searches in the dictionary for the best pair of atom/activity that minimizes the intermediate reconstruction error $r(t)$, such as:

$$r(t) = I - \sum_{n=1}^{N} \sum_{m=1}^{M} \hat{a}_{m,n}(t)\phi_{m,n} \tag{2}$$

where $\hat{a}_{m,n}$ is the current activity vector. Carried out N_0 times, this mechanism allow to find a set of atoms that reconstructs the signal, given the current dictionary. To prevent an atom from becoming dominant in the reconstruction process, the value of $\hat{a}_{m,n}(t)$ is transformed by $z(.)$, a homeostasis function. Thus, $z(.)$ modifies the activity of the sparse code according to its activity distribution to balance the atoms that are over or under activated. It can be described by the next equations:

$$s^* = \text{ArgMax}_{m,n} \left[z_{m,n}\left(\hat{a}_{m,n}\right) \right] \tag{3}$$

$$\text{with} \quad z_{m,n}\left(\hat{a}_{m,n}\right) \leftarrow (1 - \eta_h) \, z_{m,n}\left(\hat{a}_{m,n}\right) + \eta_h P\left(a_{m,n} \leq \hat{a}_{m,n}\right) \tag{4}$$

where s^* is the index of the selected atom and η_h is the homeostatic coefficient.

Update of Dictionary: The update of the dictionary is realized with an Hebb's rule, formulated for an atom $\phi_{m,n}$ as:

$$\begin{cases} \phi_{m,n} \leftarrow \phi_{m,n} + \eta * (\mathbf{I} - \phi\mathbf{a}) * a_{m,n} & \text{if } a_{m,n} > 0 \\ \phi_{m,n} \leftarrow \phi_{m,n} + \eta * (\mathbf{I} - \phi\mathbf{a}) * h(r, \mathbf{s}) & \text{otherwise} \end{cases} \tag{5}$$

where η is the learning rate, s is the list of atoms that were selected during the encoding, r is the current atom position and $h(.)$ the function that defines the neighbourhood membership of an atom. $h(.)$ computes the smallest distance between the current atom's position and each atom selected in the encoding process, as described in the next equation:

$$h(r,s) = \exp\left(-\frac{Min_{s\in \mathbf{s}}(||l-s||)}{2\sigma^2(t)}\right) \tag{6}$$

with $||.||$ a distance function and σ the neighbourhood coefficient. Thus, a neuron is updated in two cases: if it has contributed to the reconstruction of the signal $(a_{m,n} > 0)$ or if it is in the neighbourhood of one of them.

4 SMP Model

The Sparse Max-Pi (SMP) model is an unsupervised neural architecture aimed at solving the problem of visual localization for autonomous vehicle (Fig. 1). It uses the vehicle's visual information and absolute orientation[1] to builds a neural representation of an environment. In particular, the model simulates place cells, a specific king of neurons found in the HS of mammals. Like biological ones, these neurons respond with high activity for a given place in the environment and have shown interesting properties of robustness in complex environments [2]. The SMP model was initially proposed to resolve the computational cost issues of the LPMP model on which it is strongly based. Unlike the original model, it does not use a log polar to encode visual information but a topological sparse dictionary. This allows the SMP model to use much smaller visual descriptors, strongly reducing its computational cost[2].

To locate an image, the SMP model starts by searching for the position of its N_p most significant landmarks. To do so, a saliency map is built by successively convolving the image with two filters (a Deriche filter and a Difference of Gaussians (DoG) filter) to highlight its curvature points. The landmarks are then sorted and selected via a local competition, a bio-inspired mechanism which allows to keep only the most significant landmark. Then, two information streams are processed in parallel for each detected landmark:

1. The *visual identity* (or *what pathway*), corresponding to the encoding of a local view centered on the position of the landmark. To compress the visual information, the system uses a topological sparse dictionary followed by a max-pooling layer of 2×2.
2. The *azimuth information* (or *where pathway*), corresponding to the encoding of the absolute direction of the landmark in the environment. This information is computed using the vehicle absolute orientation and the PoI coordinate in the image.

---

[1] Absolute orientation can be obtained from a magnetic or visual compass [2].
[2] The model must compare the current image with all images stored in memory to localize a place. The smaller the code, the faster the memory search.

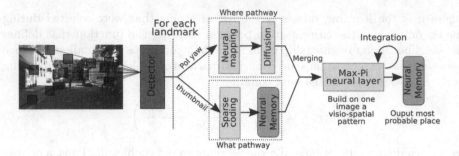

Fig. 1. Scheme of the SMP model. To locate a place, the SMP model encodes the visual identity and absolute orientation of each landmark in an image, and merges them into a Max-Pi layer to build a visuo-spatial model. These two information are encoded for each landmark through two pathways: the "what pathway", where a sparse dictionary is used to encodes the landmarks and store them in a memory; And the "where pathway", where the model encodes the absolute orientation of the landmarks in arrays of neurons.

Finally, the visual identity and the azimuth information of each landmark are merged and accumulated in a Max-Pi neural layer. This structure allows to build a visuo-spatial code which is characteristic of the vehicle current position (see [2] for a more complete description). This visuo-spatial code is then sent to a neural memory called Winner Memory, to be either memorized or searched through the known locations.

5   Materials and Methods

5.1   Dataset

Among the different datasets available, we decided to use the *Oxford-car dataset* [5] to evaluate the performance of the SMP model. This dataset has the advantage of being very complete, giving access to a hundred driving sequences on the same road in various conditions (lighting, traffic, or weather). As each sequence is 9 km long, we decided to subdivide the dataset into several test sequences (Table 1). To do so, we divided the dataset into different routes through different environments (*city-center*, *boulevard* and *forest*), as proposed in previous work [2]. For each route, 3 different trajectories have been selected, taken at different times. The sequences were selected to present favorable weather conditions, but different levels of human activity. Moreover, the different dictionaries tested were learned from a dataset of 54000 landmarks, generated using the visual system of SMP. They are extracted from the sequence "2014/07/14 14:49:50", outside the areas of performance evaluation.

5.2   Metrics

To evaluate the TSC algorithm and the SMP model, we selected four metrics:

Table 1. Trajectories selected from the *Oxford-car dataset*. This table presents the trajectories selected in the dataset to assess the performances of the SMP model. Three different environments were selected to vary the localization conditions.

Env.	Images	Distance (meters)	Duration (seconds)	Sequence date	Reference index
Boulevard	1401	625	89	2014/07/14 14:49:50	2820–4220
Boulevard	1159	624	74	2015/07/29 13:09:26	5928–7086
Boulevard	1572	626	101	2015/08/4 14:54:57	5665–7236
City-center	1521	532	104	2015/05/19 14:06:38	6199–7719
City-center	2227	527	143	2015/07/29 13:09:26	7210–9436
City-center	2134	585	140	2015/05/22 11:14:30	7728–9861
Forest	927	292	61	2014/07/14 14:49:50	5190–6116
Forest	566	286	38	2015/05/19 14:06:38	7827–8392
Forest	595	287	37	2015/05/22 11:14:30	10211–10805

- **Reconstruction error:** The reconstruction error of a dictionary is the difference between a data pattern and its reconstructed image after encoding.
- **Population kurtosis:** This metric measures the distribution of dictionary responses to a single stimulus. It has been described as the best metric for measuring the sparsity of a dictionary [10].
- **Precision/recall:** The localization performances were evaluated using standard precision/recall measurements. To do so, we followed the classical method for evaluating VPR systems, which consists of characterising the distance between the coordinate of an image to localize and the coordinates of the image that the model best recognises [2]. These results are summarized by their Area Under Curves (AUC) and the recall at 100% precision.
- **Response frequency:** It was assessed by measuring the average frequency that each model takes to answer a query, depending of the number of locations learned.

5.3   Evaluation Methodology

To study the SMP model, three types of experiments were performed:

- **Learning experiments:** The first type of experiment is performed to study the evolution of the code generated by the SMP model during training. For this purpose, the training of the SMP model is interrupted at regular intervals in order to test it's dictionary on a subset of the training dataset. This subset is then encoded via its sparse dictionary and evaluated using the population Kurtosis and the reconstruction error.
- **Localization performance experiments:** The second type of experiment allows the study of the localization performance of the VPR model under different conditions. It is measured using standard precision/recall measurements in cross validation. Thus, for a given configuration (learning sampling

rate or dictionary size), 3 tests are performed to address every configuration of learning and test sequence. Moreover, for the test sequences, one image per meter is tested to see to what extent a vehicle using this model would be able to locate itself along all the path.

- **Computational cost experiments:** This experiment allows the study to measure the computational cost of a model in different conditions. To do so, we evaluated the average time taken by a model to respond to a query. To limit the influence of code optimization on the experiment, the models were evaluated using only one CPU and no GPU.

5.4   Implementation Details

The performance of the SMP model relies on the tuning of two important parts: the visual system which influences the quality of the PoI (stable position, attachment on characterising landmarks) and the encoding system which influences the amount of information kept by the model. In this paper, we have focused our analyses on the encoding system, being the major novelty brought to the model. Thus, excepted for the dictionary, the parameters of the SMP model are the same than those use in the LPMP model [2]. Moreover, to compare SMP with CoHog and NetVLAD, we used the original implementation provided by their authors. Thus, we used the best pre-trained model for NetVLAD (VGG-16+whitening+Pittsburgh). Furthermore, experiments on localization performance were realized using an AMD Ryzen Threadripper 2990wx (3.7 GHz) and experiments on computational cost carried out using an Intel Core i9-9880H (2.3 GHz).

6   Results

6.1   Properties of TSC During Learning

The Fig. 2 shows the evolution of the mean reconstruction error and the mean population Kurtosis during the training of a $30 * 30$ dictionary. Thus, the first graph shows that during learning, the dictionary improves its ability to reconstruct the landmarks that are presented to it. The second graph on the other hand shows an increase in the mean population Kurtosis during the learning. This indicates that the sparsity of the code generated by the TSD increases, despite the addition of a topology constraint. These results seem to indicate that the algorithm does converge towards a solution that better encodes visual information and that is more sparse.

6.2   Evaluation of Configuration/Performance

The Fig. 3 shows the evolution of the SMP model's localization performance, according to its configuration[3]. They were computed on the first 250 m of the *Boulevard* dataset with a sampling rate of 5 m. Thus, the two graphs show that:

---

[3] To facilitate the notation of the dictionary configuration used during an experiment, the SMP model using a dictionary of size $n * n$ is called $SMP - n$.

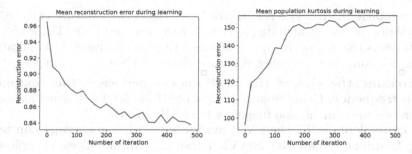

Fig. 2. Evolution of a topological sparse code during its learning process. Evolution of mean reconstruction error (left) and mean population kurtosis (right) at regular intervals during the learning process a 30 * 30 dictionary.

- **Increasing the number of atoms of the SMP model tends to improve its localization performance.** Moving from SMP-12 to SMP-30 improves the mean AUC by 8%. However, a peak of performance is reached at SMP-30.
- **SMP-30 has an average AUC equivalent to NetVlad.** SMP-30 has a mean AUC of 0.934, very close to that of NetVlad of 0.928.
- **SMP-30 has a slightly better average AUC than CoHog.** SMP-30 has an average AUC 5% better than CoHog.
- **All configurations of the SMP model have a better recall at 100% than the other models.** SMP-12, the least efficient configuration, has a recall at 100% of 0.136 against 0.063 for the CoHog model and 0.064 for the NetVlad model. This trend can also be observed in the Fig. 5 with a sampling of 5 m.

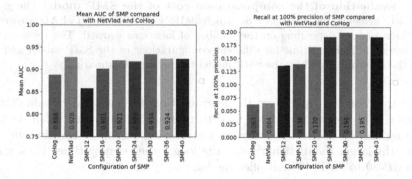

Fig. 3. Influence of SMP configuration on localization performances. The graphs presents the mean AUC (left) and the recall at 100% precision (right) of NetVlad, CoHog, and different configurations of the SMP model. The curves were computed in cross validation on the first 250 m of the *Boulevard* dataset with a sampling rate of 5 m.

To complete the previous results, the Fig. 4 shows the influence of the SMP configuration on the computational cost and the learning time. The graph on the left shows the average frequency at which the models answer to localization queries, according to the number of learned places. It allows us to conclude that:

- **Increasing the size of the SMP model decreases the computation frequency.** Going from SMP-20 to SMP-30 for 100 learned locations decreases the computation frequency from 4 Hz to 3 Hz.
- **At equivalent AUC, the SMP model has a higher average computing frequency than the NetVlad model.** SMP-30 allows to achieve a gain of ×60 on the computation frequency with NetVlad-1-CPU[4] and a gain of ×3 with NetVlad-4-CPU.
- **At equivalent AUC, the SMP model also has a higher average computation frequency than the CoHog model.** SMP-18 allows to achieve a gain of ×2 on the computation frequency for 100 learned locations. However, unlike the SMP model and NetVlad, the CoHog model does not require learning to operate.

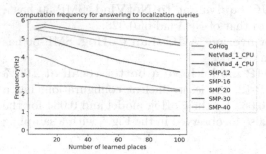

Model	Learning time	Descriptor size
SMP-12	215s	36
SMP-16	387s	64
SMP-20	538s	100
SMP-30	481s	225
SMP-36	1376s	324
SMP-40	1632s	400

Fig. 4. Evaluation of the computational cost of the SMP model The graph on the left presents the frequency at which SMP, CoHog and NetVLAD answer to localization queries depending on the number of locations learned. The table on the right shows the learning time for different configurations of the SMP model and the size of the descriptor used by the SMP model to encode a landmark.

The table on the right gives the learning time for each SMP configuration and the size of the feature vector used to represent a landmark. It shows that increasing the size of the dictionary has a strong impact on the learning time. In general, the larger the dictionary size, the longer the learning time. Thus, going from SMP-30 to SMP-40 multiplies the learning time by 5.

6.3 Evaluation of Localization Performances with the State of the Art

The Fig. 5 shows the average performance SMP-30, CoHog and NetVlad according to the three environments and three sampling distances: 3 m, 5 m and 10 m.

---

[4] The NetVlad model run at an average frequency of 0.05 Hz with one CPU.

The graphs on top show the mean AUC of the precision-recall curves and the graphs below show the mean recall at 100%. Each value was computed in cross validation on the first 500 m of each environment.

- **The SMP model has better localization performance than the CoHog model in almost all cases.** This difference is generally of 5% for the mean AUC, but is much larger for the recall at 100% precision. CoHog only exceeds SMP in the city-centre environment with a sampling distance of 2 m.
- **The SMP model has competitive localization performance with the NetVlad model.** The SMP model has slightly better performance than the NetVlad model at a sampling distance of 2 m and 5 m but the NetVlad model is better at a sampling distance of 10 m.

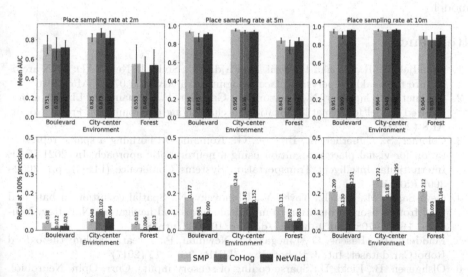

Fig. 5. Localization performances of SMP-30, CoHog and NetVLAD models. The performances are evaluated by computing precision/recall curves, summarized by their Area Under Curves and their recall at 100% precision. The evaluation was made in cross-validation on each environment and each place sampling rate.

7   Discussion and Conclusion

In this paper, we proposed the TSC algorithm, a new method of sparse coding that allows to build an organized sparse dictionary. This method, contrary to the classic sparse coding method, allows to build a more "coherent" dictionary i.e. with closer codes for two similar images. We have thus demonstrated that TSC have a strong interest in the context of visual localization to encode visual information. In particular, we demonstrated that the SMP model, based on the use of TSC, is competitive with two state-of-the-art models: CoHog and NetVlad.

Moreover, the experiments carried out demonstrated the interest of sparse coding for large-scale localization. In particular, we have seen that the model allows to strongly compress the visual information while keeping very high localization performances. The performances obtained can thus allow us to hope for meeting the real-time constraints of a localisation system on an autonomous vehicle. Tests have been undertaken on real vehicles and have shown encouraging first results.

Finally, this proposal is in line with previous work, in particular the HSD model, an encoding model based on the use of several layers of sparse dictionaries [3]. Unlike the previous model, the TSC algorithm directly integrates the topology into the update rule. This writing of the algorithm results in a better sparse dictionaries, which perform more efficiently when used with a VPR model. Thus, further work has been undertaken to chain several TSC to further improve the performance of the model, in the same way as proposed in the HSD model.

References

1. Arandjelović, R., Gronat, P., Torii, A., Pajdla, T., Sivic, J.: NetVLAD: CNN architecture for weakly supervsied place recognition. arXiv:1511.07247, May 2016
2. Colomer, S., Cuperlier, N., Bresson, G., Gaussier, P., Romain, O.: LPMP: a bioinspired model for visual localization in challenging environments. Front. Robot. AI **8** (2022)
3. Colomer, S., Cuperlier, N., Bresson, G., Romain, O.: Forming a sparse representation for visual place recognition using a neurorobotic approach. In: 2021 IEEE International Intelligent Transportation Systems Conference (ITSC), pp. 3002–3009 (2021)
4. Geva-Sagiv, M., Las, L., Yovel, Y., Ulanovsky, N.: Spatial cognition in bats and rats: from sensory acqusiition to multsicale maps and navigation. Nat. Rev. Neurosci. **16**, 94–108 (2015). https://doi.org/10.1038/nrn3888
5. Maddern, W., Pascoe, G., Linegar, C., Newman, P.: 1 year, 1000km: the oxford RobotCar dataset. Int. J. Robot. Res. (IJRR) **36**, 3–15 (2017)
6. Olshausen, B., Field, D.: Sparse coding of sensory inputs. Curr. Opin. Neurobiol. **14**, 481–487 (2004). https://doi.org/10.1016/j.conb.2004.07.007
7. Perrinet, L.U.: An adaptive homeostatic algorithm for the unsupervsied learning of visual features. Vision **3**(3), 47 (2019). https://doi.org/10.3390/vsiion3030047
8. Rolls, E.T., Wirth, S.: Spatial representations in the primate hippocampus, and their functions in memory and navigation. Prog. Neurobiol. **171**, 90–113 (2018)
9. Serre, T., Wolf, L., Bileschi, S., Riesenhuber, M., Poggio, T.: Robust object recognition with cortex-like mechansims. IEEE Trans. Pattern Anal. Mach. Intell. **29**, 411–426 (2007). https://doi.org/10.1109/TPAMI.2007.56
10. Willmore, B., Tolhurst, D.: Characterizing the sparseness of neural codes. Netw. Comput. Neural Syst. **12**(3), 255–270 (2001)
11. Yurtsever, E., Lambert, J., Carballo, A., Takeda, K.: A survey of autonomous driving: common practices and emerging technologies. IEEE Access **8**, 58443–58469 (2020). https://doi.org/10.1109/ACCESS.2020.2983149
12. Zaffar, M., Ehsan, S., Milford, M., McDonald-Maier, K.: CoHOG: a light-weight, compute-efficient, and training-free visual place recognition technique for changing environments. IEEE Robot. Autom. Lett. **5**, 1835–1842 (2020)

Contribution of the Retrosplenial Cortex to Path Integration and Spatial Codes

Mingda Ju[(✉)] and Philippe Gaussier

ETIS UMR8051, CY Université, ENSEA, CNRS, 2 Avenue Adolphe-Chauvin
BP 222, 95000 Cergy, France
{mingda.ju,gaussier}@ensea.fr

Abstract. In the proposed model, we suppose the retrosplenial cortex (RSC) conveys path integration (PI) information to the hippocampal system. Our model shows the potential of the PI field in reproducing diverse neuronal activities involved in the spatial representation of animals. We explain the absence of places cells in the RSC because of the difficulty of neurons to access the whole PI field. The simulated activity with only local connections fits with the recorded activities in the RSC. Moreover, we emphasize the importance of the entorhinal cortex (EC) as a hub to merge the different afferent cortical activities in order to build an efficient hash code for complex pattern recognition and novelty detection at the level of the hippocampus. The grid cells could be a by-product of this compression mechanism in the EC.

Keywords: Path integration · Retrosplenial cortex · Entorhinal cortex · Head direction cell · Place cell · Grid cell

1 Introduction

Path integration (PI) is the estimation of distance and direction as a function of velocity and time. It enables animals to return to a starting point even in the absence of visual cues. Many different species, from insects [1] to mammals [2], have the ability to perform PI. However, it remains unknown where and how this information is integrated. Various recordings in the retrosplenial cortex (RSC) [3–5] suggest that the RSC might play an important role in PI. The place cell-like activity found in the RSC [6] could also be a sign of the PI information conveying via the RSC. Many prior models [7,8] propose that PI is performed in the hippocampus. Some of the models adapted to the findings of grid cells and head direction (HD) cells in the entorhinal cortex (EC) by reclaiming that the PI takes place inside the EC. Grid cell models including oscillatory interference model [9,10] and attractor models [11,12] rely on velocity input consisting of the movement direction and the linear speed . These models take the movement direction calculated from sequential positions in the experimental data comprising the velocity input, rather than the HD at each position while citing HD recordings as the justification for velocity input [9–11]. Recordings in the EC

L. Cañamero et al. (Eds.): SAB 2022, LNAI 13499, pp. 165–176, 2022.
https://doi.org/10.1007/978-3-031-16770-6_14

[13] indicate that coding of MD is not prominent in the medial EC, and HD cannot directly replace MD in the mentioned models using PI to build the grid cells. Cortices such as RSC and the parietal cortex could be candidates for the seeking of the moving directional tuning and as the potential origin of the PI. Our model of the PI is independent on the hippocampus nor the HD cells in the EC. We suppose grid cells [14] are the result of a generic compression mechanism of the cortical activities when applied on PI fields primarily computed outside the hippocampus [15,16]. The hippocampus could play a role of indexing or building hash codes of the cortical activity [17] in order to detect new events or patterns that have to be stored in the cortex [18,19]. In this research, we used a simple learning rule (classical conditioning) [20] as a low path filtering to directly compute PI from movement direction cells. Following the biological recordings of the place cell-like activity in the retrosplenial cortex [6] which has been successfully simulated using our PI model [16], our model of PI is also able to account for diverse neuronal activities in the corticohippocampal circuit including activities of place cells, grid cells and movement direction-modulated cells. We emphasized in our simple model the potential of the PI as the substrate of the spatial representation of animals and the richness of the spatial information conveyed by the PI might have been under-estimated.

2   Computational Model

The preliminary inputs to our PI model are the HD cells simulated by an one-directional ring attractor [21] with the presumption that the moving direction is consistent with the HD while recordings [13] proved the contrary. We thereby replace the HD cells by the movement direction cells as the input to our model and hypothesize that the MD cells share common properties as the HD cells. To simplify, the potential MD cells are simulated by the one-directional ring attractor.

The activity of MD cells is represented as a bump of activity of a ring of neurons: $G_i(\theta) = e^{-\frac{(\theta - \theta_i)^2}{2\sigma^2}}$ where σ determines the width of the firing range of MD cells and θ_i is the absolute orientation of the animal.

Input of the model (Fig. 1) is the absolute orientation and the linear velocity of the animal. We suppose that a group of neurons is equally distributed to represent $360°$ in order to simulate MD cells. Each neuron has a preferred direction depending on the number (N) of neurons. The interval between each preferred direction is $360°$ divided by N. This group of neurons can represent $360°$ with a good precision if we have enough neurons. Visual place recognition of the starting location for PI is used to reset the PI field and limit the error accumulation. Each time the animal is coming back in the vicinity of this location the reset is performed. There is no lateral interaction or adjacency among neurons on the PI field.

Now we will describe how a simple condition mechanism can be used to perform path integration if the input activity is a bump of activity of a ring of neurons. Starting from the linear velocity of the animal V and a field of neurons

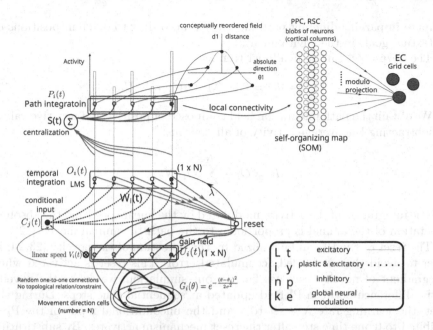

Fig. 1. Computation model of path integration (PI) in the retrosplenial cortex. Since there is no need of lateral interaction between the neurons on the PI field, the global bump of activation is only visible if neurons are reordered according to their preferred direction. Self organization properties in RSC with local connections to some neurons in the PI field allow to build different spatial signatures. Compression of this information at the level of EC allows the building of a compact code (grid cells). Hippocampal neurons having a global access to the whole PI field from EC grid cells can recognize associated places to PI information.

$G_i(\theta)$ representing the M cells, conjunctive cells are used to build the field U_i defined as $V \cdot G_i(\theta)$. U_i is used as the unconditional stimulus to perform temporal integration on O_i neurons.

$$O_i(t) = f(\sum W_{ij} \cdot C_j) \text{ , with } f(x) = \begin{cases} 0 & \text{if } x < 0 \\ x & \text{if } 0 \leq x < 1 \\ 1 & \text{if } x > 1 \end{cases} \qquad (1)$$

The update of the synapses dW_{ij} is subject to the least mean square algorithm which is identical to a classical conditioning [20]:

$$dW_{ij} = \lambda \cdot (U_i - O_i) \cdot C_j \qquad (2)$$

where λ is the learning rate of the classical conditioning. C_j is a binary value associated to a spatial context j (the conditional input). To simplify, we maintain the environmental context which is the conditional stimulus C_j constant and equal to 1 during the simulations in this work. However, replacing this constant neuron by a set of neurons representing different contexts might be used to compute in parallel different path integration according to different positions or contextual goals in the environment.

The output O_i can be finally written as:

$$O_i(t + dt) = (1 - \lambda) \cdot O_i(t) + \lambda \cdot U_i \qquad (3)$$

We obtain the path integration field composed of positive and negative values by subtracting the average activity of all neurons:

$$P_i = O_i - \sum_{i=0}^{N} O_i/N \qquad (4)$$

The integration of the activity modulated by the linear speed and the absolute orientation of the animal is proportional to the path the animal moved [22].

The reset of the PI can be realized by the detection of the novelty [23,24] in order to avoid the overloaded accumulated error. This reset is activated when the gradient of novelty becomes flat. In our simulation, we define the novelty as the difference between PI field updated at sequential time steps. During the reset, the learning rate λ is set to 1 and the unconditional input of the PI is inhibited to 0 one time step after the reset mechanism activates. By substituting the parameters in (Eq. 3) with their reset values, we have $O_i(t + dt) = U_i$ so that PI is reset to 0 in one time step.

The activity of PI field is projected to a set of Kohonen self-organizing maps (SOM) (blobs on Fig. 1). Each neuron on the PI field projects selectively to every neurons on the SOM depending on the connectivity (local or global) from PI field to the SOM. The activity of neuron k on the SOM is the following:

$$E_k = \left(\frac{\sum P_i(t) \cdot W_{ik}(t)}{\sqrt{\sum P_i(t)^2 \cdot \sum W_{ik}(t)^2}} \right), k \in [1, .., M] \qquad (5)$$

The index of the winner neuron k^w is defined as:

$$k^w(t) = arg\ max\ (E_k)\,, k \in [1, .., M] \qquad (6)$$

M is the number of neurons on the SOM. The synaptic weights between neurons on the input field P_i and neurons on the SOM is updated by:

$$W_{ik}(t + dt) = \lambda_{som} \cdot (P_i(t) - W_{ik}(t)) \cdot S_k(t) \qquad (7)$$

λ_{som} is the learning rate of the self-organization. The potential of neurons on the self-organizing map is subject to a Mexican hat function $h_{kk^w}(t)$ such as:

$$S_k(t) = h_{kk^w}(d_k) \cdot S_{k^w}(t),\ k \in [1, Q]\ \text{with}$$

$$h_{kk^w}(d_k) = (\frac{1}{\sigma_1 \cdot \sqrt{2 \cdot \pi}} \cdot exp^{-\frac{d_k^2}{2 \cdot \sigma_1^2}} - \frac{1}{\sigma_2 \cdot \sqrt{2 \cdot \pi}} \cdot exp^{-\frac{d_k^2}{2 \cdot \sigma_2^2}}) \cdot 15 \qquad (8)$$

Here we take σ_1 equals to 3 and σ_2 equals to 6 for the SOM containing 32 neurons. $S_k(t)$ is the potential of the k-th neuron with Q the size of the Mexican hat. d_k represents the distance between the winner neuron k^w and other neurons k on the SOM.

In the next section, we discuss in details the potential of our PI model to simulate diverse neuronal activity related to the PI in the RSC according to the size of the neuron receptive field and to the learning rate used.

3   Experiment and Results

In the following simulations without special indication, the animal moves freely in a two metres by two metres square arena for 40000 time steps. One iteration in the simulation corresponds to 0.1 s. The product of the learning rate λ and its associated time constant τ equals to 0.1 s in order to scale the simulation from time steps to seconds. The moving pattern of the animal is adjusted to be biologically plausible. The acceleration of linear and angular speed has been introduced. The linear speed varies from 10 cm/s to 40 cm/s. The acceleration of linear speed is 20 cm/s^2 while the angular speed of the animal's body is 90°/s.

The (x, y) coordinate of the animal are updated as follow:

$$x(t + dt) = x(t) + d.cos(\theta(t))$$
$$y(t + dt) = y(t) + d.sin(\theta(t)) \qquad (9)$$

with $\theta(t)$ the animal's MD according to an absolute referential and $d = v \cdot dt$ with v its instantaneous speed.

Simulations are conducted using bumps of activity of MD cells as the input. The bump is simulated by a Gaussian function with $\sigma = 60°$. MD is analyzed with a 6° bin width. The metric to characterize the MD cells [25] is the directional information rate:

$$MD_{score} = \sum_{i}^{N} p_i \frac{\lambda_i}{\lambda} log_2 \frac{\lambda_i}{\lambda} \qquad (10)$$

where N equals to 60, λ_i is the mean firing rate of a neuron in the i-th bin, λ is the overall mean firing rate, and p_i is the probability that the animal's MD pointed to the direction which is represented by the i-th bin. The spatial information rate is calculated to characterize the place cells:

$$PC_{score} = \sum_{j}^{M} p_j \frac{\lambda_j}{\lambda} log_2 \frac{\lambda_j}{\lambda} \qquad (11)$$

where the environment is divided into 100 non-overlapping spatial bins which means M equals to 100, p_j is the occupancy probability of bin j, λ_j is the mean firing rate of bin j, and λ is the overall firing rate of the cell.

The sparsity of cells [26] measures the fraction of the environment in which a cell is active:

$$Sparsity = \sum (p_j \cdot \lambda_j)^2 / \sum p_j \cdot \lambda_j^2 \qquad (12)$$

Intuitively, a sparsity of 0.1 means that the place field of the cell occupies 1/10 of the area the rat traverses. The selectivity measure is equal to the spatial maximum firing rate divided by the mean firing rate of the cell. The more tightly concentrated the cell's activity, the higher the selectivity is. A cell with no spatial tuning at all will have a selectivity of 1. The main variable modulated during all the simulations is the learning rate λ used for the temporal integration of the gain field in Fig. 1 and in Eq. 2, 3. The performance of the PI model with learning rates ranging from 0.1 to 0.001 (τ from 1 s to 100 s) will be tested.

3.1   Recording ot Neurons Learning MD Activities in RSC

The first simulation tests the capability of our path integration to retrieve the activity of MD or HD cells by using a high learning rate λ equal to 0.1. The activity of one neuron on a SOM showing MD cell's activity is recorded in Fig. 2.

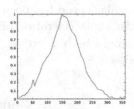
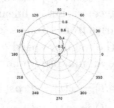

(a) activity of one neuron as a function of MD

(b) activity of the same neuron as a function of MD in polar coordinates

(c) winner position of the same along the trajectory

Fig. 2. Example of one activated neuron showing MD cell activity on the SOM when λ equals to 0.1

The mean values of the directional and spatial information rate are 2.35 and 2.43 with STD of 0.73 and 1.41 respectively. MD cells present high directional information rate but very random spatial information rate. The high standard derivation in the spatial information rate is related to the freely moving pattern in which the probability of the animal facing to each direction can be different. The width of the bump of activity of MD cells before the competition depends on the shape of the bump of activity of the initial MD cells which are the input to our model. The dependency between the retrieval MD cells and the original MD cells as the input to the PI model leads to a hypothesis that the HD or potential MD cells in the RSC could be homogeneous to the ones found in the hippocampus. A high learning rate leads to the early saturation of the PI field and realizes the retrieval of the MD cells homogeneous to the input MD cell.

3.2   Building Place Cells from PI Information

The involvement of the spatial information conveyed by the PI in the generation of place cells is tested using a comparatively low learning rate equal to 0.001

with neurons fully connected to the virtual PI field. The activity of one neuron on a SOM is shown in Fig. 3.

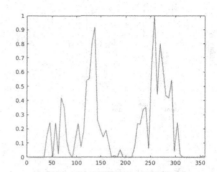

(a) winner position of one neuron along the trajectory

(b) activity of the same neuron as a function of MD in polar coordinates

Fig. 3. Example of one activated neuron showing place cell activity on the SOM when λ equals to 0.001 when using connections to the whole path integration field

The mean values of the directional and spatial information rate are 1.08 and 4.44 with STD of 0.62 and 0.66 respectively. No MD cell's activity is observed. By accessing to the whole PI field, our model is able to build place cells activity by simply using a low learning rate. The classical conditioning thereby plays a role of a short-term memory or a low pass filter.

The average directional and spatial information rates of the activity of neurons using different learning rate is shown in Fig. 4. Our PI model is capable of building a wide range of neuronal activity by exclusively modulating the learning rate as long as the downstream region get full access to the upstream cortex conveying the PI information.

Notably, no place cell in an open environment was found in RSC. It means the connectivity from the PI field to the SOM in RSC is not global but only local as it is the case for classical cortical column.

3.3 Robustness of the Model

High Frequency Recalibration. To test the robustness of our model, the uniform white noise with the amplitude of 10% of the value of linear and angular speed is implemented at the stage of gain field. The learning rate is fixed to 0.001. The animal is forced to go through the recalibration point once per 10 s. The activity of neurons is recorded when the animal moves freely in a two metres by two metres environment for 7500 s (1 iteration = 0.1 s).

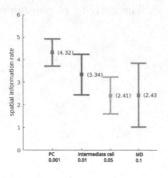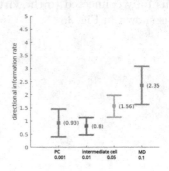

(a) spatial information rate   (b) directional information rate

Fig. 4. The average directional and spatial information rates of the activity of neurons using different learning rates. The square indicates the mean value. The interval of STD is represented by horizontal lines.

The equation of the gain field in Fig. 1 can be rewritten as:

$$U_i(t) = speed(t) \cdot (1 + speed\_noise) \cdot f_{\theta_i}(\theta(t))$$
$$\text{with } \theta(t+1) = \theta(t) + angular\_s \cdot (1 + angular\_noise) \tag{13}$$

This noise will accumulate during the PI until the animal moves to a point of recalibration. The activity of one neuron is illustrated in Fig. 5 top.

The mean values of the directional and spatial information rate are 1.19 and 4.16 with STD of 0.83 and 0.92 respectively.

Low Frequency Recalibration. To test the limit of our model, the frequency of the recalibration is decreased tenfold to once per 100 s. The duration of the free movement of the animal is still 7500 s. The activity of one neuron is illustrated in Fig. 5. bottom.

The mean values of the directional and spatial information rate are 1.12 and 3.27 with STD of 0.99 and 1.71 respectively. The spacial information rate decreases significantly along with the destruction of the place cells activity.

Under a high frequency recalibration, the mean activity and the standard deviation of neurons are consistent with the values obtained without the interference of the noise. Our model is robust to convey information of different spatially related neuronal activity using different learning rates even under the interference of the considerable noise. Nevertheless, the generation of the spatial activity is destructed due to the accumulated error of the PI causing by the lack of a solid recalibration mechanism. The recalibration of the path integration field could be realized by visual cues or other sensory input such as olfactory or tactile stimuli.

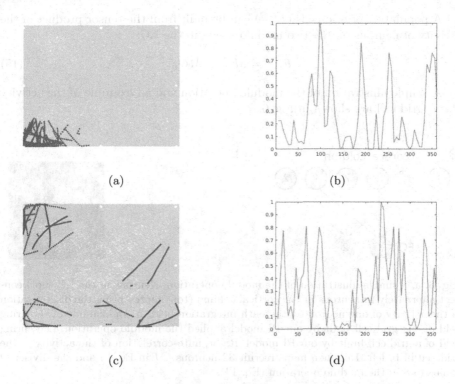

(a)   (b)

(c)   (d)

Fig. 5. Activity of two neurons under the situation of High (top) and low (bot) frequency recalibration. a and c show the winner position of the two neurons along the trajectory. b and d show the activity of the same two neurons as a function of MD in polar coordinates.

Grid Cells in EC from RSC Activities. We have shown in our prior works the capability of reproducing the place cell-like activity [6] in the RSC when the animal runs on a treadmill using our PI model [16]. Notably, place cells can be obtained even in a 2D environment with a global connections from the PI field to a SOM. However, biologists didn't find place cells in the RSC when the animal moves freely instead of running in a fixed direction on a treadmill. We thereby suppose the connectivity between neurons performing PI and the SOM is local and define blobs of neurons working as local Kohonen maps. Neurons in the EC could have global access to the PI field and compress the PI information using a simple modulo operation. To build grid cells, one pair of neurons (P_{i1}, P_{i2}) distant from $60°$ ($i2 = i1 + [\frac{N}{360} \cdot 60]$) on the path integration field is selected as the input to two kohonen maps (E_j and E_k calculated by Eq. 5) which are compressed by two modulo layers (MO_l and MO_n) according to the equation:

$$MO_l = \begin{cases} 1 & \text{if } l = 1 + argmax(E_j) \ mod \ Q \\ 0 & \text{else} \end{cases} \tag{14}$$

A population of grid cells (F^{GC}) can be built from the tensor product of the activity of neurons on the two modulo layers in the EC:

$$F^{GC} = MO_l \otimes MO_n \tag{15}$$

A simple illustration of the modulo operation and an example of the activity of one grid cell are shown in Fig. 6.

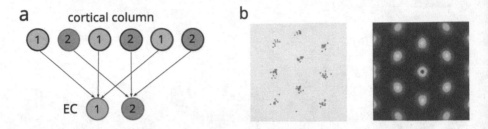

Fig. 6. a, a simple illustration of the modulo operation. Neurons in the EC (bot) connect alternately to neurons in one cortical column (top) representing the discretization of the activity of one neuron on the path integration field. b, an example of the firing field of one grid cell built by our PI model applied the modulo operation. Left, firing field of a grid cell built by our PI model. Right, auto-correlation of the activity of the grid cell in b. left. Kohonen maps recruit 32 neurons (M in Eq. 5) and the divisor Q equals to 8 in the modulo operation (Eq. 14).

For sake of simplicity, self organization of the Kohonen maps used to discretize the path integration field was done during a long random walk limited to the arena. It is therefore normal the same cell is activated 4 times (compression ratio $Cr = M : Q$) in the diagonal direction (longest distance in our environment) when Kohonen maps recruit 32 neurons (M) and the divisor Q equals to 8 in the modulo operation.

It is known that one of the most important role of hippocampus is the detection of the novelty and the recognition of complex states, but the number of neurons in the hippocampus is very limited. The EC could play the role of a compression mechanism providing the hippocampus the capability to detect and learn quickly complex cortical patterns.

4   Conclusion and Perspective

The potential of the PI to convey spatial information is studied in this work. Our simulations show that if some RSC neurons had global connections to the whole PI fields, RSC neurons should always exhibit place cell activities. Due to the local connectivity, the place cell-like activity can be only observed in the RSC when the animal moves in one direction on the treadmill with its head fixed [6]. A wide range of spatially related neuronal activities has been produced by our PI model assuming the RSC has full access to upstream brain areas where the PI originates. Producing place cells in the EC from the RSC activity could be possible with one to all connections from RSC to EC. However, it is not biologically plausible considering the limited number of synaptic connections of each neuron (typically 10000 connections per neuron). We thereby propose that the EC including perirhinal and parahippocampal regions could play the role of a hub to compress the cortical information involved in navigation, vision and other recognition tasks. The EC could maintain the global feature of the cortical information with a sparse connectivity to the afferent cortices owing to the modulo operation. The grid cells activity in the EC could be a by-product of this general compression mechanism.

We will present in our future work how the reciprocal connectivity between the hippocampus and the EC could play a crucial role in the self-organization of grid cells. The place cells activity from the hippocampus could be the teaching signal to the EC [12] during the early development. At this stage, place cells could also emerge based on the detection of novelty taking non grid activity of immature EC grid cells which have random synaptic connections with the cortical columns in the PPC or the RSC. The modulo projection learned from a local learning rule maximizing the independence of the output neurons in the EC will be detailed in an ongoing paper.

References

1. Collett, T.S., Baron, J., Sellen, K.: On the encoding of movement vectors by honeybees. Are distance and direction represented independently? J. Comp. Physiol. A **179**(3), 395–406 (1996)
2. Etienne, A.S., Jeffery, K.J.: Path integration in mammals. Hippocampus **14**(2), 180–192 (2004)
3. Cooper, B.G., Mizumori, S.J.Y.: Retrosplenial cortex inactivation selectively impairs navigation in darkness. Neuroreport **10**(3), 625–630 (1999)
4. Czajkowski, R., et al.: Encoding and storage of spatial information in the retrosplenial cortex. Proc. Natl. Acad. Sci. **111**(23), 8661–8666 (2014)
5. Elduayen, C., Save, E.: The retrosplenial cortex is necessary for path integration in the dark. Behav. Brain Res. **272**, 303–307 (2014)
6. Mao, D., et al.: Sparse orthogonal population representation of spatial context in the retrosplenial cortex. Nat. Commun. **8**(1), 1–9 (2017)
7. McNaughton, B.L., et al.: Deciphering the hippocampal polyglot: the hippocampus as a path integration system. J. Exp. Biol. **199**(1), 173–185 (1996)
8. Redish, A.D., Elga, A.N., Touretzky, D.S.: A coupled attractor model of the rodent head direction system. Netw. Comput. Neural Syst. **7**(4), 671 (1996)
9. Burgess, N., Barry, C., O'keefe, J.: An oscillatory interference model of grid cell firing. Hippocampus **17**(9), 801–812 (2007)
10. Hasselmo, M.E.: Grid cell mechanisms and function: contributions of entorhinal persistent spiking and phase resetting. Hippocampus **18**(12), 1213–1229 (2008)
11. McNaughton, B.L., et al.: Path integration and the neural basis of the 'cognitive map'. Nat. Rev. Neurosci. **7**(8), 663–678 (2006)
12. Bonnevie, T., et al.: Grid cells require excitatory drive from the hippocampus. Nat. Neurosci. **16**(3), 309–317 (2013)

13. Raudies, F., et al.: Head direction is coded more strongly than movement direction in a population of entorhinal neurons. Brain Res. **1621**, 355–367 (2015)
14. Hafting, T., et al.: Microstructure of a spatial map in the entorhinal cortex. Nature **436**(7052), 801–806 (2005)
15. Gaussier, P., et al.: A model of grid cells involving extra hippocampal path integration, and the hippocampal loop. J. Integr. Neurosci. **6**(03), 447–476 (2007)
16. Ju, M., Gaussier, P.: A model of path integration and representation of spatial context in the retrosplenial cortex. Biol. Cybern. **114**(2), 303–313 (2020)
17. Teyler, T.J., Rudy, J.W.: The hippocampal indexing theory and episodic memory: updating the index. Hippocampus **17**(12), 1158–1169 (2007)
18. Eichenbaum, H., Otto, T., Cohen, N.J.: Two functional components of the hippocampal memory system. Behav. Brain Sci. **17**(3), 449–472 (1994)
19. Buzsáki, G., Moser, E.I.: Memory, navigation and theta rhythm in the hippocampal-entorhinal system. Nat. Neurosci. **16**(2), 130–138 (2013)
20. Rescorla, R.A.: A theory of Pavlovian conditioning: variations in the effectiveness of reinforcement and nonreinforcement. Curr. Res. Theory 64–99 (1972)
21. McNaughton, B.L., Chen, L.L., Markus, E.J.: "Dead reckoning," landmark learning, and the sense of direction: a neurophysiological and computational hypothesis. J. Cogn. Neurosci. **3**(2), 190–202 (1991)
22. Alexander, A.S., Nitz, D.A.: Retrosplenial cortex maps the conjunction of internal and external spaces. Nat. Neurosci. **18**(8), 1143–1151 (2015)
23. Markou, M., Singh, S.: Novelty detection: a review-part 2: neural network based approaches. Signal Process. **83**(12), 2499–2521 (2003)
24. Jauffret, A., et al.: How can a robot evaluate its own behavior? A neural model for self-assessment. In: The 2013 International Joint Conference on Neural Networks (IJCNN). IEEE (2013)
25. Taube, J.S., Muller, R.U., Ranck, J.B.: Head-direction cells recorded from the postsubiculum in freely moving rats. I. Description and quantitative analysis. J. Neurosci. **10**(2), 420–435 (1990)
26. Skaggs, W.E., et al.: Theta phase precession in hippocampal neuronal populations and the compression of temporal sequences. Hippocampus **6**(2), 149–172 (1996)

Flexible Path Planning in a Spiking Model of Replay and Vicarious Trial and Error

Jeffrey L. Krichmar[1](✉)(iD), Nicholas A. Ketz[2,3], Praveen K. Pilly[3], and Andrea Soltoggio[4]

[1] Department of Cognitive Sciences, Department of Computer Science, University of California, Irvine, Irvine, CA 92697-5100, USA
jkrichma@uci.edu
[2] Colossal Biosciences, Madison, WI, USA
nick@colossal.com
[3] Center for Human-Machine Collaboration, Information and Systems Sciences Laboratory, HRL Laboratories, Malibu, CA 90265, USA
pkpilly@hrl.com
[4] Computer Science Department, Loughborough University, Loughborough LE11 3TU, UK
a.soltoggio@lboro.ac.uk

Abstract. Flexible planning is necessary for reaching goals and adapting when conditions change. We introduce a biologically plausible path planning model that learns its environment, rapidly adapts to change, and plans efficient routes to goals. Our model addresses the decision-making process when faced with uncertainty. We tested the model in simulations of human and rodent navigation in mazes. Like the human and rat, the model was able to generate novel shortcuts, and take detours when familiar routes were blocked. Similar to rodent hippocampus recordings, the neural activity of the model resembles neural correlates of Vicarious Trial and Error (VTE) during early learning or during uncertain conditions and preplay predicting a future path after learning. We suggest that VTE, in addition to weighing possible outcomes, is a way in which an agent may gather information for future use.

Keywords: Cognitive map · Hippocampus · Navigation · Preplay · Spiking neural network

1 Introduction

Flexible planning is an important aspect of cognition that is especially useful when achieving a goal under uncertain conditions. Multi-step planning can be

Supported by the Air Force Office of Scientific Research (AFOSR) Contract No. FA9550-19-1-0306, by the National Science Foundation (NSF-FO award ID 2024633), and by the United States Air Force Research Laboratory (AFRL) and Defense Advanced Research Projects Agency (DARPA) under Contract No. FA8750-18-C-0103.

L. Cañamero et al. (Eds.): SAB 2022, LNAI 13499, pp. 177–189, 2022.
https://doi.org/10.1007/978-3-031-16770-6_15

thought of as a process that uses a cognitive map to guide a sequence of actions towards a goal [12]. In the context of spatial navigation, humans and other animals have the ability to choose alternate routes when necessary. Moreover, they can express spatial knowledge in the form of novel shortcuts over locations not previously explored [3].

Neural correlates of planning have been observed in rodent hippocampus place cell responses. In hippocampal replay, plans are formed by reactivating place cells of previously experienced location sequences [4,13]. Computational models have shown how hippocampal preplay, which is sometimes called forward replay, can plan paths towards new goals in familiar environments and replan when familiar paths are no longer viable [11,15]. However, these models of preplay do not address the decision-making process when faced with uncertainty, and they may not explain how knowledge of never experienced locations can be stored and expressed.

In the mid-twentieth century, Edward Tolman described the flexible, intelligent behavior observed in animals as a cognitive map [16]. One aspect of a cognitive map was Vicarious Trial and Error (VTE), which is the ability to weigh one's options before taking decisive action. Similar to hippocampal preplay, neural correlates of VTE have been observed in hippocampal CA1 where neurons with place-specific firing exhibit "sweeps" of activity representing the locations at which the animal considers its left versus right turn choice [8,14]. VTE seems to occur when the animal is uncertain about which path to take. After experience, hippocampal preplay occurs for the path the animal intends to take, but not the alternatives.

In this paper, we introduce a computational model of path planning that demonstrates VTE during early learning or when environmental conditions change. We further show that this model can acquire knowledge about never experienced paths, and rapidly adapt to express this knowledge when challenged. We suggest this activity is comparable to VTE observed in animals and that VTE may assist in the acquisition of knowledge that can be later expressed as novel shortcuts or rapid re-routing.

2 Methods

2.1 Spiking Wave Propagation

Spiking wavefront propagation is a neuromorphic navigation algorithm inspired by neuronal dynamics and connectivity of neurons in the brain [7]. The algorithm is loosely based on the responses of place cells in the hippocampus during preplay. The spiking wavefront propagation algorithm learns by adjusting axonal delays. This was inspired by biological evidence suggesting that the myelin sheath, which wraps around and insulates axons, may undergo a form of activity-dependent plasticity [5]. These studies have shown that the myelin sheath becomes thicker with learning motor skills and cognitive tasks. A thicker myelin sheath implies faster conduction velocities and improved synchrony between neurons. In the present work, adjusting axonal delays fits better with the idea behind wave propagation than the more commonly used synaptic weight updates.

The spiking wavefront propagation algorithm assumes a grid representation of space. Each grid unit corresponds to a discretized area of physical space, and connections between units represent the ability to travel from one grid location to a neighboring location. Each unit in the grid is represented by a single neuron with spiking dynamics, which are captured with a model described by the equations below. Further description of model can be found in [7].

The membrane potential of neuron i at time $t + 1$ is represented by Eq. 1:

$$v_i(t + 1) = u_i(t) + I_i(t + 1) \tag{1}$$

in which $u_i(t)$ is the recovery variable and $I_i(t)$ is the synaptic input at time t, which denotes the advancement of the path planning algorithm and is not related to clock time. In practice, the algorithm is lightweight and t is much shorter than real time.

The recovery variable $u_i(t + 1)$ is described Eq. 2:

$$u_i(t + 1) = \begin{cases} -5 & if \ v_i(t) = 1 \\ min(u_i(t) + 1, 0) & otherwise \end{cases} \tag{2}$$

such that immediately after a membrane potential spike, the recovery variable starts as a negative value and linearly increases toward a baseline value of 0.

The synaptic input I at time $t + 1$ is given by Eq. 3:

$$I_i(t + 1) = \sum_{j=1}^{N} \begin{cases} 1 & if \ d_{ij}(t) = 1 \\ 0 & otherwise \end{cases} \tag{3}$$

such that $d_{ij}(t)$ is the delay counter of the signal from neighboring neuron j to neuron i. This delay is given by Eq. 4:

$$d_{ij}(t + 1) = \begin{cases} D_{ij} & if \ v_j(t) \geq 1 \\ max(d_{ij}(t) - 1, 0) & otherwise \end{cases} \tag{4}$$

which behaves as a timer corresponding to an axonal delay with a starting value of $D_{ij}(t)$, counting down until it reaches 0.

The value of $D_{ij}(t)$ depends on the environmental cost associated with traveling between the locations associated with neurons i and j. Synaptic input comes from neighboring connected neurons. When a neighboring neuron spikes, the synaptic input I_i is increased by 1. This triggers the neuron to spike. After the spike, the recovery variable u_i is set to -5, then gradually recovers back to 0, modeling the refractory period. Also, immediately after spiking, all delay counters d_{ij} for all neighbor neurons j are set to their current values of D_{ij}. In the present paper, and in contrast to [7], D_{ij} are set to some initial value (10 in the experiments described in Sect. 3.1 and 5 in the experiments described in Sect. 3.2) and then change based on the agent's observations in the environment with the learning rule described in Sect. 2.2.

2.2   E-Prop and Back-Propagation Through Time

The E-Prop algorithm was introduced to learn sequences in spiking recurrent neural networks [2]. Learning was dictated by a loss function related to the desired output. The credit assignment problem was resolved by subjecting each neuron to an eligibility trace based on the neuron's recent activity. Weights between neurons were updated based on the loss and the value of the eligibility trace. In this way, the E-Prop algorithm resembled Back-Propagation Through Time (BPTT).

In the present model, E-Prop is used to learn sequences of movements through an environment based on the traversal cost. The active neurons during the wave propagation are eligible to be updated. Once eligible, they are subject to an exponential decay due to an eligibility trace. The most eligible neurons are those most recently active relative to when the wave reaches the goal destination. After the path is calculated, E-Prop is applied to weights projecting from neurons along the calculated path. Since these weights are connected to locations adjacent to the path, we assume the agent can observe the features (e.g., traversal cost) at these map locations. In this way, E-Prop solves the credit assignment problem by rewarding paths that lead to goal locations, while also learning about the environmental structure of nearby map locations.

Weights denote the axonal delay in sending an action potential or spike from the pre-synaptic neuron to the post-synaptic neuron. We apply the E-Prop algorithm to these weights so that the spiking neural network learns an axonal delay corresponding to environmental features observed in map_{xy}, which is the spatial location at Cartesian coordinates (x, y) of the map. The values of D_{ij} are updated when the agent reaches the goal destination. The learning rule is described by Eq. 5:

$$D_{ij}(t+1) = D_{ij}(t) + \delta(e_i(t)(map_{xy} - D_{ij}(t))) \tag{5}$$

where δ is the learning rate, set to 0.5, $e_i(t)$ is an eligibility trace for neuron i, and map_{xy} represents the observed cost for traversing the location (x, y), which corresponds to neuron i. This rule is applied for each of the neighboring neurons, j, of neuron i. By using this method of axonal plasticity, the agent can simultaneously explore and learn, adapting to changes in the environment. The loss in Eq. 5 is map_{xy} - D_{ij}.

The eligibility trace for neuron i is given by Eq. 6:

$$e_i(t+1) = \begin{cases} 1 & if \ v_j(t) \geq 1 \\ e_i(t) - \frac{e_i(t)}{\tau} & otherwise \end{cases} \tag{6}$$

where τ is the rate of decay for the eligibility trace. The setting of τ will be explored in Sect. 3.1.

2.3   Extracting a Path from the Spike Wavefront Algorithm

We illustrate the spiking wavefront algorithm with a simple example (Fig. 1). In this example, there is a 4 × 4 spiking neural network that has converged to a learned representation of the space (Fig. 1A). The inner section of the environment contains an obstacle that is twice as costly to traverse than the outer section.

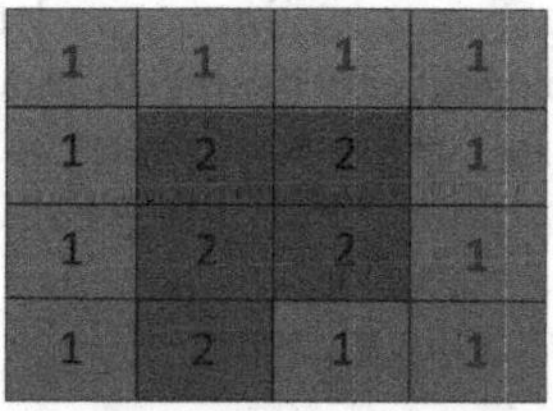

B.

time	neuron id
1	(1, 1)
2	(2, 1)
2	(1, 2)
3	(3, 1)
3	(2, 2)
3	(1, 3)
4	(4, 1)
4	(3, 2)
4	(2, 3)
4	(1, 4)
5	(4, 2)
5	(2, 4)
6	(3, 4)
7	(3, 3)
7	(4, 4)

A.

1	1	1	1
1	2	2	1
1	2	2	1
1	2	1	1

Fig. 1. Simple example with a 4×4 neural network. A neuron is connected to its 4 neighbors (North, South, East, West). The numbers denote the learned axonal delays between each neuron and its neighbors. The task is to find a path from (1,1) to (4,4). The resulting path found by the spike wave propagation algorithm is denoted in red font. A. 4×4 neural network representing a simple environment. The delays, which correspond to a cost map of the environment, are numbered. B. Example of using the spike table for extracting a path from (1,1) to (4,4). The extracted path is shown in red font. (Color figure online)

To extract a path from these learned delay-encoded costs, the neuron corresponding to the current location (1,1) is induced to spike. This causes an input current to be sent to neighboring neurons, starting a traveling wave of activity across the area covered by the grid. As each neuron spikes, the spike index and the time of spike are logged in a table. Figure 1B illustrates how this information is used to trace a path from the start to the goal location (4,4). To extract a path from the spike table, a list of neuron IDs is maintained, starting with the goal neuron. The first spike time of the goal neuron is found (see Fig. 1B). Then, the timestamps are decremented until the spiking of a neuron neighboring the goal neuron is found. The process then continues by finding spikes of neurons neighboring the most recent neuron. The process is repeated until the start neuron is found. The result is an optimal path between the start and goal (see red font in Fig. 1B).

3   Results

The spiking wave propagation algorithm with E-Prop learning was tested in two different environments: 1) Human navigation in a virtual maze [3], and 2) Rodent navigation in the Tolman detour maze [1]. We simulated their experimental protocols and compared the simulation results with the human and rodent experimental results.

3.1   Simulating Human Navigation and Taking Novel Shortcuts

In [3], human participants navigated through a virtual hedge maze where they first took several laps on a fixed path, which we will refer to as the "learned route" in the remainder of the paper, and then were tested by how well they could navigate between locations (Fig. 2). Along the learned route, there were landmarks, such as a chair, mailbox, potted plant, and picnic table. During the test phase, participants were placed at one landmark and told to navigate to another landmark. Some subjects took learned routes to landmarks, and others took novel shortcuts to landmarks. In another experiment, participants were told to take the shortest path to a landmark. This resulted in more participants taking novel shortcuts, and suggested that participants had survey knowledge, an allocentric mental map of the environment, even if they had previously not chosen to express this knowledge.

Fig. 2. Maps derived from a virtual environment used in human navigation studies [3]. A. Map is a 13 × 13 grid. Yellow denotes the border, orange denotes untraversable areas, and blue denotes traversable areas. B. Green denotes the fixed route learned by participants. C. Green denotes landmark locations. (Color figure online)

We converted the virtual maze into a 13 × 13 grid of Cartesian coordinates, which corresponded to a spiking neural network of the same size. Similar to [3], we forced the model to take a fixed tour of the environment by presenting the path planning algorithm with starting and ending locations that were close by and along a straight line. The weights of the spiking neural network, which correspond to axonal delays, were initially set to 10. Through repeated application of E-Prop learning, the weights began to reflect the costs associated with maze features (i.e., traversable regions, boundaries, and obstacles).

The performance of the spike wave propagation algorithm with E-Prop learning is dependent on the amount of training and how long neurons are eligible for updates. We tested the sensitivity of the algorithm by varying the number of loops on the learned route and the time constant of the eligibility trace (τ in Eq. 6). Similar to the human study, after these training loops, starting and goal locations, which corresponded to landmarks (Fig. 2C), were presented to the algorithm. We chose 24 starting and goal pairs. Navigation errors were defined as the number of times the path calculated by the algorithm attempted to navigate over untraversable regions, such as obstacles or outside the maze borders.

These errors indicated how well the spiking neural network learned the maze layout. With some training and a long enough time constant, the neural network learned the maze well enough that there were little or no navigation errors. Based on these exploratory results, we used 6 loops over the learned route and a time constant τ equal to 25 for the remainder of the simulations.

During experience on the learned route, the activity of the spiking neural network reflected the uncertainty of maze features. This could be observed in the number of neurons eligible for updates. For example on the first loop, more neurons were activated during path planning than on the sixth loop (Fig. 3). The path planning algorithm propagated a wave of neural activity based on the weights corresponding to axonal delays. Therefore, early in the training experience, when features of the maze were unknown, more neurons became active and eligible (see Eq. 6). However, later in the training, these eligible neurons were confined to the learned route, as well as regions near the learned route that could lead to novel shortcuts.

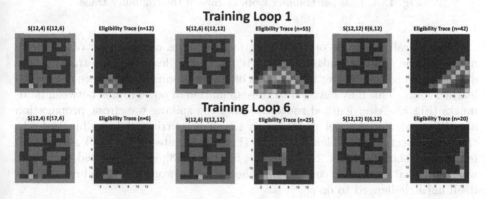

Fig. 3. Left panels. Path calculated by the spike wave algorithm for segments of the learned route. The text S(row,col) and E(row,col) above each figure denotes the starting and ending locations, respectively. Right panels. Active neurons during the path planning. The pixels denote neurons with hotter colors corresponding to more recently active neurons according to the eligibility trace. Dark blue pixels denote inactive neurons. The number of eligible neurons is denoted by n in the text above the figure. (Color figure online)

As learning progressed, the total loss (map_{xy} - D_{ij} in Eq. 5) decreased, which meant the network was learning the maze features, and the number of eligible neurons decreased (Fig. 4). We suggest that the eligibility trace is qualitatively similar to VTE and hippocampal preplay. When the agent was uncertain about the path, there were more neurons active, reflecting a number of alternative routes. This is somewhat like the neural correlates of VTE that have been observed in rodent hippocampus during early exposure to an environment [8,14]. After exposure, the neural activity was mostly confined to the route taken.

This is somewhat like preplay activity observed in rodent hippocampus when the animal is familiar with an environment [13,14].

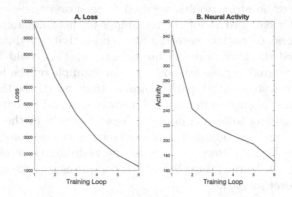

Fig. 4. A. Loss per training loop. B. Size of the eligibility trace.

The neural correlates of VTE may facilitate the construction of cognitive maps and the ability to take novel shortcuts. During learned route training, the eligible neurons spilled over into regions of the environment that were not on the learned route. This may have led to the calculation of novel routes between landmarks (Fig. 5). After learned route training, the spiking wavefront propagation algorithm calculated novel shortcuts on 12 out of 24 trials. Adding blockades to the middle section of the learned route (i.e., coordinates $(2,7)$, $(7,7)$ and $(12,7)$) led to more shortcuts (i.e., 15 out of 24). Similar to [3], this suggested that there was additional knowledge contained in the neural network, which did not express itself until challenged to do so.

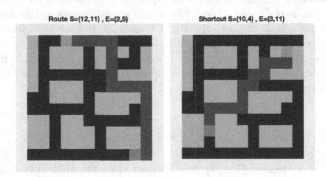

Fig. 5. Paths calculated between landmarks. Left. Path along the learned route. Right. Novel shortcut.

3.2   Simulating Rodent Navigation in Tolman Detour Task

In the Tolman detour task, rats were required to choose detours when well-known paths were blocked. Initially, rats were trained to run along a straight corridor from a start location to a goal location (from A to B in Fig. 6A). After training, rats needed to plan a detour path when barriers were placed along the original path. If the barrier was placed at P1, the rat could only use the long detour to get from A to B. But if the barrier was placed at P2, the rat might choose either the long detour on the right or the short detour on the left.

We constructed an environment to simulate the Tolman maze. The corridors had a cost of 1 (blue regions in Fig. 6A), the maze borders had a cost of 120 (yellow regions in Fig. 6A). During the detour test, the barriers, P1 or P2, were placed at (5,7) and (7,7), respectively and the cost was set to 120. The weights in the neural network were initialized to 5.

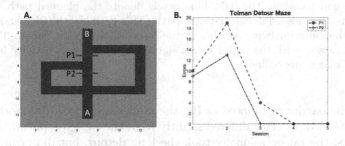

Fig. 6. Tolman detour maze task. A. The maze used in the rodent and modeling experiments. The agent is trained to go from A to B. After training, a barrier is placed at P1 or P2. B. Errors during navigation with barriers at P1 or P2. Each session denotes 4 trials from A to B.

During training, the spiking wave propagation algorithm with E-Prop learned a path from A to B over 20 trials. After training, a barrier was placed at P1 or P2. Then the spike wave propagation algorithm underwent 20 additional trials to plan paths from A to B.

The spiking wave propagation algorithm with E-Prop quickly learned the best detour given the barrier (Fig. 6B). Each session contained 4 trials where the spike wave propagation planned a path from A to B. Errors were whenever the planned path went outside the corridor or attempted to traverse through a barrier. Backtracking and re-routing after an error occurred was not simulated. After the first 2 sessions, the agent planned mostly error-free paths.

Similar to rodent experiments [1], when the barrier was placed at P1, the agent took the longer detour (left panels of Fig. 7). Like the rat, the agent attempted to travel straight from A to B when the barrier was introduced. By the 10th trial, the agent took the longer detour to reach its goal. Note how the number of timesteps (TS), the path length (PL), and the loss (see Eq. 5) decreased with the number of trials.

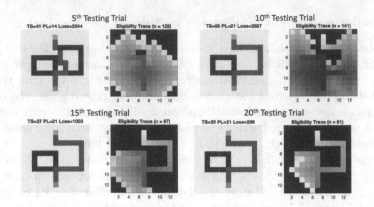

Fig. 7. Tolman detour maze task with barrier placed at P1. Left panels. The path planned by the agent. The cyan pixel denotes the start location, and the green pixel denotes the end location. The light blue pixels denote the planned path. Title text contains timesteps needed to calculate the path (TS), path length (PL), and loss when comparing the neural network weights to the maze values. Right panels. The eligible neurons are shown, with the hotter colors signifying more recent activity in the path planning. (Color figure online)

When the barrier was placed at P2, the model agent took the shorter detour (left panels of Fig. 8). This differed slightly from the rat experiments. In the rat experiments, the rat occasionally took the long detour, but did favor the short detour. This could be simulated by including prior preferences or adding noise to the model. By trial 10, the spiking wave propagation algorithm exclusively planned paths along the shorter detour. Similar to when the barrier was placed at P1, the timesteps (TS), path length (PL), and loss decreased as trials progressed.

Introducing a barrier forced the agent to learn alternative routes. This uncertainty was reflected in the eligibility trace of the neural network model (right panels of Fig. 7 and Fig. 8). In the first few trials, the model was exploring possible alternatives. We suggest this neural activity is comparable to VTE in the hippocampus. By trial 15 and later, activity was mainly confined to the path to be taken by the agent. We suggest that this is more akin to preplay in the hippocampus. Taken together, these results show how the spiking wave propagation algorithm with E-Prop can rapidly adapt and re-route when changes occur. Furthermore, the uncertainty and consideration of alternative routes can be observed in the neural network activity.

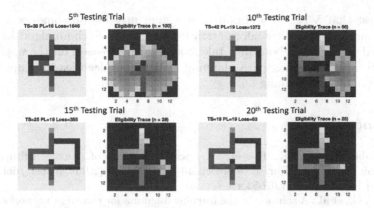

Fig. 8. Tolman detour maze with barrier placed at P2. Notations same as in Fig. 7.

4 Discussion

A hallmark of cognitive behavior is flexible planning [12]. In the present study, we show that a path planning algorithm from robotics, coupled with a biologically plausible learning rule, could demonstrate flexible path planning, and generate neural correlates of assessing alternatives when faced with uncertainty. The spiking wavefront propagation path planner presented here has been used for robot navigation [7], and to simulate human navigation [10]. Unlike other path planners, the spiking wavefront algorithm is a network of spiking neurons that is compatible with power efficient neuromorphic hardware, as was shown its implementation on the IBM TrueNorth NS1e [6]. Although evidence suggests that these activations occur sequentially [14], wavefront propagation operates in parallel, which can speed up processing. This has practical applications for autonomous systems operating at the edge and may be of interest to follow up experimentally now that more neurons can be recorded simultaneously.

The present work explores how a biologically plausible learning rule [2], specifically designed for spiking neural networks, could extend the spiking wavefront propagation algorithm. Rather than having learning be related to changes in synaptic efficacy, the present algorithm changed the delays between pre- and post-synaptic neurons. This was inspired by evidence suggesting that the myelin sheath, which wraps around and insulates axons, undergoes a form of activity-dependent plasticity [5]. Although, we are not suggesting that hippocampal learning is solely due to changes in conductance velocity, it is an intriguing form of plasticity rarely applied to neural networks that also provides a simple and effective method of explainability and uncertainty quantification.

The spiking wavefront propagation path planner presented here has activity similar to neural correlates of VTE: 1) It is more prominent during early learning and when faced with environmental challenges or uncertainty. 2) The wave of activity propagates to alternative choices, and 3) After experience, the wave of activity more resembles preplay in that it becomes confined to the future choice.

We suggest that VTE, in addition to weighing possible outcomes is a way in which an agent may gather information for future use. Such an algorithm could be applied to mobile robots that take cost, which is based on the application goals, into account during path planning rather than deep learning approaches that require off-line training [9].

References

1. Alvernhe, A., Save, E., Poucet, B.: Local remapping of place cell firing in the Tolman detour task. Eur. J. Neurosci. **33**(9), 1696–705 (2011). https://doi.org/10.1111/j.1460-9568.2011.07653.x
2. Bellec, G., et al.: A solution to the learning dilemma for recurrent networks of spiking neurons. Nat. Commun. **11**(1), 3625 (2020). https://doi.org/10.1038/s41467-020-17236-y
3. Boone, A.P., Maghen, B., Hegarty, M.: Instructions matter: individual differences in navigation strategy and ability. Mem. Cogn. **47**(7), 1401–1414 (2019). https://doi.org/10.3758/s13421-019-00941-5
4. Dragoi, G., Tonegawa, S.: Preplay of future place cell sequences by hippocampal cellular assemblies. Nature **469**(7330), 397–401 (2011). https://doi.org/10.1038/nature09633
5. Fields, R.D.: A new mechanism of nervous system plasticity: activity-dependent myelination. Nat. Rev. Neurosci. **16**(12), 756–67 (2015). https://doi.org/10.1038/nrn4023
6. Fischl, K.D., Fair, K., Tsai, W., Sampson, J., Andreou, A.: Path planning on the truenorth neurosynaptic system. In: 2017 IEEE International Symposium on Circuits and Systems (ISCAS), pp. 1–4 (2017). https://doi.org/10.1109/ISCAS.2017.8050932
7. Hwu, T., Wang, A.Y., Oros, N., Krichmar, J.L.: Adaptive robot path planning using a spiking neuron algorithm with axonal delays. IEEE Trans. Cogn. Develop. Syst. **10**(2), 126–137 (2018). https://doi.org/10.1109/Tcds.2017.2655539
8. Johnson, A., Redish, A.D.: Neural ensembles in CA3 transiently encode paths forward of the animal at a decision point. J. Neurosci. **27**(45), 12176–89 (2007). https://doi.org/10.1523/JNEUROSCI.3761-07.2007
9. Kahn, G., Abbeel, P., Levine, S.: BADGR: an autonomous self-supervised learning-based navigation system. arXiv:2002.05700 (2020)
10. Krichmar, J.L., He, C.: Importance of path planning variability: a simulation study. Top. Cogn. Sci. (2021). https://doi.org/10.1111/tops.12568
11. Mattar, M.G., Daw, N.D.: Prioritized memory access explains planning and hippocampal replay. Nat. Neurosci. **21**(11), 1609–1617 (2018). https://doi.org/10.1038/s41593-018-0232-z
12. Miller, K.J., Venditto, S.J.C.: Multi-step planning in the brain. Curr. Opin. Behav. Sci. **38**, 29–39 (2021). https://doi.org/10.1016/j.cobeha.2020.07.003
13. Pfeiffer, B.E., Foster, D.J.: Hippocampal place-cell sequences depict future paths to remembered goals. Nature **497**(7447), 74–9 (2013). https://doi.org/10.1038/nature12112
14. Redish, A.D.: Vicarious trial and error. Nat. Rev. Neurosci. **17**(3), 147–59 (2016). https://doi.org/10.1038/nrn.2015.30

15. Stachenfeld, K.L., Botvinick, M.M., Gershman, S.J.: The hippocampus as a predictive map. Nat. Neurosci. **20**(11), 1643–1653 (2017). https://doi.org/10.1038/nn.4650
16. Tolman, E.C.: Cognitive maps in rats and men. Psychol. Rev. **55**(4), 189–208 (1948). https://doi.org/10.1037/H0061626

Affective and Social Cognition
and Collective Intelligence

Impact of the Update Time
on the Aggregation of Robotic Swarms
Through Informed Robots

Antoine Sion[1]($\boxtimes$) , Andreagiovanni Reina[2] , Mauro Birattari[2] ,
and Elio Tuci[1]

[1] Faculty of Computer Science, University of Namur, Namur, Belgium
{antoine.sion,elio.tuci}@unamur.be
[2] IRIDIA, Université Libre de Bruxelles, Brussels, Belgium
{andreagiovanni.reina,mauro.birattari}@ulb.be

Abstract. Self-organised aggregation is one of the basic collective
behaviours studied in swarm robotics. In this paper, we investigate an
aggregation problem occurring on two different sites. Previous studies
have shown that a minority of robots, informed about the site on which
they have to aggregate, can control the final distribution of the entire
robot swarm on the sites. We reproduce this strategy by adapting the
previous probabilistic finite-state machine to a new simulated robotic
platform: the Kilobot. Our simulation results highlight that the update
time (i.e., the amount of time a robot waits before making a decision on
leaving a site) impacts the dynamics of the aggregation process. Namely,
a longer update time lowers the number of robots wandering in the arena,
but can slow down the dynamics when the target final distribution is far
from the one initially formed. To ensure a low number of wandering
robots while maintaining a quick convergence towards the target final
distribution of the swarm, we introduce the concept of a dynamic update
time increasing during the aggregation process.

1 Introduction

Swarm robotics studies the coordination of decentralised robot swarms displaying self-organised collective behaviours emerging from local interactions between
the agents. The goal is to design swarms that are robust to the loss of robots,
scalable in size, and flexible to different environments and tasks [2]. Several basic
collective behaviours have been identified and studied in robotic swarms such
as collective motion, task allocation, pattern formation, or consensus [16,25]. In
this paper, we study an aggregation behaviour. This collective behaviour is often
a prerequisite used to group a part or the totality of the swarm physically before
starting another behaviour requiring the proximity of the robots [27]. Two types
of control systems have been used to achieve aggregation in swarms of robots:
probabilistic finite-state machines and artificial neural networks. The first one
is inspired by biology studies that investigate the aggregation behaviours of

L. Cañamero et al. (Eds.): SAB 2022, LNAI 13499, pp. 193–204, 2022.
https://doi.org/10.1007/978-3-031-16770-6_16

animals like cockroaches [17] or bees [28] and have been adapted to robotic systems [14,27]. The second one employs neural networks as controllers to generate aggregation behaviours through training in simulation [7,13].

The controller used in this paper is a probabilistic finite-state machine composed of simple states such as leaving a site or exploring the environment (see Fig. 1a). We study an aggregation problem on two distinct sites where a swarm of robots is equipped with the controller of Fig. 1a. A minority of robots in the swarm are informed about which of the two sites they have to aggregate on. Black-informed robots selectively avoid to aggregate on the white site and only aggregate on the black site, and white-informed robots avoid the black site and only aggregate on the white site. By adjusting the ratio of informed robots choosing to aggregate exclusively on the black or the white site, the designer can bias the entire swarm to reach a target distribution (e.g., 70% of robots on the black site and 30% on the white site). This method used to steer the group dynamic of the aggregation process is inspired by collective behaviours observed in biology where a minority of individuals aware of pertinent environmental information dictate the group behaviour [3,5]. The concept of informed robots has already been applied to a number of diverse collective behaviours in swarm robotics such as flocking [4,8,9], collective decision making [6,22] or, as in our study, self-organised aggregation [10–12,15].

Firat et al. [10,11] originally introduced informed robots in an aggregation task on two sites in order for the entire swarm to aggregate on only one of them. Informed robots in this study were programmed to aggregate on only one of the two sites. This was extended by another study [12] allowing informed robots to be divided in two groups reflecting the target final distribution on the two sites. In parallel, an analytical model for this problem was developed by Gillet et al. [15], showing that the quantity of informed robots needed to have an effect on the final distribution was dependent of the site carrying capacity. In subsequent work [26], we simplified the controller designed by Firat et al. [12] by employing a memoryless reactive controller based on a simpler communication protocol, and we conducted a comparative study showing that the novel controller resulted in a more flexible behaviour of the swarm, together with equal or better performance compared to the original controller.

Our end goal is to implement this controller on physical robots on a different robotic platform than the one used in [26] to show that the controller is not robot-specific but generic for other mobile robots capable of minimal motion and minimal communication. Moreover, in swarm robotics, the validation of the simulated controller on the physical robots is of paramount importance due to the so-called reality gap. This gap generally translates in a performance drop when porting the control software on the physical robots due to the differences between the simulation and the real world [19]. In this paper, we adapt the controller to the new robotic platform by taking into account the different sensors, actuators and programming language while keeping the same individual behaviour found in [26]. Then, we recreate the experimental setup in simulation to validate our modifications. In this study, we also investigate the impact of the update time on the aggregation dynamics of the swarm: our results indicate a trade-off between the speed of the aggregation process and the number of robots not aggregating on any of the two sites when the system has reached a stable final distribution. Finally, we propose a new simple method acting on the update time to avoid a slowdown of the dynamics while keeping the number of robots wandering in the arena low; fast convergence of the number of robots on the sites is indeed required to stay inside the limits of the robots' battery autonomy. Our methodology is presented in Sect. 2 along the robotic platform and our results in Sect. 3.

2   Materials and Methods

The scenario we consider investigates the aggregation process of a swarm of 50 robots inside a squared arena containing a black and a white site (see Fig. 1b). We control the aggregation by introducing a bias in the swarm through the use of a minority of informed robots. Informed robots are robots that are programmed to selectively aggregate on one of the two sites only. With a swarm of size N containing N_{sb} black-informed robots only aggregating on the black site and N_{sw} white-informed robots only aggregating on the white site, we can define the proportion of informed robots in the swarm by $\rho_I = \frac{N_{sb}+N_{sw}}{N}$. In a similar manner, the proportion of black-informed robots and white-informed robots relative to the total number of informed robots are defined as $\rho_{sb} = \frac{N_{sb}}{N_{sb}+N_{sw}}$ and $\rho_{sw} = \frac{N_{sw}}{N_{sb}+N_{sw}}$, respectively. Starting from positions and orientations randomly chosen in the arena following a uniform distribution, the swarm should redistribute itself on the aggregation sites to obtain a final distribution of the robots approaching $N \times \rho_{sb}$ on the black site and $N \times \rho_{sw}$ on the white site.

The robotic platform used for the implementation of our controller is the Kilobot [24], which is a low-cost robot designed to facilitate the testing of collective behaviours requiring a large number of robots (see Fig. 1c). Two vibrations motors are used for locomotion, allowing a forward speed of $1\,\mathrm{cm/s}$ and a rotation speed of $45\,°/\mathrm{s}$. The robot is also equipped with an infrared LED emitter and an infrared photodiode receiver which allow communication between robots up to $10\,\mathrm{cm}$ by sending light that reflects on the ground. There is also a visible light sensor on the top of the robot and a three-colour LED to visualise the state in which the robot is. These robots are widely employed also because they can easily be programmed in batches using an overhead controller that sends infrared messages.

While it is user friendly, the Kilobots are limited by the simplicity of their sensors. This restricts the types of experiments that can be performed with the robots as they can not get feedback on their physical environment (other than with the light sensor). To overcome this problem, solutions have been proposed such as the ARK system [23] which allows the use of virtual sensors through an overhead controller and a camera tracking system. In this paper, we equip the Kilobots with virtual sensors using the Kilogrid [29]; an electronic table made of a grid of infrared modules allowing communication to and from the Kilobots. Each module ($10\,\mathrm{cm} \times 10\,\mathrm{cm}$) is divided equally into four cells, each capable of

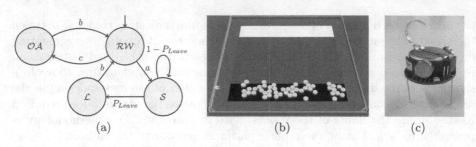

(a)   (b)   (c)

Fig. 1. (a) The probabilistic finite-state machine controller composed of four states: Random Walk ($\mathcal{RW}$), Stay ($\mathcal{S}$), Leave ($\mathcal{L}$) and Obstacle Avoidance ($\mathcal{OA}$). Letters in lowercase represent events triggering the transition between states: a is finding a suitable site for aggregating, b is getting out of a site or the obstacle area, and c is entering the obstacle area. P_{Leave} is the probability to leave the site as described in Eq. (2). (b) The simulated Kilogrid with a swarm of 50 Kilobots, an aggregation site in white, an aggregation site in black, the obstacle area in red and a neutral area in blue. (c) The Kilobot robot. (Color figure online)

communicating with the Kilobots above them. Each cell is also equipped with two RGB LEDs that can be colored to inform the user. The Kilogrid monitors continuously the position and state of each Kilobot, and allows the implementation of virtual sensors measuring different values in each cell (e.g. to measure the humidity or the temperature of a virtual environment). The Kilobots are also able to modify the environment by sending messages to the current cell that will be processed as actions.

Experiments were performed using the ARGoS simulator [21] with the ARGoS-Kilobot plugin to model the Kilobots [20], and the ARGoS-Kilogrid plugin [1] which allow the use of identical code in simulation and on the real Kilobots and Kilogrid. In our previous experimental scenario [26], the arena was a circle with two circular aggregation sites. Here, we test a different environment with a squared arena of $100 \times 100 \, cm^2$ (Fig. 1b) allowing experimentation with swarms of 50 Kilobots. The two aggregation sites are stripes positioned symmetrically at the edges of the arena. One stripe stands for the white site and the other one for the black site. Each stripe is composed of 16×3 Kilogrid cells, corresponding to $80 \times 15 \, cm^2$. We added a red zone with a width of 2 Kilogrid cells (10 cm) around the perimeter of the arena which acts as an obstacle for the Kilobots. Once in the red area, the robots enter a state of obstacle avoidance until they get back inside the arena. The use of the Kilogrid enhances the capabilities of the Kilobots with virtual ground sensors: each cell broadcasts continuously its colour which is received by the robots present at the location.

We reproduced the controller from [26] which is a probabilistic finite-state machine composed of three states and we added a state of obstacle avoidance for the walls of the arena (Fig. 1a). The robot can be in the state: ($\mathcal{RW}$) random walk during which it explores the environment, ($\mathcal{S}$) stay during which it aggregates on a site, ($\mathcal{L}$) leave during which it gets out of a site, and ($\mathcal{OA}$) obstacle avoidance during which it gets out of the obstacle area. Different from [26], in our experimental setup, the Kilobots are not equipped with physical sensors capable of detecting the position of other close robots or obstacles. Therefore, the controller used in this paper does not implement a collision avoidance scheme between the robots. However, to keep the robots from getting stuck on the walls of the arena, we added the $\mathcal{OA}$ state which triggers as soon as the robots enter the red area surrounding the environment and allows the robot to get out of it. This differs from [26] where robots can directly detect close obstacles with their physical sensors and avoid them while in any state of the probabilistic finite-state machine.

The initial state is random walk ($\mathcal{RW}$); in this state, the robot explores the environment following an isotropic random walk with turning angles obtained from a wrapped Cauchy distribution [18] with the following density function:

$$f_\omega(\theta, \mu, \rho) = \frac{1}{2\pi} \frac{1 - \rho^2}{1 + \rho^2 - 2\rho \cos(\theta - \mu)}, 0 < \rho < 1, \tag{1}$$

with μ the average value of the distribution and ρ the skewness. At $\rho = 0$, the distribution becomes uniform and the turning angles of the robot are not correlated. At $\rho = 1$, the distribution becomes a Dirac distribution and the robot's path is a straight line. In this paper, we use $\rho = 0.5$. We define a fixed step length by taking a step duration of $10\,\mathrm{s}$ (the Kilobot average speed is $1\,\mathrm{cm/s}$). If the robot enters a valid aggregation site (any site if it is non-informed, the white site if it is white-informed or the black site if it is black-informed), it transitions from state $\mathcal{RW}$ to state $\mathcal{S}$. During this transition, it continues to move straight during $10\,\mathrm{s}$ to avoid aggregating on the border of the site.

While in state $\mathcal{S}$, the robot stops moving and signals its presence to other robots by broadcasting infrared messages containing its unique ID. At the same time, it receives messages from other robots resting in the nearby neighbourhood (the maximum communication range of the Kilobot is $10\,\mathrm{cm}$). Each time the robot receives a message with a new ID, it stores this ID in an array. Periodically, every update period of length T_{update}, it estimates n, the local number of robots, by counting the total number of unique messages received. This number is then used to compute the probability to leave the site:

$$P_{Leave} = \begin{cases} \alpha e^{-\beta n} & \text{for non-informed robots} \\ 0 & \text{for informed robots} \end{cases} \tag{2}$$

where $\alpha = 0.5$ and $\beta = 2.25$. The higher is the number of robots in the local neighbourhood, the higher is the probability to stay on the site. Informed robots do not leave their site after finding it. After sampling the probability, the robot stays in state $\mathcal{S}$ or transitions to state $\mathcal{L}$.

In state $\mathcal{L}$, the robot tries to leave the aggregation site by moving forward. Once out, it transitions to state $\mathcal{RW}$. In some cases where the robot is encircled by a cluster of other robots, it will not be able to get out of the site. To avoid a situation where the robot tries to go forward indefinitely but cannot get out of the cluster, we implemented a timer limiting the time spent in state $\mathcal{L}$. If after $30\,\mathrm{s}$, the robot is not outside the site, it transitions back to state $\mathcal{S}$.

The robot can also transition from state $\mathcal{RW}$ to state $\mathcal{OA}$ by entering the obstacle area near the surrounding walls. In state $\mathcal{OA}$, the robot first turns left for 4 s, then moves straight for 10 s. Once the robot is out of the obstacle area, it transitions to state $\mathcal{RW}$. If not, it repeats the operation. Our simulation experiments show that this simple method is sufficient to allow the Kilobots to exit the obstacle area.

3 Results

This section discusses the impact of the update time on the dynamics of the swarm for all configurations of the parameters found in Table 1. We run 50 trials for each combination of these parameters. The swarm size is set to $N = 50$ robots and the proportion of informed robots in the swarm to $\rho_I = 0.3$. We vary the update time $T_{update} = \{2\,\text{s}, 8\,\text{s}\}$ for different proportions of black/white informed robots: $\rho_{sb} = \{0.5, 0.7, 1\}$, and $\rho_{sw} = 1 - \rho_{sb}$. The robots are randomly placed at the start of the simulation in the neutral area (the blue area in Fig. 1b) following a uniform distribution. The time length of the simulation experiments is set to 5 h to capture the slow convergence of the system occurring in some cases, even if the battery autonomy of the real robots is limited to 2.5 h. After discussing the obtained results, we also propose a simple method to drive the convergence of the swarm towards the target final distribution in a shorter time while limiting the number of wandering robots in the arena.

Table 1. Parameters values

Experiment parameters	Values
Swarm size (N)	$\{50\}$
Proportion of informed robots (ρ_I)	$\{0.3\}$
Proportion of black informed robots (ρ_{sb})	$\{0.5, 0.7, 1\}$
Update time (T_{update})	$\{2, 8\}$ s

Figure 2 shows the evolution of the numbers of robots aggregated on the white site and the black site as well as the number of robots wandering in the arena in function of the time. In all graphs, the solid black lines are the median and the interquartile range of the number of robots aggregated on the black site over the 50 trials. The same applies for the number of robots aggregated on the white site in grey and the number of wandering robots in blue. We set T_{update} to 2 s in Figs. 2a, 2c, 2e and to 8 s in Figs. 2b, 2d, 2f. The proportion of informed robots staying on the black site is set to $\rho_{sb} = 0.5$ in Figs. 2a and 2b, to $\rho_{sb} = 0.7$ in Figs. 2c and 2d and to $\rho_{sb} = 1$ in Figs. 2e and 2f. The target final distributions of the swarm at the end of the experiment for these proportions are, respectively, 25 robots on each site; 35 robots on the black site and 15 on the white site; 50 robots on the black site.

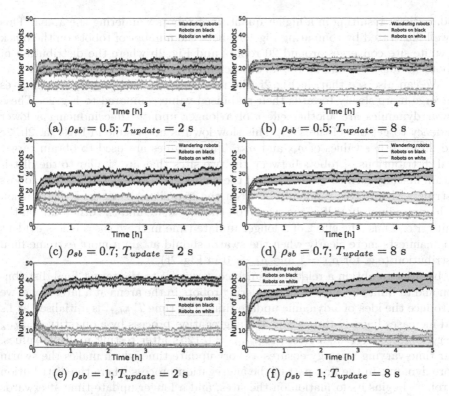

(a) $\rho_{sb} = 0.5$; $T_{update} = 2$ s

(b) $\rho_{sb} = 0.5$; $T_{update} = 8$ s

(c) $\rho_{sb} = 0.7$; $T_{update} = 2$ s

(d) $\rho_{sb} = 0.7$; $T_{update} = 8$ s

(e) $\rho_{sb} = 1$; $T_{update} = 2$ s

(f) $\rho_{sb} = 1$; $T_{update} = 8$ s

Fig. 2. Evolution over time of the number of robots over 50 trials for $\rho_I = 0.3$. $T_{update} = 2$ s on the graphs of the first column and $T_{update} = 8$ s on the graphs of the second column. $\rho_{sb} = 0.5$ in the first row, $\rho_{sb} = 0.7$ in the second row and $\rho_{sb} = 1$ in the third row. The solid grey lines represent the median and the interquartile range of the number of robots aggregated on the white site. The same applies to the black lines corresponding to the number of robots aggregated on the black site and the blue lines corresponding to the number of wandering robots.

The dynamics of the system are the following. The numbers of robots aggregated on the sites increase rapidly in the first phase of the simulation. Afterwards, they vary slowly before stabilising around a certain value. In the graphs of the left column of Fig. 2, the median of the number of robots not aggregated on any of the two sites and wandering in the environment decreases quickly (as a consequence of robots aggregating on the two sites), and then remains stable throughout the simulation around a value of 10 robots. The same occurs for the graphs of the right column of Fig. 2 but the number of wandering robots stabilises around 5. This effect is due to the longer update time of 8 s which improves the total number of robots staying on the sites. A robot with a short update time has more occasions to sample the probability to leave the site in a given time frame, compared to a robot having a longer update time. Thus, the proportion of robots staying at a site that choose to leave is higher for shorter update time, resulting in a higher quantity of robots wandering the arena. This is well illustrated by comparing Fig. 2a where the number of robots on the black or white site converges around 20 robots and Fig. 2b where the distribution of robots stabilises around 22 robots on each site.

We can also see that, in Fig. 2f, the numbers of robots staying on the sites converge more slowly towards their stabilised value compared to Fig. 2e. These slower dynamics are another effect of a longer update time inducing a lower tendency to get out of the sites. This slowdown is not visible in Figs. 2a, 2b, 2c and 2d for other values of ρ_{sb} and ρ_{sw}. These values are used to obtain target final distributions of robots between the two sites that are similar to the distribution initially formed at the start of the aggregation process, where the robots distribute themselves randomly between the two sites, hence in a distribution with approximately half of the swarm on the black site and the other half on the white site. Thus, the effect of a longer update time in these cases is less evident but manifests more clearly when the swarm should attain a more extreme final distribution (e.g. for $\rho_{sb} = 1$ and $\rho_{sw} = 0$ in Fig. 2f).

In order to obtain a relatively quick convergence to the target final distribution and to limit the number of wandering robots in the arena at a later stage, we introduce the idea of a dynamic update time. The time T_{update} is initialised at 1 s and increases linearly throughout the aggregation process by a quantity Δ_{update} every minute. Here we selected $\Delta_{update} = 0.125$ s after testing multiple values. Our time-varying strategy ensures a short update time which makes the swarm more dynamic in the first part of the aggregation process where the distribution of robots begins its formation on the sites, and a longer update time afterwards which lowers the probability of robots getting out of the sites and makes the swarm more static. Results for the same parameters described in Table 1 are shown in Fig. 3. For all graphs, the median of the number of wandering robots gradually decreases to attain a value of 5. Figure 3a shows a convergence of the median of the number of robots on both sites around a value of 22. In Fig. 3b, the median of the number of robots aggregated on the black site stabilises around 31 and the one for the white site around 14. In Fig. 3c, the median of the number of robots aggregated on the black site converges to 45 and the median of the number of robots aggregated on the white one to 0.

These results show that the performance of the swarm at attaining the target final distributions is improved by the use of our strategy of dynamic update time. In all studied cases, the number of wandering robots remain close to 5, as it was the case for a update time of 8 s. In addition, the use of a dynamic update time cancels the slow dynamics observed with a longer update time when the target final distribution was far from the one initially formed in the first phase of the aggregation process. The numbers of robots aggregated on the two sites stay stable after 2 h which will allow us to test our controller on the physical robots with an experiment time that do not exceed the Kilobot's battery autonomy.

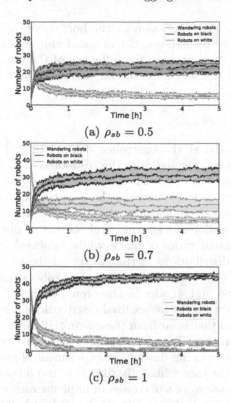

(a) $\rho_{sb} = 0.5$

(b) $\rho_{sb} = 0.7$

(c) $\rho_{sb} = 1$

Fig. 3. Evolution over time of the number of robots over 50 trials for $\rho_I = 0.3$, and different proportions of informed black robots: (a) $\rho_{sb} = 0.5$, (b) $\rho_{sb} = 0.7$ and (c) $\rho_{sb} = 1$ with a linear increase of the update time. The solid grey lines represent the median and the interquartile range of the number of robots aggregated on the white site. The same applies to the black lines corresponding to the number of robots aggregated on the black site and the blue lines corresponding to the number of wandering robots. (Color figure online)

In all the graphs, there is a small number of robots that do not aggregate on the sites. Visual inspection of the simulations show that this could be due to the nature of the robots used and the shape of the arena. No collision avoidance scheme is implemented on the Kilobots. When the aggregation has occurred and the numbers of robots aggregated on the sites are high, there is a higher probability for the remaining robots trying to enter a site to push other robots out of the site while entering. Furthermore, robots choosing to leave an already heavily populated site also have a higher probability to push other robots out of the site while getting out of it. This could explain the constant remaining number of wandering robots at the end of the experiment: even if new robots manage to aggregate on the sites, a small amount of aggregated robots are constantly being pushed out of the sites. Another cause could also be that the entrance of the few remaining robots into the already populated sites is hindered by the physical barrier formed by clusters of robots near the borders of the sites. Nevertheless, while we recognise that a small number of wandering robots always subsist at the end of the aggregation process, the influence of the informed robots on the dynamics is clearly visible as well as the impact of the update time.

4   Conclusions

We successfully reproduced the controller defined in [26] in simulation and adapted it to a second robotic platform, the Kilobot [24]. Namely, we introduced an obstacle avoidance state to avoid the edges of the arena and we removed the collision avoidance scheme between the robots. Through simulations, we conducted an empirical study showing the impact of the update time on the dynamics of the aggregation of a swarm of robots on two distinct sites. This was realised for three different ratios of black/white informed robots in the swarm targeting three final distributions of the swarm on the sites. Our results show that a longer update time reduces the number of robots that do not aggregate on any of the two sites and wander in the arena. However, this also induces a slower convergence towards the target final distributions when the swarm needs to attain a distribution that is far from the one initially formed in the first phase of the aggregation process. To solve this problem, we introduced a dynamic update time linearly increasing during the experiment. This resulted in a quick convergence towards the target final distributions and an overall low number of wandering robots. Future work will consist of implementing our controller on the physical robots in order to validate our results and evaluate its ability to cross the reality gap.

Acknowledgements. This work was supported by Service Public de Wallonie Recherche under grant n° 2010235 - ARIAC by DIGITALWALLONIA4.AI; by the European Research Council (ERC) under the European Union's Horizon 2020 research and innovation programme (grant agreement No. 681872); and by Belgium's Wallonia-Brussels Federation through the ARC Advanced Project GbO (Guaranteed by Optimization). AR and MB acknowledge the financial support from the Belgian F.R.S.-FNRS, of which they are Chargé de Recherches and Directeur de Recherches, respectively.

References

1. Aust, T., Talamali, M.S., Dorigo, M., Hamann, H., Reina, A.: The hidden benefits of limited communication and slow sensing in collective monitoring of dynamic environments. In: Swarm Intelligence (ANTS 2022). LNCS, vol. 13491. Springer (2022)
2. Brambilla, M., Ferrante, E., Birattari, M., Dorigo, M.: Swarm robotics: a review from the swarm engineering perspective. Swarm Intell. **7**(1), 1–41 (2013)
3. Calvo Martín, M., Eeckhout, M., Deneubourg, J.L., Nicolis, S.C.: Consensus driven by a minority in heterogenous groups of the cockroach periplaneta americana. iScience **24**(7), 102723 (2021)

4. Çelikkanat, H., Şahin, E.: Steering self-organized robot flocks through externally guided individuals. Neural Comput. App. **19**(6), 849–865 (2010)
5. Couzin, I.D., Krause, J., Franks, N.R., Levin, S.A.: Effective leadership and decision-making in animal groups on the move. Nature **433**, 513–516 (2005)
6. Masi, G.D., Prasetyo, J., Zakir, R., Mankovskii, N., Ferrante, E., Tuci, E.: Robot swarm democracy: the importance of informed individuals against zealots. Swarm Intell. **15**(4), 315–338 (2021). https://doi.org/10.1007/s11721-021-00197-3
7. Dorigo, M., et al.: Evolving self-organizing behaviors for a swarm-bot. Autonom. Robots **17**(2), 223–245 (2004)
8. Ferrante, E., Turgut, A.E., Huepe, C., Stranieri, A., Pinciroli, C., Dorigo, M.: Self-organized flocking with a mobile robot swarm: a novel motion control method. Adapt. Behav. **20**(6), 460–477 (2012)
9. Ferrante, E., Turgut, A.E., Stranieri, A., Pinciroli, C., Birattari, M., Dorigo, M.: A self-adaptive communication strategy for flocking in stationary and non-stationary environments. Natural Comput. **13**(2), 225–245 (2013). https://doi.org/10.1007/s11047-013-9390-9
10. Firat, Z., Ferrante, E., Cambier, N., Tuci, E.: Self-organised aggregation in swarms of robots with informed robots. In: Fagan, D., Martín-Vide, C., O'Neill, M., Vega-Rodríguez, M.A. (eds.) TPNC 2018. LNCS, vol. 11324, pp. 49–60. Springer, Cham (2018). https://doi.org/10.1007/978-3-030-04070-3_4
11. Firat, Z., Ferrante, E., Gillet, Y., Tuci, E.: On self-organised aggregation dynamics in swarms of robots with informed robots. Neural Comput. App. **32**(17), 13825–13841 (2020). https://doi.org/10.1007/s00521-020-04791-0
12. Firat, Z., Ferrante, E., Zakir, R., Prasetyo, J., Tuci, E.: Group-size regulation in self-organized aggregation in robot swarms. In: Dorigo, M., Stützle, T., Blesa, M.J., Blum, C., Hamann, H., Heinrich, M.K., Strobel, V. (eds.) ANTS 2020. LNCS, vol. 12421, pp. 315–323. Springer, Cham (2020). https://doi.org/10.1007/978-3-030-60376-2_26
13. Francesca, G., Brambilla, M., Trianni, V., Dorigo, M., Birattari, M.: Analysing an evolved robotic behaviour using a biological model of collegial decision making. In: Ziemke, T., Balkenius, C., Hallam, J. (eds.) SAB 2012. LNCS (LNAI), vol. 7426, pp. 381–390. Springer, Heidelberg (2012). https://doi.org/10.1007/978-3-642-33093-3_38
14. Garnier, S., Gautrais, J., Asadpour, M., Jost, C., Theraulaz, G.: Self-organized aggregation triggers collective decision making in a group of cockroach-like robots. Adapt. Behav. **17**(2), 109–133 (2009)
15. Gillet, Y., Ferrante, E., Firat, Z., Tuci, E.: Guiding aggregation dynamics in a swarm of agents via informed individuals: an analytical study. In: The 2019 Conference on Artificial Life: A Hybrid of the European Conference on Artificial Life (ECAL) and the International Conference on the Synthesis and Simulation of Living Systems (ALIFE), pp. 590–597. MIT Press (2019)
16. Hamann, H.: Swarm Robotics: A Formal Approach (2018)
17. Jeanson, R., et al.: Self-organized aggregation in cockroaches. Animal Behav. **69**(1), 169–180 (2005)
18. Kato, S., Jones, M.: An extended family of circular distributions related to wrapped Cauchy distributions via Brownian motion. Bernoulli **19**(1), 154–171 (2013)
19. Ligot, A., Birattari, M.: Simulation-only experiments to mimic the effects of the reality gap in the automatic design of robot swarms. Swarm Intell. **14**(1), 1–24 (2019). https://doi.org/10.1007/s11721-019-00175-w

20. Pinciroli, C., Talamali, M.S., Reina, A., Marshall, J.A.R., Trianni, V.: Simulating Kilobots Within ARGoS: models and experimental validation. In: Dorigo, M., Birattari, M., Blum, C., Christensen, A.L., Reina, A., Trianni, V. (eds.) ANTS 2018. LNCS, vol. 11172, pp. 176–187. Springer, Cham (2018). https://doi.org/10.1007/978-3-030-00533-7_14
21. Pinciroli, C., et al.: ARGoS: a modular, parallel, multi-engine simulator for multi-robot systems. Swarm Intell. **6**(4), 271–295 (2012)
22. Prasetyo, J., De Masi, G., Ferrante, E.: Collective decision making in dynamic environments. Swarm Intell. **13**(3), 217–243 (2019)
23. Reina, A., Cope, A.J., Nikolaidis, E., Marshall, J.A.R., Sabo, C.: ARK: augmented reality for Kilobots. IEEE Robot. Autom. Lett. **2**(3), 1755–1761 (2017)
24. Rubenstein, M., Ahler, C., Nagpal, R.: Kilobot: a low cost scalable robot system for collective behaviors. In: 2012 IEEE International Conference on Robotics and Automation, pp. 3293–3298 (2012)
25. Schranz, M., Umlauft, M., Sende, M., Elmenreich, W.: Swarm robotic behaviors and current applications. Front. Robot. AI **7**, 36 (2020)
26. Sion, A., Reina, A., Birattari, M., Tuci, E.: Controlling robot swarm aggregation through a minority of informed robots. In: Swarm Intelligence (ANTS 2022). LNCS, vol. 13491. Springer (2022)
27. Soysal, O., Şahin, E.: Probabilistic aggregation strategies in swarm robotic systems. In: Proceedings 2005 IEEE Swarm Intelligence Symposium, 2005. SIS 2005, pp. 325–332 (2005)
28. Szopek, M., Schmickl, T., Thenius, R., Radspieler, G., Crailsheim, K.: Dynamics of collective decision making of honeybees in complex temperature fields. PLOS ONE **8**(10), 1–11 (2013)
29. Valentini, G., et al.: Kilogrid: a novel experimental environment for the kilobot robot. Swarm Intell. **12**(3), 245–266 (2018)

On the Adaptive Value of Mood and Mood Contagion

Elpida Tzafestas[✉]

Laboratory of Cognitive Science, Department of History and Philosophy of Science, National
and Kapodistrian University of Athens, University Campus, 15771 Ano Ilisia, Greece
etzafestas@phs.uoa.gr

Abstract. We are presenting a study on mood that purports to contribute to an understanding of its evolution as a personal strategy and as a prosocial automatic contagion-based mechanism that both improve decision making. We present an environment where an agent interacts with objects of varying difficulty and where its mood is both a dispositional factor that influences its decision making and an information variable that aligns with the history of its interactions. We show that for very competent and very incompetent agents the mood has a positive effect on their obtained performance and that on average for the whole population the mood mechanism would be selected by evolution. We also examine a mechanism of automatic mood contagion that favors all but the most incompetent agents and on average the whole population and we show that contagion would again be selected by evolution. We delineate the implications of our model for further research on moods.

Keywords: Mood · Mood contagion · Decision making · Learning · Evolution

1 Introduction

Emotion and affect are significant for intelligent behavior and as important as reasoning and rationality for general cognition. After the precursor work of Vygotsky [1], there has been a growing trend in the research on the relation between emotion and cognition that has culminated in the late nineties and the early millennium both for psychology with the emergence of new journals (such as Emotion, since 2001) and for nouvelle artificial intelligence with dedicated special issues and workshops (such as the 24(5): 2016 issue of Adaptive Behavior). Some pioneering works relevant to the history of emotional modeling are Sloman's CogAff project [2], Marvin Minsky's "Emotion Machine" [3]. Typical more recent modeling works include [4, 5].

We are interested in understanding the evolution of affective behavior in a prosocial context, by studying its evolutionary advantage for motivated individuals that need to make decisions and learn in their environment [6–8] More specifically, we are studying the concept of mood which is defined as a relatively long lasting affective state that is experienced without concurrent awareness of its origins [9] and that arises when negative or positive experience in one context or time period alters the individual's response propensity and actual response to potentially negative or positive events in subsequent contexts or time periods. Unlike emotions, mood has a longer-lasting, global and diffuse effect on the individual's behavior and, like emotions but unlike feelings, mood is expressed by the individual and not just experienced internally and personally [10, 11].

We adopt a synthetic approach combining a dispositional view to mood [12, 13] with elements from the theory of mood as information [14, 15]. The dispositional view states that mood influences behavior, especially decision-making and learning, independently of the external context and stimuli. On the other hand, mood is a sort of information that reflects the cumulative impact of differences between reward outcomes and expectations and is used by the individuals as such anticipatory information. Both functions of mood are identified in various studies [16–22]. Many authors have provided combined views of dispositional mood with informative mood, for example [23–25]. In such views, mood and the mood mechanism influence directly decision-making, action selection and learning and are in turn affected or receive feedback from their outcome and the performance of the individual in the environment.

We are interested in modeling this interplay and its various forms as well as understanding both its origins and its consequences. For now, we only consider the very basic functions of mood, leaving for the future issues such as mood regulation (for direct mood management and hedonic balance [26, 27]), relation with temperament and personality [28] and mood instability, dysfunction and disorders [29, 30].

We are also interested in including in our models the social dimension of mood [31]. At present, we are studying mood contagion [32–35] as an automatic, uninformed mechanism of transfer of mood across individuals with the only role of acting as an additional input to the dispositional and informational function of mood. The more advanced functions concerning social cohesion [36] through collective information and disposition and its relation to social learning are left for a later stage of this research.

This paper is structured as follows. In Sect. 2, we are presenting the agent model and all about its motivation, mood, personality and learning. Next, in Sect. 3 we report the results of experiments with the basic model that show the value of mood for the agents and its positive effect on their performance. In Sect. 4 we present an evolutionary study that demonstrates that the mood mechanism has an evolutionary advantage and would be selected by evolution. In Sects. 5 and 6 we do the same with a mechanism of automatic contagion: we show its value for agents as individuals in a population and present an evolutionary study that shows that mood contagion would be selected by evolution. Final thoughts are given in the last section.

2   Agent Model

An agent is an artificial symbolic entity that exists in an abstract, spaceless environment that presents to it objects of various types, one at a time. An agent has different processing abilities for the various object types and decides whether to interact with an object or not. Each object has a flat processing cost independently of outcome and a gain if the outcome is successful. Agents start with an initial wealth of 100 and play for 1000 cycles (i.e., they are presented with 1000 random objects in order). Abilities are represented as probabilities of success (thus normalized between 0 and 1). Moreover, agents have a self-estimate for each object type ability which is initialized at 0.5 when there is no prior information available and may be updated after every trial with the object upward toward 1 or downward toward 0 according to whether processing has been successful or not. Thus learning, in the form of learning oneself, may take place.

An agent decides to interact with the presented object if its wealth is over the required cost and a randomly drawn number is less than the "knowledge" of the agent for the given type (*interact if random < knowledge*)–this knowledge is taken to be the average between the self-estimate of the agent and the actual success rate for the given object type so far, *knowledge = (success rate + self-estimate)/2* (the random number should also be greater than 0.1 to avoid taking the risk of interacting with an object with such a low probability of success). The interaction is successful if another random number is again greater than 0.1 and less than the actual ability of the agent for the given type (*successful if random < ability*). Learning by default takes place in the direction of the outcome (success or failure) with a constant learning rate, thus *new self-estimate = old self-estimate + rate * (Target value – self-estimate)*, where Target value = 1 or 0 for success or failure, respectively.

Mood is represented as a multiplication factor between *MinMood = 0.5* (low mood) and *MaxMood = 1.5* (high mood) during interaction triggering by knowledge (*interact if random < mood * knowledge*). Agents that do not use mood correspond to constant mood of 1 (neutral value). With this setup, agents with high mood (over 1) have higher probabilities of deciding to interact with objects because *knowledge * mood > knowledge* and agents with low mood (below 1) have lower probabilities of deciding to interact with objects because *knowledge * mood < knowledge*. Thus, the value of mood directly influences the agent's perception of the situation [12], so that high mood is risk-prone and low mood is risk-aversive [15, 37, 38].

After each interaction of the agent with an object, the mood is updated up or down according to success or failure, thus *new mood = old mood + rate * (Target value – mood)*, where Target value = MaxMood (1.5) or MinMood (0.5) for success or failure, respectively. Agents that use mood learn differently than those without mood [24, 39], possibly because of differences in resource mobilization [9]: if the outcome matches their mood (success for positive mood or failure for negative mood) learning toward the corresponding target value is fast (that is, learning rate is max) otherwise (in cases of success for negative mood and failure for positive mood) learning is slow (that is, learning rate is min). As is obvious from the above setup, mood represents globally the state of success or failure of the agent and its value affects directly the decision to interact with the various types of objects in an intricate way. For example, an agent may refrain from interacting with objects for which it has high ability because of repeated failed interactions with other types of objects in the past which have led to low mood. Vice versa, it may proceed with interacting with objects for which it has low ability because of repeated successful interactions with other types of objects in the past which have led to high mood.

We use the following parameters and values in the experiments of the following sections:

Agents	
Initial agent wealth	100
Default learning rate (no mood agents)	0.15
Max learning rate (mood agents)	0.15
Min learning rate (mood agents)	0.05
Mood update rate	0.1
Initial self estimate for each object type	0.5
Object types A,B,C	
Gains (for A,B,C, respectively)	{6, 10, 18}
Costs (for A,B,C, respectively)	{2, 4, 8}
Probabilities of encounter (for A,B,C, respectively)	{0.5, 0.3, 0.2}

We have also defined 6 fixed agent profiles with varying abilities for the various object types. The total ability may be computed as the sum of *prob.encounter x (ability * gain − cost)* for all object types. The profiles are described below. For example, for profile 4, total ability = 0.5 * (0.1 * 6 − 2) + 0.3 * (0.2 * 10 − 4) + 0.2 * (0.9 * 18 − 8) = 0.34. As may be observed from the rightmost column, profile 6 is the highest ability profile (well over 1), profiles 2 and 3 are the lowest ability profiles (well below 0) and profiles 1, 4 and 5 are intermediate ability profiles (around 0 and below 1).

	Abilities	Total ability
Profile 1	{0.7, 0.5, 0.3}	0.88
Profile 2	{0.4, 0.3, 0.2}	−0.98
Profile 3	{0.1, 0.2, 0.2}	−2.18
Profile 4	{0.1, 0.2, 0.9}	0.34
Profile 5	{0.8, 0.2, 0.2}	−0.08
Profile 6	{0.8, 0.7, 0.9}	3.94

The above parameters of the model and the details of the agent profiles have been worked out by Vazoukis [40] whose work focuses on mood temperament and dysfunction and not on mood evolution. The resulting values have been tuned to allow visible differences between agents and relatively fast mood stabilization.

3   Reference Mood Experiments

We have run simulation experiments to evaluate whether agents with mood end up wealthier than agents without mood. In all the experiments of the present and the following sections we study societies of agents that are either uniform with one of the basic 6 agent profiles (usually 50 agents) or with the "mix profile" (50 agents for every profile, thus 300 in total) or, finally, with the general profile (50 agents with random abilities between 0 and 1 for each of the object types). In all cases, we measure and compare the average wealth in the society after 1000 cycles, the average mood for mood agents and the average *self-confidence* of the agents (*self-confidence = self estimate - actual ability*, hence positive self-confidence means self-estimate higher than actual ability).

In the following experiment, we compare agents with mood and agents without mood for the 8 types of society presented above. The agents run independently for 1000 cycles, i.e. they run without interacting with one another in any way.

	Without mood			With mood			
	Num	Wealth	S.Conf.	Num	Wealth	S.Conf.	Mood
Profile 1	50	621.563	−0.13	50	632.789	−0.065	1.034
Profile 2	50	1.646	−0.128	50	19.274	−0.154	0.674
Profile 3	50	0.386	−0.012	50	9.65	−0.008	0.6
Profile 4	50	1382.738	−0.041	50	1380.41	0.002	1.252
Profile 5	50	923.035	−0.079	50	939.052	0.008	1.195
Profile 6	50	2865.146	−0.049	50	3729.085	0.105	1.266
Mix 1–6	300	966.192	−0.073	300	1119.086	−0.019	1.004
General	50	1214.658	−0.083	50	1346.425	−0.013	1.068

We immediately observe that with mood, the agents have equal or higher wealth on average than without mood, with high gains in the case of very high or very low ability agents (profiles 6 and 2,3, respectively). This goes hand in hand with the higher self-confidence values for higher scoring agents. Furthermore, the mood is positive (above 1) for high scoring agents and negative (below 1) for low scoring agents. This aligns with the agents' abilities and shows that the mood mechanism functions on the one hand as stimulation for the high ability agents to dare act and on the other hand as protection for low ability agents to avoid excessive risks. Thus the value of mood brings information about the environment that in turn defines disposition toward the environment.

We also compare these experiments with a fixed mood case, where mood is fixed at various levels from 0.5 to 1.5. We present indicative results below to show that high and medium ability profiles (profiles 1, 4, 5, 6) function best with high mood, close to 1.5, while low ability profiles (profiles 2, 3) function best with low mood, close to 0.5. The mix and the general profile function well with almost any positive mood, as expected from the average population composition, but fixed mood is not as good as regular variable mood.

	Wealth	S.Conf.	Mood
Profile 1 (Default)	632.789	-0.065	1.034
Mood = 0.5	395.987	-0.188	0.5
Mood = 1.5	679.791	0.013	1.5
Profile 2 (Default)	19.274	-0.154	0.674
Mood = 0.5	22.478	-0.115	0.5
Mood = 1.5	0.712	0.012	1.5
Profile 3 (Default)	9.65	-0.008	0.6
Mood = 0.5	13.648	0.008	0.5
Mood = 1.5	0.215	0.086	1.5
Profile 4 (Default)	1380.41	0.002	1.252
Mood = 0.5	912.987	-0.042	0.5
Mood = 1.5	1362.313	-0.015	1.5
Profile 5 (Default)	939.052	0.008	1.195
Mood = 0.5	588.296	-0.093	0.5
Mood = 1.5	824.405	-0.017	1.5
Profile 6 (Default)	3729.085	0.105	1.266
Mood = 0.5	1830.058	-0.169	0.5
Mood = 1.5	3339.986	0.03	1.5
Mix 1-6 (Default)	1119.086	-0.019	1.004
Mood = 0.5	628.288	-0.1	0.5
Mood = 0.9	775.095	-0.122	0.9
Mood = 1.1	1044.265	0.02	1.1
Mood = 1.2	1051.105	0.019	1.2
Mood = 1.5	1034.397	0.019	1.5
General (Default)	1346.425	-0.013	1.068
Mood = 0.5	771.914	-0.121	0.5
Mood = 0.9	1011.693	-0.142	0.9
Mood = 1.1	1306.3	0.016	1.1
Mood = 1.5	1326.114	0.015	1.5

All these results are an indication that a "mood gene" would spread in a population given a uniform or, more realistically, a rather balanced composition of abilities. We test this prediction in the following section.

4 Evolution of Mood

In the following experiment, we run a society of 100 agents, 50 of them without mood and 50 with mood for the 8 types of society presented above (300 and 300 agents, respectively, in the case of the mix profile). Unlike the experiments of the previous section, this experiment is evolutionary, that is a number of generations are run, each one corresponding to one run (1000 cycles) of the previous type. After a generation is complete, the agents are sorted according to final score (wealth) and the new population consists of agents that are initialized with 90% probability with the mood/no-mood value of one of the former top ranking 50% agents and with 10% probability with the mood/no-mood value of one of the former low ranking 50% agents. We report below the final average number of agents of each type, as well as the average wealth, the average self confidence and the average mood, as before. In all cases, the number of mood agents rises from the initial 50 to a very high value and the wealth, self confidence and mood averages are as obtained in the earlier experiments. It is also noteworthy that the mood gene fully dominates in the population (100%) for the profiles 2, 3 and 6 (very low and very high, respectively) that have been found before to profit the most from the mood mechanism.

	Without mood			With mood			
	Num	Wealth	S.Conf.	Num	Wealth	S.Conf.	Mood
Profile 1	6.14	139.884	−0.03	93.86	607.7	−0.063	0.993
Profile 2	0	0	0	100	19.567	−0.154	0.673
Profile 3	0	0	0	100	9.66	−0.007	0.6
Profile 4	6.88	413.435	−0.013	93.12	1391.262	0.002	1.257
Profile 5	0.94	56.119	−0.005	99.06	939.147	0.009	1.196
Profile 6	0	0	0	100	3724.78	0.104	1.263
Mix 1–6	149.02	949.694	−0.072	450.98	1120.279	−0.019	1.005
General	19.84	512.766	−0.039	80.16	1331.555	−0.013	1.048

5 Mood Contagion

Until here, we have studied mood as a personal strategy that interacts with action selection and learning toward higher scores. But mood is also, and perhaps more importantly, a social mechanism that promotes social coherence and stability. In this section we examine how and when a mood contagion mechanism may also be advantageous for the individuals in terms of personal achievement.

We report below the results of an experiment that compares regular mood agents with mood agents with an added contagion mechanism. Contagion functions like this: after all agents have executed individually, each one meets another random agent, "reads" its mood and updates itself accordingly. By default, an agent updates itself by adopting as its new mood value the average between its own and the other agent's mood values. No other interaction takes place between the agents. As is obvious in the results reported below, mood contagion is on average better for all but the worst ability agents.

	With mood				With added contagion			
	Num	Wealth	S.Conf.	Mood	Num	Wealth	S.Conf.	Mood
Profile 1	50	632.789	−0.065	1.034	50	751.96	0.031	1.076
Profile 2	50	19.274	−0.154	0.674	50	16.909	−0.163	0.751
Profile 3	50	9.65	−0.008	0.6	50	8.823	−0.009	0.624
Profile 4	50	1380.41	0.002	1.252	50	1411.717	0.011	1.244
Profile 5	50	939.052	0.008	1.195	50	937.762	0.049	1.179
Profile 6	50	3729.085	0.105	1.266	50	3766.406	0.109	1.267
Mix 1–6	300	1119.086	−0.019	1.004	300	1143.298	0.065	1.181
General	50	1346.425	−0.013	1.068	50	1401.468	0.095	1.147

It is known that neither mood expression nor mood internalization are fixed and uniform across a population, but there exist big differences among agents, and more specifically there are "mood givers or transmitters" and "mood catchers or receivers" [41]. We report below the results of an experiment that compares a society of 100 mood agents where some or all are mood givers and some or all are mood receivers with a regular society where all 100 agents are both receivers and givers. We have examined all cases with half or all receivers (R = 50 or 100), half or all givers (G = 50 or 100) and independent 50% probabilities for each agent to be a giver and/or a receiver (R,G 0/1). It can be observed that any type of R/G contagion is at least as good in terms of final score as no contagion (mood only), except again for the cases of low scoring profiles 2 and 3. The mix and the general profile are again rather unstable, as expected from the very diversified population composition.

	Wealth	S.Conf.	Mood
Profile 1 (Mood only)	632.789	-0.065	1.034
Default (R=G=100)	751.96	0.031	1.076
R=50, G=100	750.149	0.016	1.077
R,G 0/1	656.214	-0.057	1.041
Profile 2 (Mood only)	19.274	-0.154	0.674
Default (R=G=100)	16.909	-0.163	0.751
R=50, G=50	16.995	-0.162	0.745
R,G 0/1	20.599	-0.154	0.67
Profile 3 (Mood only)	9.65	-0.008	0.6
Default (R=G=100)	8.823	-0.009	0.624
R=100, G=50	9.122	-0.008	0.621
R,G 0/1	9.902	-0.007	0.603
Profile 4 (Mood only)	1380.41	0.002	1.252
Default (R=G=100)	1411.717	0.011	1.244
R=50, G=50	1412.729	0.01	1.241
R,G 0/1	1403.038	0.006	1.252
Profile 5 (Mood only)	939.052	0.008	1.195
Default (R=G=100)	937.762	0.049	1.179
R=50, G=50	954.742	0.035	1.193
R,G 0/1	953.272	0.021	1.196
Profile 6 (Mood only)	3729.085	0.105	1.266
Default (R=G=100)	3766.406	0.109	1.267
R=100, G=50	3769.894	0.109	1.268
R,G 0/1	3742.36	0.106	1.267
Mix 1-6 (Mood only)	1119.086	-0.019	1.004
Default (R=G=100)	1143.298	0.065	1.181
R=50, G=50	1142.84	0.035	1.186
R,G 0/1	1070.217	-0.024	1.026
General (Mood only)	1346.425	-0.013	1.068
Default (R=G=100)	1401.468	0.095	1.147
R=100, G=50	1416.495	0.075	1.154
R,G 0/1	1345.295	0.002	1.086

These results are analogous to the results of Sect. 3 and they represent an indication that once a "mood gene" is in place, a "mood contagion gene" would spread in a population. We test this prediction in the following section.

6   Evolution of Mood Contagion

In the following experiment, we run a society of 50 agents, each one of them having a 50% probability to be initialized as a giver and an independent 50% probability to be initialized as a receiver (300 agents in the case of the mix profile). As in Sect. 4, this experiment is evolutionary, that is a number of generations are run, each one corresponding to one run (1000 cycles) of the original type. After a generation is complete, the agents are sorted according to final score (wealth) and the new population consists of agents that are initialized with 90% probability with the giver and receiver values of one of the former top ranking 50% agents or with 10% probability with the giver and receiver values of one of the former low ranking 50% agents. We report below the final average number of givers and receivers, as well as the average wealth, the average self confidence and the average mood, as before. In medium and high scoring profiles, an overwhelming proportion of agents end up as givers and about half of them as receivers, which can be interpreted as an evolutionary trend to become socially expressive but prudent in mood internalization and empathy, whereas in low scoring profiles most of the agents end up as non receivers or non givers, that is even more prudent and self-restrained. The mix and general case are like before more unstable, but overall more contagious than the starting point.

	Wealth	S.Conf.	Mood	Givers	Receivers
Profile 1	687.046	−0.022	1.051	0.98	0.44
Profile 2	19.097	−0.155	0.683	0.5	0.28
Profile 3	9.696	−0.008	0.601	0.16	0.38
Profile 4	1400.274	0.007	1.248	0.92	0.48
Profile 5	939.239	0.025	1.185	0.92	0.42
Profile 6	3742.185	0.106	1.262	0.88	0.5
Mix 1–6	1125.369	0.005	1.062	0.42	0.642
General	1375.004	0.034	1.099	0.64	0.6

Thus mood that has evolved as a personal mechanism in the first place can then become contagious. We note that this is a very simple and automatic contagion mechanism that is neither congruent (dependent on valence) nor reward-dependent (dependent on self performance). Such advanced contagion mechanisms are the object of a further envisaged study.

7   Discussion

We have shown that a mood mechanism that has a dual dispositional-informational nature and that interacts with decision making and learning can be advantageous for the average individual in a population. We have also shown that contagion of mood can be advantageous for the average individual as well. Moreover, in evolutionary experiments, it was found that both these individual mood and mood contagion mechanisms would be selected by evolution. Thus we have found a possible evolutionary pathway for mood to emerge in the behavior of humans and other species.

A number of open issues remain to be tackled in the immediate future. Firstly, although it looks obvious that mood has to evolve before mood contagion evolves, this is not necessarily the case. It could be that a pre-existing but irrelevant contagion mechanism would be recruited and exploited for the emergence of mood. Secondly, we have found that medium competence individuals do not really profit from mood and their behavior is rather unstable. It might be hasty to dismiss this as the price to pay for a generic evolved trait, because it could instead just be the proof that some other mechanism ensures behavioral stability in this middle range, for example one involving mood regulation and explicit pleasure-seeking. In the same way, extremely incompetent individuals do not seem to profit from mood contagion. Again, instead of being ignored, this could be an indication that contagion is less automatic and more informed if necessary, for example through mood congruency or reward dependency, as mentioned in the end of the previous section. Or, that mood contagion triggers additional learning, of the social type. Last but not least, it would be straightforward to study the effect of various dysfunctions and disorders of mood (such as depression), both for the individual and for the population it belongs to.

References

1. Vygotsky, L.S.: Théorie des émotions - Etude historico-psychologique. L'Harmattan (1984/2000)
2. https://www.cs.bham.ac.uk/research/projects/cogaff/
3. Minsky, M.: The Emotion Machine. Simon & Schuster (2006)
4. Morén, J., Balkenius, C.: Emotional learning: a computational model of the amygdala. Cybern. Syst. 32(6), 611–636 (2000)
5. Cos, I., Cañamero, L., Hayes, G.M., Gillies, A.: Hedonic value: enhancing adaptation for motivated agents. Adapt. Behav. 21(6), 465–483 (2013)
6. Nesse, R.M.: Evolutionary explanations for mood and mood disorders. In: Stein, D.J., Kupfer, D.J., Schatzberg, A.F. (eds.) The American Psychiatric Publishing Textbook of Mood Disorders, pp. 159–175 (2006)
7. Nettle, D., Bateson, M.: The evolutionary origins of mood and its disorders. Curr. Biol. 22(17), R712–R721 (2012)
8. Trimmer, P., Paul, E., Mendl, M., McNamara, J., Houston, A.: On the evolution and optimality of mood states. Behav. Sci. 3(3), 501–521 (2013)
9. Gendolla, G.H.E., Brinkmann, K.: The role of mood states in self-regulation: effects on action preferences and resource mobilization. Eur. Psychol. 10(3), 187–198 (2005)
10. Beedie, C., Terry, P., Lane, A.: Distinctions between emotion and mood. Cogn. Emot. 19(6), 847–878 (2005)
11. Davidson, R.J., Goldsmith, H., Scherer, K.R.: Handbook of Affective Sciences. Oxford University, Press (2003)
12. Siemer, M.: Moods as multiple-object directed and as objectless affective states: an examination of the dispositional theory of moods. Cogn. Emot. 19(6), 815–845 (2005)
13. Siemer, M.: Mood experience: implications of a dispositional theory of moods. Emot. Rev. 1, 256–263 (2009)
14. Schwarz, N., Clore, G.L.: Mood as information: 20 years later. Psychol. Inq. 14(3–4), 296–303 (2003)
15. Isen, A.M., Reeve, J.: The influence of positive affect on intrinsic and extrinsic motivation: facilitating enjoyment of play, responsible work behavior, and self-control. Motiv. Emot. 29(4), 295–323 (2005)
16. Bower, G.H., Monteiro, K.P., Gilligan, S.G.: Emotional mood as a context for learning and recall. J. Verbal Learn. Verbal Behav. 17(5), 573–585 (1978)

17. Esses, V.M.: Mood as a moderator of acceptance of interpersonal feedback. J. Pers. Soc. Psychol. **57**(5), 769–781 (1989)
18. Thayer, R.E.: The Biopsychology of Mood and Arousal. Oxford University Press, New York (1990)
19. Pekrun, R.: The impact of emotions on learning and achievement: towards a theory of cognitive/motivational mediators. Appl. Psychol. **41**(4), 359–376 (1992)
20. Forgas, J.P.: Mood and judgment: the affect infusion model (AIM). Psychol. Bull. **117**(1), 39–66 (1995)
21. Schwarz, N.: Emotion, cognition, and decision making. Cogn. Emot. **14**(4), 433–440 (2000)
22. Lewis, P.A., Critchley, H.D.: Mood-dependent memory. Trends Cogn. Sci. **7**(10), 431–433 (2003)
23. Gendolla, G.H.E.: On the impact of mood on behavior: an integrative theory and a review. Rev. Gen. Psychol. **4**(4), 378–408 (2000)
24. Fiedler, K., Nickel, S., Asbeck, J., Pagel, U.: Mood and the generation effect. Cogn. Emot. **17**(4), 585–608 (2003)
25. Eldar, E., Rutledge, R.B., Dolan, R.J., Niv, Y.: Mood as representation of momentum. Trends Cogn. Sci. **20**(1), 15–24 (2016)
26. Morris, W.N.: Some Thoughts about mood and its regulation. Psychol. Inq. **11**(3), 200–202 (2000)
27. Larsen, R.J.: Toward a science of mood regulation. Psychol. Inq. **11**(3), 129–141 (2000)
28. Watson, D.: Mood and Temperament. Guilford Press (2000)
29. Lane, A.M., Terry, P.C.: The nature of mood: development of a conceptual model with a focus on depression. J. Appl. Sport Psychol. **12**(1), 16–33 (2000)
30. Eldar, E., Niv, Y.: Interaction between emotional state and learning underlies mood instability. Nature Commun. **6**(1) (2015)
31. Olson, K.R.: A literature review of social mood. J. Behav. Financ. **7**(4), 193–203 (2006)
32. Hatfield, E., Rapson, R.L., Le, Y.-C.L.: Emotional contagion and empathy. In: Decety, J., Ickes, W. (eds.) The Social Neuroscience of Empathy, pp. 19–30 (2009)
33. Neumann, R., Strack, F.: "Mood Contagion": the automatic transfer of mood between persons. J. Pers. Soc. Psychol. **79**(2), 211–223 (2000)
34. Marx, A.K.G.:.\ Advancing Research on Emotional Contagion, PhD Thesis, Ludwig-Maximilians-Universität München (2020)
35. Barsade, S.G.: The ripple effect: emotional contagion and its influence on group behavior. Adm. Sci. Q. **47**, 644–675 (2002)
36. Mackie, D.M., Smith, E.R.: Intergroup Emotions Theory: Production, Regulation, and Modification of Group-Based Emotions, Advances in Experimental Social Psychology, vol. 58, chap. 1, pp. 1–69 (2018)
37. Kavanagh, D.J., Bower, G.H.: Mood and self-efficacy: impact of joy and sadness on perceived capabilities. Cogn. Ther. Res. **9**(5), 507–525 (1985)
38. Wright, W.F., Bower, G.H.: Mood effects on subjective probability assessment. Organ. Behav. Hum. Decis. Process. **52**(2), 276–291 (1992)
39. Forgas, J.P.: Don't worry, be sad! On the cognitive, motivational, and interpersonal benefits of negative mood. Curr. Dir. Psychol. Sci. **22**(3), 225–232 (2013)
40. Vazoukis, P.: Interaction Between Action Selection and Mood. M.Sc. Thesis, Cognitive Science Laboratory, University of Athens (2022)
41. Isabella, G., Carvalho, H.C.: Emotional contagion and socialization: reflection on virtual interaction. In: Tettegah, S.Y., Espelage, D.L. (eds.) Emotions, Technology, and Behaviors, chap. 4, pp. 63–82 (2016)

Author Index

Printed in the United States
by Baker & Taylor Publisher Services

Printed in the United States
by Baker & Taylor Publisher Services